AUTODESK®
3DS MAX® 2015
ESSENTIALS

Randi L. Derakhshani

Dariush Derakhshani

AUTODESK.
Official Press

SYBEX®
A Wiley Brand

Acquisitions Editor: Mariann Barsolo
Development Editor: Kim Beaudet
Technical Editor: Jon McFarland
Production Editor: Rebecca Anderson
Copy Editor: Linda Recktenwald
Editorial Manager: Pete Gaughan
Vice President and Executive Group Publisher: Richard Swadley
Associate Publisher: Chris Webb
Book Designer: Happenstance Type-O-Rama
Compositor: Cody Gates, Happenstance Type-O-Rama
Proofreader: Jennifer Bennett, Word One New York
Indexer: Ted Laux
Project Coordinator, Cover: Lauren Buroker
Cover Designer: Wiley
Cover Image: Courtesy of Randi L. Derakhshani

Copyright © 2014 by John Wiley & Sons, Inc., Indianapolis, Indiana
Published simultaneously in Canada
ISBN: 978-1-118-86721-1
ISBN: 978-1-118-86753-2 (ebk.)
ISBN: 978-1-118-86770-9 (ebk.)

For general information on our other products and services or to obtain technical support, please contact our Customer Care Department within the U.S. at (877) 762-2974, outside the U.S. at (317) 572-3993 or fax (317) 572-4002.

Wiley publishes in a variety of print and electronic formats and by print-on-demand. Some material included with standard print versions of this book may not be included in e-books or in print-on-demand. If this book refers to media such as a CD or DVD that is not included in the version you purchased, you may download this material at http://booksupport.wiley.com. For more information about Wiley products, visit www.wiley.com.

Library of Congress Control Number: 2014931923

10 9 8 7 6 5 4 3 2 1

Dear Reader,

Thank you for choosing *Autodesk 3ds Max Essentials 2015*. This book is part of a family of premium-quality Sybex books, all of which are written by outstanding authors who combine practical experience with a gift for teaching.

Sybex was founded in 1976. More than 30 years later, we're still committed to producing consistently exceptional books. With each of our titles, we're working hard to set a new standard for the industry. From the paper we print on to the authors we work with, our goal is to bring you the best books available.

I hope you see all that reflected in these pages. I'd be very interested to hear your comments and get your feedback on how we're doing. Feel free to let me know what you think about this or any other Sybex book by sending me an email at contactus@sybex.com. If you think you've found a technical error in this book, please visit http://sybex.custhelp.com. Customer feedback is critical to our efforts at Sybex.

Best regards,

CHRIS WEBB
Associate Publisher, Sybex

To Max Henry

Acknowledgments

Education is an all-important goal in life and should always be approached with eagerness and earnestness. We would like to show appreciation to the teachers who inspired us; you can always remember the teachers who touched your life, and to them we say thanks. We would also like to thank all of our students, who taught us a lot during the course of our many combined academic years.

Special thanks go to Mariann Barsolo, Kim Beaudet, Rebecca Anderson, and Pete Gaughan, our editors at Sybex who have been professional, courteous, and ever patient. Our appreciation also goes to technical editor Jon McFarland, who worked hard to make sure this book is of the utmost quality. We could not have done this revision without their help.

In addition, thanks to Dariush's mother and brother for their love and support, not to mention the life-saving babysitting services.

Writing on the HP EliteBook

Having a good computer system is important with this type of work, so a special thank you goes to HP for keeping us on the cutting edge of workstation hardware by providing us with a fully decked-out EliteBook 8760w, which was our primary computer in writing this book. What struck us about the laptop was that it was not only portable, making it easy for a writing team to collaborate; it was also powerful enough to run truly demanding tasks. It takes a special machine to run graphics-intensive applications, such as the Autodesk® 3ds Max® software, and we were thrilled to write this book on the HP EliteBook.

Running an Intel i7 CPU with 16GB of RAM and an NVidia Quadro 5010M (with a whopping 6GB of memory) gave us the muscle we needed to run multiple applications alongside 3ds Max splendidly. Dual 320GB hard drives gave us plenty of space for Windows 7 Professional and its applications, and still left lots of room for renders. We opted out of the RAID option to mirror the drives (you can also stripe them for performance), but that doesn't mean we neglected our backup duties with this machine! The 8760w was easily integrated into a Gigabit network in the home office, and on fast Wi-Fi everywhere else, so we had constant access to the home network and the hundreds upon hundreds of files necessary to write this book (and all their backups!).

And since we are so very image-conscious (as in the screen!), we wondered if the images we created and captured for this book would be done justice on "just a laptop screen." The EliteBook has a stunning 17-inch, 30-bit IPS display panel that put those questions to rest very quickly! The HP EliteBook screen is no less than professionally accurate and calibrated for optimum image clarity and correct color. Barely a handful of high-end mobile workstations could even come close to meeting the demands image professionals put on their gear. But this notebook HP DreamColor display is remarkable—there's just no other way to put it—going as far as besting any of our desktop screens in color and vibrancy.

With performance at such a high level, and in a nice portable form, we were easily convinced that we should perform all of our intensive work for this book on the EliteBook. Going back to a desk-bound tower quickly became a non-option. Thanks, HP!

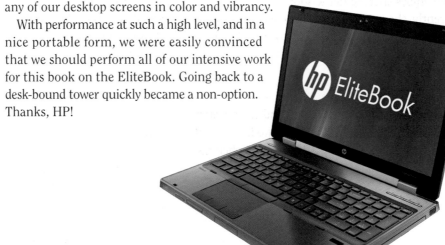

About the Authors

Randi L. Derakhshani is an Autodesk-Certified Instructor. She began working with computer graphics in 1992 and was hired by her instructor to work at Sony Pictures Imageworks, where she developed her skills with the Autodesk® 3ds Max® program and Shake, among many other programs. A teacher since 1999, Randi enjoys sharing her wisdom with young talent and watching them develop. Currently, she teaches a wide range of classes, from Autodesk 3ds Max, Autodesk® Maya®, and ZBrush to compositing with The Foundry's Nuke. Juggling her teaching activities with caring for a little boy makes Randi a pretty busy lady.

Dariush Derakhshani is an Autodesk-Certified Instructor and Certified Evaluator, a visual-effects supervisor, a writer, and an educator in Los Angeles, California, as well as Randi's husband. Dariush used Autodesk® AutoCAD® software in his architectural days and migrated to using 3D programs when his firm's principal architects needed to visualize architectural designs in 3D on the computer. Dariush started using Alias PowerAnimator version 6 when he enrolled in USC Film School's animation program, and he has been using Alias/Autodesk animation software for the past 14 years. He received an MFA in film, video, and computer animation from the USC Film School in 1997. He also holds a BA in architecture and theater from Lehigh University in Pennsylvania. He worked at a New Jersey architectural firm before moving to Los Angeles for film school. He has worked on feature films, music videos, and countless commercials as a 3D animator, as a CG/VFX supervisor, and sometimes as a compositor. Dariush also serves as an editor, and is on the advisory board of *HDRI 3D*, a professional computer graphics magazine from DMG Publishing.

Contents at a Glance

Contents

INTRODUCTION

Welcome to Autodesk® 3ds Max® 2015 Essentials. The world of computer-generated (CG) imagery is fun and ever changing. Whether you are new to CG in general or are a CG veteran new to 3ds Max designing, you'll find this book the perfect primer. It introduces you to the Autodesk 3ds Max software and shows how you can work with the program to create your art, whether it is animated or static in design.

This book exposes you to all facets of 3ds Max by introducing and plainly explaining its tools and functions to help you understand how the program operates—but it does not stop there. This book also explains the use of the tools and the ever-critical concepts behind the tools. You'll find hands-on examples and tutorials that give you firsthand experience with the toolsets. Working through them will develop your skills and the conceptual knowledge that will carry you to further study with confidence. These tutorials expose you to various ways to accomplish tasks with this intricate and comprehensive artistic tool. These chapters should give you the confidence you need to venture deeper into the feature set in 3ds Max, either on your own or by using any of the software's other learning tools and books as a guide.

Learning to use a powerful tool can be frustrating. You need to remember to pace yourself. The major complaints CG book readers have are that the pace is too fast and that the steps are too complicated or overwhelming. Addressing those complaints is a tough nut to crack, to be sure. No two readers are the same. However, this book offers the opportunity to run things at your own pace. The exercises and steps may seem confusing at times, but keep in mind that the more you try and the more you fail at some attempts, the more you will learn how to operate the 3ds Max engine. Experience is king when learning the workflow necessary for *any* software program, and with experience comes failure and aggravation. But try and try again. You will find that further attempts will always be easier and more fruitful.

Above all, however, this book aims to inspire you to use the 3ds Max program as a creative tool to achieve and explore your own artistic vision.

Who Should Read This Book

Anyone who is interested in learning to use the 3ds Max tools should start with this book.

If you are an educator, you will find a solid foundation on which to build a new course. You can also treat the book as a source of raw materials that you can adapt to fit an existing curriculum. Written in an open-ended style, *Autodesk 3ds Max 2015 Essentials* contains several self-help tutorials for home study as well as plenty of material to fit into any class.

What You Will Learn

You will learn how to work in CG with Autodesk 3ds Max 2015. The important thing to keep in mind, however, is that this book is merely the beginning of your CG education. With the confidence you will gain from the exercises in this book, and the peace of mind you can have by using this book as a reference, you can go on to create your own increasingly complex CG projects.

What You Need

Hardware changes constantly and evolves faster than publications can keep up. Having a good solid machine is important to production, although simple home computers will be able to run the 3ds Max software quite well. Any laptop (with discrete graphics, not a netbook) or desktop PC running Windows XP Professional, Windows 7, or Windows 8 (32- or 64-bit) with at least 2GB of RAM and an Intel Pentium Core 2 Duo/Quad or AMD Phenom or higher processor will work. Of course, having a good video card will help; you can use any hardware-accelerated OpenGL or Direct3D video card. Your computer system should have at least a 2.4 GHz Core 2 or i5/i7 processor with 2GB of RAM, a few GBs of hard-drive space available, and a GeForce FX or ATI Radeon video card. Professionals may want to opt for workstation graphics cards, such as the ATI FirePro or the Quadro FX series of cards. The following systems would be good ones to use:

> ► Intel i7, 4GB RAM, Quadro FX 2000, 400GB 7200 RPM hard disk
>
> ► AMD Phenom II, 4GB RAM, ATI FirePro V5700, 400GB hard disk

You can check the list of system requirements at the following website: www.autodesk.com/3dsmax.

FREE AUTODESK SOFTWARE FOR STUDENTS AND EDUCATORS

The Autodesk Education Community is an online resource with more than five million members that enables educators and students to download—for free (see website for terms and conditions)—the same software used by professionals worldwide. You can also access additional tools and materials to help you design, visualize, and simulate ideas. Connect with other learners to stay current with the latest industry trends and get the most out of your designs. Get started today at www.autodesk.com/joinedu.

What Is Covered in This Book

Autodesk 3ds Max 2015 Essentials is organized to provide you with a quick and essential experience with 3ds Max to allow you to begin a fruitful education in the world of computer graphics.

Chapter 1, "The 3ds Max Interface," begins with an introduction to the interface for 3ds Max 2015 to get you up and running quickly.

Chapter 2, "Your First 3ds Max Project," is an introduction to modeling concepts and workflows in general. It shows you how to model using 3ds Max tools with polygonal meshes and modifiers to create a retro alarm clock.

Chapter 3, "Modeling in 3ds Max: Architectural Model Part I," takes your modeling lesson from Chapter 2 a step further by showing you how to use some of the Architecture Engineering and Construction (AEC) tools to build an interior space using a room from an image.

Chapter 4, "Modeling in 3ds Max: Architectural Model Part II," continues with the interior space from Chapter 3 by adding some furniture. The main focus of this chapter is the Graphite Modeling Tools tab and its many tools.

Chapter 5, "Introduction to Animation," teaches you the basics of 3ds Max animation techniques and workflow by animating a bouncing ball. You will also learn how to use the Track View - Curve Editor to time, edit, and finesse your animation.

Chapter 6, "Animation Principles," rounds out your animation experience by showing the animation concepts of weight, follow-through, and anticipation when you animate a knife thrown at a target.

Chapter 7, "Character Poly Modeling Part I," introduces you to the creation of polygon mesh character model of an alien. In this chapter, you begin by blocking out the primary parts of the body.

Chapter 8, "Character Poly Modeling: Part II," continues the alien model, focusing on using the Editable Poly toolset. You will finish the body details, head, hands, and feet.

Chapter 9, "Introduction to Materials," shows you how to assign textures and materials to your models. You will learn to texture the couch, chair, and window from Chapter 4 as you learn the basics of working with 3ds Max materials and UVW mapping.

Chapter 10, "Textures and UV Workflow: The Alien," furthers your understanding of materials and textures, and introduces UV workflows in preparing and texturing the alien.

Chapter 11, "Character Studio: Rigging," covers the basics of Character Studio in creating a biped system and associating the biped rig to the alien model.

Chapter 12, "Character Studio: Animation," expands on Chapter 11 to show you how to use Character Studio to create and edit a walk cycle using the alien model.

Chapter 13, "Introduction to Lighting: Interior Lighting," begins by showing you how to light a 3D scene with the three-point lighting system. It then shows you how to use the tools to create and edit 3ds Max lights for illumination, shadows, and special lighting effects. You will light the furniture to which you added materials in Chapter 9.

Chapter 14, "3ds Max Rendering," explains how to create image files from your 3ds Max scene and how to achieve the best look for your animation by using proper cameras and rendering settings when you render the interior scene.

Chapter 15, "mental ray," shows you how to render with mental ray. Using Final Gather, you will learn how to use indirect lighting.

The companion web page to this book at www.sybex.com/go/3dsmax2015essentials provides all the sample images, movies, and files that you will need to work through the projects in *Autodesk 3ds Max 2015 Essentials*.

NOTE This book is a great primer for Autodesk 3ds Max. If you're interested in taking the Autodesk Certification exams for 3ds Max, go to www.autodesk.com/certification for information and resources.

The Essentials Series

The Essentials series from Sybex provides outstanding instruction for readers who are just beginning to develop their professional skills. Every Essentials book includes these features:

▶ Skill-based instruction with chapters organized around projects rather than abstract concepts or subjects

▶ Downloadable tutorial files showing the start and end state of each exercise

▶ Digital files (via download) so you can work through the project tutorials yourself. Please check the book's web page at www.sybex.com/go/3dsmax2015essentials for these companion downloads.

You can contact the authors through Wiley or on Facebook at www.facebook.com/3dsMaxEssentials.

CHAPTER 1

The 3ds Max Interface

The Autodesk® 3ds Max® software interface is where you view and work with your scene. This chapter explains its basic operations and tools. You can use this chapter as a reference as you work through the rest of this book, although the following chapters and their exercises will orient you to the 3ds Max user interface (UI) quickly. It's important to be in front of your computer when you read this chapter so you can try out techniques as we discuss them.

In this chapter, you will learn to:

▶ **Navigate the workspace**

▶ **Transform objects using gizmos**

▶ **Model with the Graphite Modeling Tools set**

▶ **Manage animation with the time slider and track bar**

Navigate the Workspace

Certification Objective

The following sections present a brief rundown of what you need to know about the 3ds Max user interface and how to navigate in the 3D workspace.

When you first open the program, you will see the Default workspace (Figure 1.1). The Workspace feature controls the interface, and with this menu you can define as many different workspaces as you want. You can then switch among them from the drop-down list on the Quick Access toolbar or the Current Workspaces list on the Manage Workspaces dialog.

FIGURE 1.1 Workspace drop-down menu

User Interface Elements

Figure 1.2 shows the 3ds Max UI. (See Table 1.1 for explanations of the UI elements.) At the top left of the application window is an icon called the Application button (); clicking it opens the Application menu, which provides access to many file operations. Also running along the top is the Quick Access toolbar, which provides access to common commands, and the InfoCenter, which offers access to many product-related information sources. Some of the most important commands in the Quick Access toolbar are file management commands such as Save File and Open File. If you do something and then wish you hadn't, you can click the Undo Scene Operation button () or press Ctrl+Z. To redo a command or action that you just undid, click the Redo Scene Operation button () or press Ctrl+Y.

FIGURE 1.2   The 3ds Max interface elements

TABLE 1.1   The 3ds Max interface elements*

Element	Function	
1	Application button	Opens the Application menu, which provides file management commands.
2	Quick Access toolbar	Provides some of the most commonly used file management commands as well as Undo Scene Operation and Redo Scene Operation.

(Continues)

TABLE 1.1 *(Continued)*

Element	Function	
3	InfoCenter	Provides access to 3ds Max product-related information.
4	The ribbon	Provides access to a wide range of tools to make building and editing models in 3ds Max fast and easy. In Figure 1.2, the ribbon is shown in a horizontal orientation but can be switched to vertical using the Workspace drop-down menu shown in Figure 1.1.
5	Command panel tabs	Where all the editing of parameters occurs; provides access to many functions and creation options; divided into tabs that access different panels, such as Create panel, Modify panel, etc.
6	Rollout	A section of the command panel that can expand to show a listing of parameters or collapse to just its heading name.
7	Viewport navigation controls	Icons that control the display and navigation of the viewports; icons may change depending on the active viewport.
8	Animation Time/Keying controls	Controls for animation keyframing and animation playback.
9	Coordinate display area	Allows you to enter transformation values.
10	Track bar	Provides a timeline showing the frame numbers; select an object to view its animation keys on the track bar.
11	Prompt line and status bar controls	Prompt and status information about your scene and the active command.
12	Time slider	Shows the current and total frames and allows for changing the current frame by moving (or scrubbing) the time bar.

(Continues)

TABLE 1.1 *(Continued)*

Element	Function	
13	MAXScript Mini Listener	A command-prompt window for the MAXScript programming language. The window is useful for performing interactive work and developing small code fragments.
14	Viewport Layout tab bar	This is an easy-access tab for quickly changing viewport layouts. Preset layouts can be added to the menu on the tab bar.
15	Viewports	You can choose different views to display in these four viewports as well as different layouts from the viewport label menus.
16	Main toolbar	Provides quick access to tools and dialog boxes for many of the most common tasks.
17	Menu bar	Provides access to commands grouped by category.

*The numerals in the first column refer to labels in Figure 1.2.

Just below the Quick Access toolbar is the menu bar, which runs across the top of the interface. The menus give you access to a ton of commands—from basic scene operations, such as Duplicate and Group under the Edit menu, to advanced tools such as those found under the Modifiers menu. Immediately below the menu bar is the main toolbar. It contains several icons for functions, such as the three transform tools: Select And Move, Select And Rotate, and Select And Uniform Scale (▣).

When you first open 3ds Max, the workspace has many UI elements. Each is designed to help you work with your models, access tools, and edit object parameters.

Viewports

You'll be doing most of your work in the viewports. These windows represent 3D space using a system based on Cartesian coordinates. That is a fancy way of saying "space on X, Y, and Z axes."

You can visualize X as left-right, Y as in-out (into and out of the screen from the Top viewport), and Z as up-down within the Perspective and Camera viewports. In the orthographic viewports, you can visualize Y as up-down and Z as in-out. The coordinates are expressed as a set of three numbers, such as (0, 3, –7). These coordinates represent a point that is at 0 on the X-axis, 3 units up on the Y-axis, and 7 units back on the Z-axis.

Four-Viewport Layout Tab Bar

The viewports in 3ds Max are the windows into your scene. By default, there are four views: Front, Top, Left, and Perspective. The first three—Front, Top, and Left—are called orthographic views. They are also referred to as modeling windows. These windows are good for expressing exact dimensions and size relationships, so they are good tools for sizing up your scene objects and fine-tuning their layout. The default viewport layout has the four views, but this can be changed. The Viewport Layout tab bar, which is located at the lower-left corner of the interface, allows you to switch between many different viewport layout configurations with a single click. When you click the arrow button on the tab bar, the Standard Viewport Layouts menu gives you access to choose a layout. It will then be added to the tab bar for easy access, as shown in Figure 1.3.

FIGURE 1.3 Viewport Layout tab bar

The General Viewport label menus ([+]) in the upper-left corner of each viewport provide options for overall viewport display or activation, as shown in Figure 1.4. They also give you access to the Viewport Configuration dialog box.

FIGURE 1.4 Viewport label menus showing the General Viewport, Point-of-View, and Shading Viewport menus

The Perspective viewport displays objects in 3D space using perspective. Notice in Figure 1.2 how the distant objects seem to get smaller in the Perspective viewport. In actuality, they are the same size, as you can see in the orthographic viewports. The Perspective viewport gives you the best representation of what your output will be.

To make a viewport active, click in a blank part of the viewport (not on an object). If you do have something selected, it will be deselected when you click in the blank space.

When active, the view will have a mustard-yellow highlight around it. If you right-click in an already active viewport, you will get a pop-up context menu called the quad menu. You can use the quad menu to access some basic commands for a faster workflow. We will cover this topic in the section "Quad Menus" later in this chapter.

> ▶
> You can also right-click anywhere in an inactive viewport to activate it without selecting or deselecting anything.

ViewCube

The ViewCube® 3D navigation control, shown in Figure 1.5, provides visual feedback of the current orientation of a viewport; it lets you adjust the view orientation and allows you to switch between standard and isometric views.

Home button: Resets viewport
to Home view.

Using the left mouse button, you can
switch to one of the available preset
views or rotate the current view.

Compass indicates the north direction
for the scene. You can toggle the
compass display below the ViewCube
and specify its orientation with the
compass settings.

FIGURE 1.5 ViewCube navigation tool

The ViewCube is displayed by default in the upper-right corner of the active viewport; it is superimposed over the scene in an inactive state to show the orientation of the scene. When you position your cursor over the ViewCube, it becomes active. Using the left mouse button, you can switch to one of the available preset views, rotate the current view, or change to the Home view of the model. Right-clicking the ViewCube opens a context menu with additional options.

Mouse Buttons

Each of the three buttons on your mouse plays a slightly different role when manipulating viewports in the workspace. When used with modifiers such as the Alt key, they are used to navigate your scene, as shown in Figure 1.6.

Specialized quad menus become available
when you right-click with Shift or Ctrl or Alt
in any standard viewport.

Right mouse button
brings up the quad menu.

Left mouse button

Mouse wheel and middle mouse button (MMB).
Use wheel for zooming, MMB for pan,
Alt+MMB for orbit, and Ctrl+Alt+MMB for slow zoom.

FIGURE 1.6 Breakdown of the three mouse buttons

Quad Menus

When you click the right mouse button anywhere in an active viewport, except on the viewport labels and the ViewCube, a quad menu is displayed at the location of the mouse cursor, as shown in Figure 1.7. The quad menu can display up to four quadrant areas with various commands without your having to travel back and forth between the viewport and rollouts on the command panel (the area of the interface to the right—more on this later in the section "Command Panel").

Polygon quad menu   Display/Transform   Editable Spline
                      quad menu   quad menu

FIGURE 1.7 Quad menus

The right quadrant of the default quad menu displays generic commands, which are shared among all objects. The left quadrant contains context-specific commands, such as mesh tools and light commands. You can also repeat your last quad menu command by clicking the title of the quadrant.

The quad menu contents depend on what is selected. The menus are set up to display only the commands that are available for the current selection; therefore, selecting different types of objects displays different commands in the quadrants. Consequently, if no object is selected, all of the object-specific commands will be hidden. If all of the commands for one quadrant are hidden, the quadrant will not be displayed.

Cascading menus display submenus in the same manner as context menus. The menu item that contains submenus is highlighted when expanded. The submenus are highlighted when you move the mouse cursor over them.

To close the menu, right-click anywhere on the screen or move the mouse cursor away from the menu and click the left mouse button. To reselect the last-selected command, click in the title of the quadrant of the last menu item. The last menu item selected is highlighted when the quadrant is displayed.

Some of the selections in the quad menu have a small icon next to them. Clicking this icon opens a dialog box where you can set parameters for the command.

Display of Objects in a Viewport

Viewports can display your scene objects in a few ways. If you click the viewport's name, you can switch that panel to any other viewport angle or point of view. If you click the Shading Viewport label, a menu appears to allow you to change the display driver. The display driver names differ depending on the graphics drive mode you selected when you first start 3ds Max. This book uses the default display driver Nitrous.

Wireframe Mode   Wireframe mode displays the edges of the object, as shown on the left in Figure 1.8. It is the fastest to use because it requires less computation on your video card.

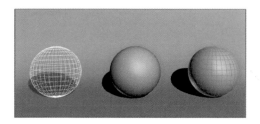

FIGURE 1.8   Viewport rendering options with the default Nitrous driver modes

Realistic Mode   Realistic mode is a shaded view in which the objects in the scene appear solid. It shows realistic textures with shading and lighting, as shown in the middle of Figure 1.8.

Edged Faces Mode   In Edged Faces mode the wireframe edges of selected objects appear along with the shaded surfaces, as shown on the right of Figure 1.8.

Each viewport displays a ground plane grid, called the *home grid*. The home grid represents one of three planes that intersect at right angles to one another at a common point called the origin; the coordinates are (0, 0, 0). It's defined by three fixed planes on the coordinate axes (X, Y, Z). The home grid is visible by default, but it can be turned on and off in the context General Viewport Label menu or by pressing the G key.

Selecting Objects in a Viewport

Click an object to select it in a viewport. If the object is displayed in Wireframe mode, its wireframe turns white while it is selected. If the object is displayed in a Realistic or Shaded mode, a white bracket appears around the object. This is set by default in the Perspective view; to toggle the selection brackets on and off use the keyboard shortcut J.

To select multiple objects, hold down the Ctrl key as you click additional objects to add to your selection. If you Alt+click an active object, you will deselect it. You can clear all your active selections by clicking in an empty area of the viewport.

Changing/Maximizing the Viewports

To change the view in any given viewport—for example, to go from a Perspective view to a Front view—click the current viewport's name. From the menu, select the view you want to have in the selected viewport. You can also use keyboard shortcuts. To switch from one view to another, press the appropriate key on the keyboard, as shown in Table 1.2.

TABLE 1.2 Viewport shortcuts

Viewport	Keyboard shortcut	Viewport	Keyboard shortcut
Top view	T	Bottom view	B
Front view	F	Left view	L
Camera view	C	Orthographic view	U
Perspective view	P		

You can also use the Alt+W keyboard shortcut to toggle between the maximized and four-viewport views.

If you want to have a larger view of the active viewport than is provided by the default four-viewport layout, click the Maximize Viewport Toggle icon () in the lower-right corner of the 3ds Max window.

Viewport Navigation

3ds Max allows you to move around its viewports by using either key/mouse combinations, which are highly preferable, or the viewport controls found in the lower-right corner of the 3ds Max UI. An example of navigation icons is shown for the Top viewport in Figure 1.9, although it's best to become familiar with the key/mouse combinations.

FIGURE 1.9 The viewport navigation controls are handy, but the key/mouse combinations are much faster to use for navigation in viewports.

Open a new, empty scene in 3ds Max. Experiment with the following controls to get a feel for moving around in 3D space. If you are new to 3D, using these controls may seem odd at first, but it will become easier as you gain experience and should become second nature in no time.

Pan   Panning a viewport slides the view around the screen. Using the middle mouse button (MMB), click in the viewport and drag the mouse pointer to pan the view.

Zoom   Zooming moves your view closer to or farther away from your objects. To zoom, press Ctrl+Alt and MMB+click in your viewport and then drag the mouse up or down to zoom in or out. The zoom will occur around the cursor location. You may also use the scroll wheel to zoom.

Orbit   Orbit will rotate your view around your objects. To orbit, press Alt and MMB+click and drag in the viewport. By default, 3ds Max will rotate about the center of the viewport.

Transforming Objects Using Gizmos

The Transform gizmos are viewport icons that let you quickly choose the axes when moving, rotating, or scaling an object. Using gizmos is a fast and effective way to transform your objects with interactive feedback. When you select a transform tool such as Select And Move, a gizmo appears on the selected object. Gizmos let you manipulate objects in your viewports interactively to transform them. Coordinate display boxes at the bottom of the screen display coordinate, angular, or percentage information on the position, rotation, and scale of your object as you transform it. The gizmos appear in the viewport on the selected object at their pivot point as soon as you invoke one of the transform tools, as shown in Figure 1.10.

The ViewCube will not display in a viewport that has been switched to a Camera or Light viewport.

Certification
Objective

Move gizmo: Use a colored handle to move in just that axis.

Rotate gizmo: Use the colored rings to rotate about a single axis. Use the center to rotate freely.

Scale gizmo: Drag in the center gizmo to scale uniformly. To perform nonuniform scaling, drag on a colored handle.

FIGURE 1.10   Gizmos for the transform tools

You can select the transform tools by clicking the icons in the main toolbar's Transform toolset ( ) or by invoking shortcut keys:

W for Select And Move

E for Select And Rotate

R for Select And Scale

In a new scene, to create a sphere, go to the menu bar at the top of the interface and choose Create ➤ Geometry ➤ Standard Primitives ➤ Sphere. Then in the perspective viewport, click and drag to create the Sphere object. Follow along as we explain the transform tools next.

Select And Move   Invoke the Select And Move tool by pressing W (or accessing it through the main toolbar), and your gizmo should look like the top image in Figure 1.10. Dragging the X-, Y-, or Z-axis handle moves an object on a specific axis. You can also click the plane handle, the box between two axes, to move the object in that two-axis plane.

Select And Rotate   Invoke the Select And Rotate tool by pressing E, and your gizmo will turn into three circles, as shown in the middle image in Figure 1.10. You can click one of the colored circles to rotate the object on the axis only, or you can click anywhere between the circles to freely rotate the selected object in all three axes.

Select And Scale   Invoke the Select And Scale tool by pressing the R key, and your gizmo will turn into a triangle, as shown in the bottom image of Figure 1.10. Clicking and dragging anywhere inside the yellow triangle will scale the object uniformly on all three axes. By selecting the red, green, or blue handle for the appropriate axis, you can scale along one axis only. You can also scale an object on a plane between two axes by selecting the side of the yellow triangle between two axes.

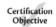

The transform tools, which are called Select And Move/Rotate/Scale, will be just called the Move, Rotate, and Scale tools in this book.

Graphite Modeling Tools Set

The ribbon interface is a toolbar containing these tabs: Modeling, Freeform, Selection, Object Paint, and Populate. Each tab comprises a number of panels and tools whose availability depends on the context. The ribbon can be oriented horizontally or vertically. The default for the ribbon is horizontal, as shown earlier in Figure 1.2. The ribbon contains additional tools for creating, selecting, and editing geometry. The Freeform tab allows for polygon painting within the viewport for modifying the polygon surface. The Selection tab contains additional tools for making selections at a sub-object level. The Object Paint tab enables you to paint objects freehand anywhere in the scene or onto specific object surfaces. The Populate tab has tools for adding animated characters quickly and easily.

Certification
Objective

Graphite Modeling Tool Set

Modeling Tab   Ribbon

FIGURE 1.11   The Modeling tab found in the ribbon

The Modeling tab, shown in Figure 1.11, provides you with a wide range of modeling tools to make building and editing models in 3ds Max fast and easy. All the available tools are organized into separate panels for convenient access:

- ▶ Polygon Modeling
- ▶ Edit
- ▶ Modify Selection
- ▶ Geometry (All)
- ▶ Subdivision
- ▶ Align
- ▶ Properties

One easy way to customize the ribbon is by using the Min/Max toggle switch, as shown in Figure 1.12. By clicking the button, you toggle the minimum/maximum options; when you maximize the ribbon, you are able to view most of the controls. The Minimize drop-down list, which is the small arrow next to the Min/Max toggle switch, gives access to different ribbon states.

— Min/Max toggle switch
— Minimize drop-down list

FIGURE 1.12   The Min/Max toggle for the Graphite Modeling Tools set

Command Panel

Certification
Objective

Everything you need to create, manipulate, and animate objects can be found in the command panel running vertically on the right side of the UI (Figure 1.2). The command panel is divided into tabs according to function. The function or toolset you need to access will determine which tab you need to click. When you encounter a panel that is longer than your screen, 3ds Max displays a thin vertical scroll bar on the right side. Your cursor also turns into a hand you can use to click and drag the panel up and down.

You will be exposed to more panels as you progress through this book. Table 1.3 is a rundown of the command panel functions and what they do.

TABLE 1.3   Command panel functions

Icon	Name	Function
✳	Create panel	Create objects, lights, cameras, etc.
◪	Modify panel	Applies modifiers to objects and edits object parameters.

(Continues)

TABLE 1.3 *(Continued)*

Icon	Name	Function
	Hierarchy panel	Adjust the hierarchy for objects and adjust their pivot points
	Motion panel	Access animation tools and functions
	Display panel	Access display options for scene objects
	Utilities panel	Access several functions of 3ds Max, such as motion capture utilities and the Asset Browser

Object Parameters and Values

The command panel and all its tabs give you access to an object's parameters. Parameters are the values that define a specific attribute of or for an object. For example, when an object is selected in a viewport, its parameters are shown in the Modify panel, where you can adjust them. When you create an object, that object's creation parameters are shown (and editable) in the Create panel.

Modifier Stack

In the Modify panel you'll find the modifier stack, as shown in Figure 1.13. This UI element lists all the modifiers that are active on any selected object. Modifiers are actions applied to an object that change it somehow, such as bending or warping. You can stack modifiers on top of each other when creating an object and then go back and edit any of the modifiers in the stack (for the most part) to adjust the object at any point in its creation. You will see this in practice in the following chapters.

Modifier Stack

FIGURE 1.13 The modifier stack in the Modify panel

Objects and Sub-objects

To edit a sub-object, you have to convert it to an editable poly object, which you will learn how to do in the following chapters.

An object or mesh in 3ds Max is composed of polygons that define the surface. For example, the facets or small rectangles on a sphere are *polygons*, all connected at common edges at the correct angles and in the proper arrangement to make a sphere. The points that generate a polygon are called *vertices*. The lines that connect the points are called *edges*. Polygons, vertices, and edges are examples of sub-objects and are all editable so that you can fashion any sort of surface or mesh shape you wish.

Time Slider and Track Bar

Certification
Objective

Running across the bottom of the 3ds Max UI are the time slider and the track bar, as shown earlier in Figure 1.2. The time slider allows you to move through any frame in your scene by scrubbing (moving the slider back and forth). You can move through your animation one frame at a time by clicking the previous frame and next frame arrows on either side of the time slider or by pressing the shortcut keys.

You can also use the time slider to animate objects by setting keyframes, which are frames in which the animator creates a pose for a character (or whatever is being animated). With an object selected, right-click the time slider to open the Create Key dialog box, which allows you to create transform keyframes for the selected object. The track bar is directly below the time slider. The track bar is the timeline that displays the timeline format for your scene. More often than not, the track bar is displayed in frames, with the gap between each tick mark representing frames. On the track bar, you can move and edit your animation properties for the selected object. When a keyframe is present, right-click it to open a context menu where you can delete keyframes, edit individual transform values, and filter the track bar display.

The Animation Playback controls in the lower right of the 3ds Max UI ( ) are similar to the ones you would find on a VCR (how old are you?) or DVD player.

File Management

Certification
Objective

Different kinds of files are saved in categorized folders under the project folder. For example, scene files are saved in a scenes folder and rendered images are saved in a renderoutput folder within the project folder. The projects are set up according to what types of files you are working on, so everything is neat and organized from the get-go.

The conventions followed in this book and on the accompanying web page (www.sybex.com/go/3dsmax2015essentials) follow this project-based system so that you can grow accustomed to it and make it a part of your own workflow. It pays to stay organized.

Setting a Project

The exercises in this book are organized into specific projects based on chapters, such as the c02_First Project that you will tackle in the next chapter. The c02_First Project should be on your hard drive or where ever you choose to store the files, and the folders for your scene files and rendered images will be in that project layout. Once you copy the appropriate projects to your hard drive, you can tell 3ds Max which project to work on by clicking the Application button and choosing Manage ➤ Set Project Folder. Doing so will send the current project to that project folder. For example, when you save your scene, 3ds Max will automatically take you to the scenes folder of the current project.

For example, if you are working on a project about a castle, begin by setting a new project called Castle. Click the Application button and choose Manage ➤ Set Project Folder, as shown in Figure 1.14. In the dialog box that opens, click Make New Folder to create a folder named Castle on your hard drive. 3ds Max will automatically create the project and its folders.

Designating a specific place on your PC or server for all your project files is important, as is having an established naming convention for the project's files and folder.

FIGURE 1.14 Choosing Set Project Folder

Once you save a scene, one of your scene filenames may look like this: c02_ex3_body_v01.max. This tells you right away it's a scene from Chapter 2, exercise 3, and that it is version 1 of the model of the body.

Version Up!

After you've spent a significant amount of time working on your scene, you will want to *version up*. This means you save your file using the same name, but you increase the version number by 1. Saving often and using version numbers are useful for keeping track of your progress and protecting yourself from mistakes and from losing your work.

To version up, you can save by clicking the Application button, choosing Save As, and manually changing the version number appended to the end of the filename. 3ds Max also lets you do this automatically by using an increment feature in the Save As dialog box. Name your scene file and click the Increment button (the + icon) to the right of the File Name input field. Clicking the Increment button appends the filename with 01, then 02, then 03, and so on as you keep saving your work using Save As and the Increment button.

NOW YOU KNOW

In this chapter, you learned the basic operation of the 3D workspace and user interface, starting with a tour of the UI and getting initial experience manipulating an object using 3ds Max Transform gizmos. Then you saw how to access the Graphite Modeling Tools set and how to control your scene with the command panel. Next, you learned how the time slider and track bar work, and lastly, you saw how to best manage files for a clean workflow using projects.

As you continue with the following chapters, you will gain experience and confidence with the UI, and many of the features that seem daunting to you now will become second nature. Meanwhile, use this chapter as a reference to help you navigate the UI as you progress in your knowledge of the 3ds Max workflow.

CHAPTER 2

Your First 3ds Max Project

In production work, setting down a plan and having clear goals for your project is very important. Without a good idea of where you need to go, you'll end up floundering and losing out on the whole experience. In any project, the beginning of the workflow starts with modeling.

Modeling in 3D programs is like sculpting or carpentry; you create objects out of shapes and forms. Even a complex model is just an amalgam of simpler parts or shapes/volumes. The successful modeler can dissect a form down to its components and translate them into surfaces and meshes. The Autodesk® 3ds Max® modeling tools are incredibly strong for polygonal modeling, so the focus of the modeling in this book is on polygonal modeling. In this chapter, you will learn modeling concepts and how to use 3ds Max modeling toolsets.

In this chapter, you will learn to:

▶ **Set up a project workflow**

▶ **Model accurately using reference material**

▶ **Build a simple model**

▶ **Create details using splines**

▶ **Create 3D from 2D using lathing, extruding, and beveling**

Set Up a Project Workflow

Certification
Objective

You will begin by modeling a clock body to develop your modeling muscles. This exercise introduces you to primitives and polygons. You will be modeling by editing the polygon component; it's called *editable-poly* modeling. Why buy a clock when you can just make one using 3ds Max tools?

Exercise 2.1: How to Set a Project

Download the c02_First Project, c02_First Project.zip, from the book's web page at www.sybex.com/go/3dsmax2015essentials. Place the files on your hard drive. Open the 3ds Max 2015 program and set a 3ds Max project. Choose the c02_First Project folder from your hard drive, flash, or network drive and follow these steps:

1. Set your project folder to the c02_First Project you just downloaded (click the Application button ( ) and choose Manage ➢ Set Project Folder).

2. Navigate to the place on the hard drive where you saved the book projects.

3. Click c02_First Project, and then click OK.

Now when you want to open a scene file, just click the Application button and choose Open, and you will automatically be in the c02_First Project scenes folder.

The Secret to Accurate Modeling: Reference Material!

Using reference materials will help you efficiently create your 3D model and achieve a good likeness in your end result. The temptation to just wing it and start building the objects is strong, especially when time is short and you're raring to go. You should always suppress this temptation in deference to a well-thought-out approach to the task. Sketches, photographs, and drawings can all be used as resources for the modeling process. Not only are references useful for giving you a clear direction in which to head, but you can also use references directly in 3ds Max to help you model. Photos, especially those taken from different sides of the intended model, can be added to a scene as background images to help you shape your model.

Go to the c02_First Project folder on your hard drive; in the sceneassets/ images subfolder you will see some additional reference images of the clock. These sample reference images will give you an idea of what kind of images will be useful for a project like the clock. Of course, if this were your clock, you would have captured tons of pictures already, right?

You're so close to modeling something! You'll want to get some sort of reference for what you're modeling. Study the photo in Figure 2.1 for the model.

FIGURE 2.1 The clock to be modeled

Exercise 2.2: Setting Up the Modeling Reference

For the best in modeling references, bring in photos of your model and use the *crossing boxes* technique, which involves placing the reference images on crossing plane objects or thin boxes in the scene.

To begin the clock body, start with a new 3ds Max file:

1. Open a new 3ds Max file by clicking the Application button (⬛) and choosing New. This clears the contents of the current scene without changing any of the system settings.

2. On the Create tab (⬛), click the Geometry icon (⬛), and in the Object Type drop-down menu, click the Plane button.

3. Make sure the Front viewport is selected by right-clicking it. This will align the plane to that viewport when it is created.

4. In the plane primitive parameters, expand the Keyboard Entry rollout.

5. Change the value in the X Position Type-In box to 0.0, the Y box to -3.0, and the Z box to 0.0, as shown in Figure 2.2. This will place the plane 5 units away from the center of the scene along the Y-axis.

FIGURE 2.2 Position and Length/Width Type-Ins in the plane Keyboard Entry rollout

6. Change Length value to **10** and the Width value to **10**, and then click the Create button (Create). This creates the image plane in the Front viewport, which you will use for the front view image plane.

7. Change the name of the Plane001 object to **Front View Image**.

8. Now right-click the Left viewport to activate it. Back in the Standard Primitives drop-down menu, select the Plane button, if it is not already active from the previous steps. Expand the Keyboard Entry rollout.

9. Change the X Position Type-In to **0.0**, Y to **0.0**, and Z to **0.0**. This will move the plane to the center and help with the alignment of the images when they are in place.

10. Change the Length parameter in the Keyboard Entry to **10** and the Width parameter to **10**, if they are not already set that way. The parameters will stay set from the previous plane that was created.

11. Click the Create button in the Keyboard Entry rollout.

12. Rename the Plane001 object **Side View Image**.

13. Go to the Viewport Label menus at the top left of the Left viewport. Click the Shading viewport label menu and choose Shaded, as shown in Figure 2.3.

> When you have an object selected, its name appears at the top of the command panel. It is a type-in that you can use to rename your object. To the right of the type-in is a small color box. Select the box and you can choose a color for your object.

> This menu lets you choose how objects are displayed in the viewport. You can also use the keyboard shortcut F3, which toggles between Shaded and Wireframe.

FIGURE 2.3 Shading viewport label menu

14. Do the same for the Front viewport.

15. Open a Windows Explorer window; navigate to the sceneassets\images folder in the c02_First Project folder that you downloaded to your hard drive. In this folder, you will find two reference JPEG images, one for each of the two image planes you just created in the scene.

16. Select the front view reference image called Front.jpg, drag it into the Front viewport, and then drop it onto the Front View Image plane. This automatically places the image onto the plane, so the image is viewable in the viewport.

17. Repeat the previous step to place the Side.jpg image onto the Side View Image plane in the Left viewport. Figure 2.4 shows the image planes with the reference images applied.

Use the Zoom Extents All tool on all the viewports by pressing the shortcut Ctrl+Shift+Z, or you can use the viewport navigation tool, Zoom Extents All. You may have to click and hold the icon to access the flyout, and then choose the desired tool.

FIGURE 2.4 The image planes with the clock images applied

18. To finish, click the Application button ( ) and choose Save As. Save the file; to check the progress of your work against our example, you can open c02_ex2_ref_end.max.

Building a Simple Model

Certification
Objective

When modeling any object, it is always best to study the object and break it up into smaller, easier-to-model components. To begin modeling the clock body, you will start with a cylinder because the clock body has a cylindrical shape as its base.

Exercise 2.3: Start with a Primitive

For this procedure, either continue with a file from a previous exercise or use the c02_ex3_body_start.max file. Follow these steps:

1. Select the Front viewport, which should still be set to Shaded display mode, from the previous steps.

2. Enable Edged Faces mode in the viewport by using the keyboard shortcut F4, if it isn't already set. Edged Faces places the wireframe over the shaded object, making the object easier to see when modeling.

3. Right-click the Front viewport to make it the active viewport. This will align the cylinder to the Front viewport when it is created.

4. In the command panel, choose the Create tab, click the Geometry icon, and make sure Standard Primitives is selected.

5. In the Object Type rollout, click Cylinder, and select the Keyboard Entry rollout to expand the parameters.

6. Leave the X, Y, and Z values at 0, but enter **5.0** for Radius and **–5.0** for Height, and then click the Create button.

7. Open the Modify panel (); this is where you go to edit the parameters of an object.

8. Change Height Segments to **1** and Sides to **30**; then press Enter on your keyboard to set the new parameter. Leave all the remaining parameters at the default.

9. To turn on See-Through mode, use the keyboard shortcut Alt+X. See-Through mode will ghost out the cylinder and allow you to see through it to the image planes.

Save the file and to check the progress of your work against our example, open c02_ex3_body_end.max.

> Alternatively, you could select Cylinder from the Create panel, and in the Front viewport click and drag to create the cylinder, eyeballing the size from the Front and Left viewports.

Exercise 2.4: Modeling in Sub-Object Mode

To start the process of modeling the clock, you need to access the cylinder's components. All 3D objects are at their core made up of three main components: vertices, edges, and polygons. These components are the basis of polygon modeling. To access the components of any object, you need to convert it to an editable poly, which means a polygon that allows access to the components. There are many ways to do this; we will be using the Graphite Modeling Tools set, also called the *ribbon*. For this procedure, use the c02_ex4_body_start.max file or the file that you saved in the previous section. Follow these steps:

1. Select the cylinder; go to the Ribbon ➤ Modeling tab ➤ Polygon Modeling select the Convert to Poly button, as shown in Figure 2.5.

FIGURE 2.5 Converting the cylinder to an editable poly

2. Turn on Edged Faces in the Front, Left, and Perspective viewports using the keyboard shortcut F4, if it isn't already enabled. This will allow you to see the wireframe while modeling.

3. Select the Polygon icon (▮) or press 4 on the keyboard to enter the Polygon sub-object mode.

4. In the Perspective viewport, orbit around the cylinder so you can see the back end. Do this by clicking and dragging on any part of the ViewCube, which is the icon in the upper right of the viewport. If the Front View Image is in the way, select it, and then right-click it and choose Hide Selected.

All the editable polygons have keyboard shortcuts to quickly navigate through the sub-object levels. Vertex level is 1, Edge is 2, Border is 3, Polygon is 4, Element is 5, and Ctrl+B returns you to object level.

5. Then select the back-end polygon. The polygon is shaded red to indicate it is selected, as shown in Figure 2.6. (Front viewport image plane is hidden in the figure.)

FIGURE 2.6 Select the back polygon of the cylinder; it is shaded red when selected.

6. In the Ribbon ➢ Modeling tab, go to the Polygons panel and click Outline. Click the arrow under the Outline button, and then select Outline Settings. This will open the Outline caddy, which is a dialog box to input your outline parameters.

7. Change Outline Amount to –0.75, and click the OK button (). This will scale the selected polygon smaller. Look at the cylinder in the Left viewport. You will see that end of the cylinder now fits that end of the clock on the image plane.

The SwiftLoop tool places new edges that loop around the cylinder, which subdivides the sides. The subdivisions will allow for greater control of the details to be added.

8. In the Ribbon ➢ Modeling tab, go to the Edit panel and select the SwiftLoop tool. You will add three new subdivisions, or loops, on the cylinder. To add the loops, just move your cursor over the part of the cylinder and you will see a preview loop. When the preview is where you want it, just click, and the new loop will be created.

9. View the cylinder in the Left viewport; place the loops at the positions shown in Figure 2.7. With the new loops (or edge loops) in place, you will now edit them to change the profile of the cylinder to match the clock body.

Place the
loops here.

FIGURE 2.7 Using the SwiftLoop tool, place three loops as shown.

10. In the Ribbon ➤ Modeling tab ➤ Modeling, select Edge mode (keyboard shortcut 2). When you select Edge mode, the last loop you created will be selected. If it is not selected, continue with the steps 11 and 12; if it is selected, skip to step 13.

11. Select one of the edges toward the top of the cylinder; only a single edge will be selected, not the entire loop.

12. On the Modify Selection tab of the Ribbon ➤ Modeling tab, select Loop. This will continue the selection around the cylinder. For a shortcut for the Loop tool, double-click an edge and the loop will be competed.

13. Move your cursor to the main toolbar and select the Scale tool ( ). The keyboard shortcut is R.

14. The triangle in the center of the Scale gizmo will turn yellow when active. Scale the edges up until they match the detail in the Left viewport image plane.

15. Repeat steps 11 through 14 on the other new edge loops until the cylinder matches Figure 2.8. Don't worry if it doesn't match up perfectly with the image.

FIGURE 2.8   Edges are scaled to match the image plane.

16. This is a good time to save your file. Choose Save from the Application menu. You will use this file in the next section.

Save the file and to check the progress of your work against our example, open `c02_ex4_body_end.max`.

ORBITING IN THE VIEWPORTS

Orbiting in the viewports is a skill, and the faster you learn the many ways you can do it, the more efficient you will be as a 3D artist. You can orbit using the Orbit tool ( ), which is one of the viewport navigation tools found at the lower right of the interface. Drag the mouse on or around a view rotation "trackball," which is displayed as a yellow circle with handles placed at the quadrant points. An alternative way to orbit is to use the ViewCube. It is a great way to orbit within the viewports. Simply move your cursor to the ViewCube icon in the upper-right portion of the viewport and click+drag to rotate the current viewport. You can also use one of the preset views on the ViewCube to switch a viewport to front, back, left, right, top, or bottom. Another way to orbit is to use the keyboard/mouse shortcut Alt+MMB and drag in the viewport. As the user, you need to decide which method works best for you.

Exercise 2.5: Bring on the Bevel

Now you will add detail to the front of the clock. On the Clock object there is a small edge and a depression where the clock face and hands sit. To create this edge in the cylinder, you will use the Bevel tool. Beveling involves first extruding polygons and then scaling the extruded polygons with the Outline tool. The Bevel tool has three parameters:

Bevel Type   Controls how to extrude multiple polygons at once.

Height   Specifies how much extrusion to apply, based on units.

Outline Amount   Scales the outer border of the selected polygons, depending on whether the value is positive or negative.

For the Clock object the Bevel tool creates many of the details of the body. It allows you to create a rough model that you can refine with further tools. For this procedure, use the c02_ex5_body_start.max file or the file that you saved in the previous section. Follow these steps:

1. Select the Polygon icon (▢), or use the keyboard shortcut 4 to enter the Polygon sub-object mode.

2. Select the front face of the cylinder.

3. On the Polygons panel in the ribbon, click the arrow next to the Bevel button. Then select Bevel Settings, as shown in Figure 2.9. This will open the Bevel caddy, which is a dialog box for inputting your bevel parameters.

FIGURE 2.9 Bevel Settings will bring up the caddy for parameter input.

4. In the Bevel caddy, enter the 0.0 in the Height text box, and then press Enter on your keyboard.

5. Enter −0.25 in the Outline text box and press Enter again.

6. Click the Apply and Continue button (⊕). This applies the specified settings without closing the caddy.

7. Now change the Bevel caddy parameters. Enter −1.0 in the Height box, press Enter, enter 0.0 in the Outline box, press Enter again, and then click the OK button.

The detail that you just created will be the part of the clock body where the clock face will sit. Figure 2.10 shows the clock the way it looks with the changes, shown with image planes hidden and See-Through mode turned off.

Save your file; to check the progress of your work open c02_ex5_body_end.max.

FIGURE 2.10 Clock body progress

ACCESSING MODELING TOOLS

Using the ribbon is a convenient way to access modeling tools, but it isn't the only way. In most software packages, when new tools are added, the older versions of those tools aren't removed; in previous versions of the software, all poly modeling tools were accessed through the Modify panel. Many of the same buttons and functionality can still be found in the Modify panel. You can also right-click an object to access the quad menu. The quad menu allows you to find and activate most commands without having to travel back and forth between the viewport and rollouts on the command panel or main toolbar. In this book we will be using the Graphite Modeling Tools set (the ribbon) to access the modeling tools.

Exercise 2.6: Chamfer Time

Chamfering refers to the rounding of sharp edges or corners. For the clock, the new details on the sides are too sharp. You will be using the Chamfer tool in Edge mode. For this section, you will turn off See-Through mode and hide the image planes. Use the c02_ex6_body_start.max file or the file that you saved in the previous section, and follow these steps:

1. Select the clock body; then turn off See-Through mode, using the keyboard shortcut Alt+X. To hide the image planes, you will enter Isolate Selection mode. At the bottom of the interface, below the timeline, is an icon of a light bulb ( ). The keyboard shortcut is Alt+Q.

2. Either click the icon or use the shortcut to hide all but what is selected.

3. In the ribbon, open the Polygon Modeling panel and select Edge mode (keyboard shortcut 2).

4. Select the edge shown in Figure 2.11.

FIGURE 2.11 Select the edge shown in this image.

5. In the Ribbon ➤ Modeling tab ➤ Modify Selection, select Loop. This will select the entire edge loop (or use the shortcut, which is to double-click the edge you want to loop).

6. In the main toolbar, click the Select and Move tool ( ). The keyboard shortcut is W.

7. Move the edges back toward the beveled surface, as shown in Figure 2.12.

FIGURE 2.12   Move the edges back.

8. Exit Edge mode by selecting the Ribbon ➤ Modeling tab ➤ Polygon Modeling ➤ Edge (or use the keyboard shortcut 6). This will take you to the top level and out of sub-object mode. Now you want to turn See-Through mode back on.

9. Select the clock body, and use the keyboard shortcut Alt+X to turn on See-Through mode.

10. To exit Isolate Selection mode select the light bulb icon at the bottom of the interface. The image planes will reappear.

11. On the Polygon Modeling panel in the modeling ribbon, select Edge mode (keyboard shortcut 2).

12. Looking in the Left viewport, select and loop the middle edge, as shown in Figure 2.13 (the Ribbon ➤ Modeling tab ➤ Modeling ➤ Modify Selection ➤ Loop), to select the entire edge loop.

FIGURE 2.13 Select and loop the edge to prepare for chamfer.

13. Go to the Ribbon ≻ Modeling tab ≻ Edges ≻ Chamfer, and click the arrow under the Chamfer button; then select Chamfer Settings. This will open the Chamfer caddy.

14. To Create the smooth curve from the sharp edges input 0.25 for Edge Chamfer Amount (don't forget to press Enter on keyboard!) and 4 for Connect Edge Segments, and again press Enter.

15. Then click OK (). The results are shown in Figure 2.14.

Select and loop this edge.

FIGURE 2.14 The chamfer performed on a looped edge

The chamfer will be repeated several times on different edges with different Chamfer parameters to achieve the correct smoothness for each curve.

16. On the front face of the clock, select an edge on the lip (where the clock face will be). Then hold the Ctrl key and select three more edges going toward the back of the clock, as shown in Figure 2.15 (which has See-Through mode turned off with shortcut Alt+X).

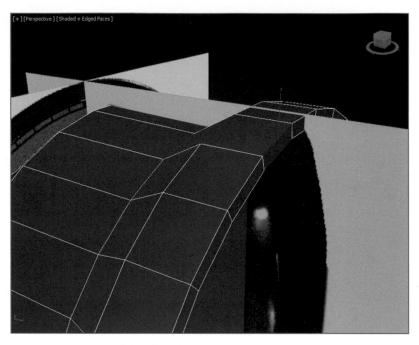

FIGURE 2.15   Select these four edges.

17. Loop the edges (the Ribbon ➢ Modeling tab ➢ Modify Selection ➢ Loop).

18. Go to the Ribbon ➢ Modeling tab ➢ Edges ➢ Chamfer, and click the arrow under the Chamfer button; then select Chamfer Settings. This will open the Chamfer caddy.

19. To create the smooth curve from the sharp edges, enter **0.05** in the Edge Chamfer Amount text box, and press Enter; then enter **2** in the Connect Edge Segments box and press Enter again.

20. Click OK (⊘). The results are shown in Figure 2.16. The back side of the clock needs some special attention; its detail is a bit more intricate. First, another SwiftLoop needs to be added, and then both edges need to be chamfered. Make sure you are still in Edge mode. If you are not, select Edge or the use the keyboard shortcut 2.

FIGURE 2.16 Chamfer result for the clock body's edge and lip.

21. In the Ribbon ➢ Modeling tab ➢ Edit, and select the SwiftLoop tool.

22. Add a SwiftLoop between the back edge of the clock and the loop that was added earlier, as shown in Figure 2.17.

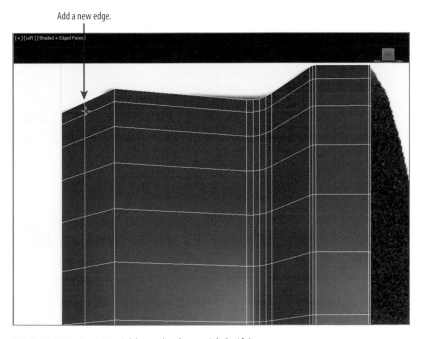

FIGURE 2.17 Add an edge loop with SwiftLoop.

23. In the main toolbar, select the Select and Uniform Scale tool (R), and scale down the edge loop until it matches the size in the image plane.

24. Hold down Ctrl and click one of the edges to the right of the new edge you just created.

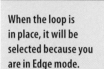

When the loop is in place, it will be selected because you are in Edge mode.

25. Select the Ribbon ➤ Modeling tab ➤ Modify Selection panel ➤ Loop; this will select that loop also.

26. Select the Ribbon ➤ Modeling tab ➤ Edges panel ➤ Chamfer. Click the arrow under the Chamfer button, and then select Chamfer Settings; this will open the Chamfer caddy.

27. Enter 0.1 in the Edge Chamfer Amount text box and 3 in the Connect Edge Segments box. Then click OK; the results are shown in Figure 2.18.

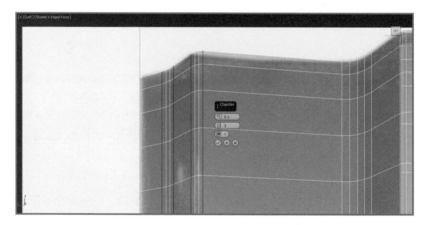

FIGURE 2.18   The two edge loops chamfered

28. To finish this section, select the cylinder and change the name to Clock Body.

29. Toggle See-Through mode off (Alt+X).

30. Save your file, and to check your progress open `c02_ex6_body_end.max`.

Creating Details Using Splines

Certification
Objective

Now that the clock body is complete, it's time to move on to some of the clock parts. The parts that will be covered in this section are the handle, the hands, and the bell. To create these objects, you will learn a modeling technique called *spline modeling.* In computer graphics, a *spline* is a group of vertices and connecting segments that form a line or curve. Splines are used to create more complex geometry than can be found in the primitives available in 3ds Max. The first clock part that you will create is the clock handle, shown in Figure 2.19.

FIGURE 2.19   The clock handle

Exercise 2.7: Building the Handle

Follow these steps:

1. Open c02_ex7_handle_start.max from the scenes folder of the Clock project on this book's companion web page. This file has a full image of the front of the clock, loaded onto an image plane.

2. Start by accessing the Create panel (   ), and choose the second icon from the row of icons, Shapes (   ), and from there choose Line. The following apply when you use the Line tool:

    ▶ A single click in a viewport creates a point with a linear segment.

    ▶ A click and drag creates a curved segment when you let go of the mouse.

    ▶ Holding the Shift key will constrain your movement to 90-degree angles; this can be very helpful in creating straight lines.

    ▶ A right-click exits the Line command.

    Creating a line using this method can be difficult; it is easier to start with a simple shape and add more detail later. Figure 2.20 shows a simplified line that represents the clock handle.

First Vertex

Last Vertex
Right-click to exit the Line command.

FIGURE 2.20   **The intended cross section for the clock handle.**

3. In the Front viewport, click to set a vertex and let go (refer to the first vertex in Figure 2.20).

4. Continue to click and move, following the handle around until you reach the seventh vertex; then right-click to exit the Line command. Now that the rough line is finished, it needs to be smoothed out and refined.

5. With the line selected, in the Modify panel's modifier stack, click the plus sign (+) to expand the list of sub-objects.

6. Select Vertex, as shown in Figure 2.21.

FIGURE 2.21   **From the three sub-objects of the Line command, select Vertex.**

7. In the Front viewport, right-click the middle vertex.

8. In the upper-left quadrant of the quad menu, choose Bezier, as shown in Figure 2.22.

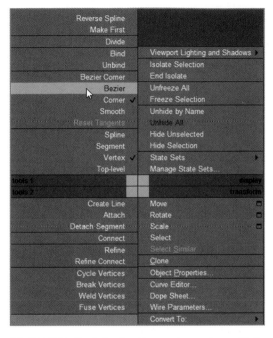

FIGURE 2.22 Use the quad menu to modify the vertex type.

VERTEX TYPES

When working on splines, you may want to change the vertex type:

Smooth   Has a smooth continuous curve without tangent handles to edit

Corner   Has sharp corners without tangent handles to edit

Bezier   Has adjustable tangent handles that are locked

Bezier Corner   Has adjustable tangent handles that are unlocked or broken and can adjust the curve entering and exiting the vertex independently

There are now tangent handles coming from the vertex; the tangent handles control the amount of curve in the line. Tangents are edited using the Move tool.

9. Choose the Select and Move tool (W), and then grab one of the green boxes on either side of the vertex at the end of the tangent handle, and move it until the curve matches the handle in the image plane.

10. Right-click the selected vertices and change their vertex type to Bezier.

11. Adjust the tangent handles to smooth out the remaining vertices on the spline except the first and last, as shown in Figure 2.23.

Moving the handle up or down moves the segment attached to the handle in the same direction. Moving the handle closer to the vertex creates a tighter curve, and moving it farther away creates a looser curve.

FIGURE 2.23   The line for the handle with all but the first and last vertices adjusted

12. In the Rendering rollout in the Modify panel, check the boxes Enable In Renderer and Enable In Viewport.

13. Change Thickness to 0.35 and leave the rest at the default, as shown in Figure 2.24.

The Rendering rollout parameters control the renderability of the line, allowing you to specify thickness in the viewports and the rendered scene. The default is Radial, which creates a cylindrical object along the path of the handle.

FIGURE 2.24   Rendering enabled on the clock handle line, set to Radial

14. Use See-Through mode (Alt+X) to ghost out the handle model; this will allow you to see the clock on the image plane.

15. In the Ribbon ➢ Modeling tab, open the Polygon Modeling panel and choose Convert to Poly. This will keep the radial thickness and allow for component manipulations.

16. Click the Select Object tool () (Q) and switch to Vertex mode. The handle has the correct shape, but the area where the handle is between the bell and the bolt needs to be scaled down.

17. To make this simpler, in the main toolbar, click and hold down the Rectangular Selection Region tool; this will bring up a flyout.

18. Choose the Fence Selection Region, as shown in Figure 2.25.

FIGURE 2.25 On the Selection Region flyout, choose the Fence Selection Region.

19. Drag a custom selection from the end of the handle line past the seventh row of vertices, as shown in Figure 2.26. To close the selection, click the part of the selection where you started.

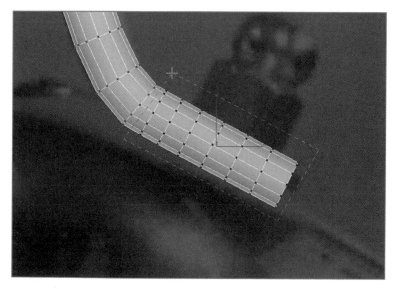

FIGURE 2.26 Use the Fence Selection Region to draw a selection around the desired vertices.

20. Select the Select and Scale tool (R). In the main toolbar, to the right of the Scale tool is the Reference Coordinate System drop-down menu.

21. Click the arrow and choose Local from the list.

22. Move your cursor over the Y-axis of the Scale gizmo. Scale the vertices down until they match the image.

23. Continue selecting and scaling vertices until they match the image. Use the Select and Move tool if necessary.

24. Exit Vertex mode and then repeat the same process on the left side of the handle, as shown in Figure 2.27. When finished, name the object **Handle**.

FIGURE 2.27   The finished handle

25. Time to save the file, but this time choose Save As and name the file Clock_Handle_End.max. To check your progress, open c02_ex7_handle_end.max.

UNDERSTANDING THE 3D COORDINATE SYSTEMS

A 3D environment is defined in terms of 3D Cartesian coordinates. In 3ds Max, the main coordinate space is used to describe the scene as a whole and is known as the coordinate system. To scale the vertices correctly, you need to change the coordinate system. By default, 3ds Max uses the View hybrid coordinate system. In the View coordinate system, all orthographic views use the Screen coordinate system, while perspective views use the World coordinate system. That is all fine and good, but it won't work for vertex selection. To allow for the proper gizmo orientation for the scale, change the coordinate system to Local, which defines the coordinates of the object or sub-object's local center.

Lathing, Extruding, and Beveling to Create 3D from 2D

Now that the body of the clock and the handle are done, it's time to make the bells. You will use splines and a few surface creation tools that are new to your workflow. You are going to create a profile of the bell and then rotate the profile around its axis to form a surface. This technique is known as *lathe*, not to be mistaken for *latte*, which is a whole different deal and not covered in this book.

Exercise 2.8: Lathe to Make a Whole

Open c02_ex8_bell_start.max from the scenes folder of the Clock project on the companion web page. You are going to create a cross section of the bell. To build the bell, follow these steps:

1. Select Create ➤ Shapes ➤ Line. Figure 2.28 shows the cross section with the vertices numbered according to their creation order.

FIGURE 2.28 The bell's profile line with the vertices numbered according to their creation order

◄

Before moving forward with the bell profile, go to the Line Parameters on the right of the interface. In the Rendering rollout uncheck Enable In Viewport and Enable In Renderer. The parameters will retain the value of the previous use.

2. Starting at the bottom-right side of the bell image, click and let go of the mouse. This will create the first vertex as a corner (1).

3. Now move the mouse up where the bell curves and drag out a tangent to create a Bezier vertex (2).

4. Continue the drag until the line's curve follows the bell image.

5. Again, move the mouse to the left and to the middle of the bell, and click to create a corner vertex (3).

6. Right-click to end the Line tool. The profile should match Figure 2.28.

When the Lathe
modifier is added, the
profile gets revolved
360 degrees around
the center of the line.
The bell doesn't look so
good. That is because
the center of the lathe
is in the wrong place.

7. On the Modify panel, choose Lathe from the Modifier List, as shown in Figure 2.29.

FIGURE 2.29 Choose the Lathe modifier from the Modifier List.

8. To reposition the center of the lathe, open the Lathe Parameters rollout, and in the Align area, click Min. This should change the lathe to look more like a bell, as shown in Figure 2.30.

FIGURE 2.30 The bell with the lathe center in the correct place

9. To finish the bell, create a cylinder to represent its base post. Then create another cylinder to represent a bolt above the bell and a sphere for the ball at the top, as shown in Figure 2.31 and Figure 2.32. Now that all the separate pieces are created, it's time to put them together.

FIGURE 2.31 The image of the bell showing the three pieces to be created

FIGURE 2.32 The parameters for the three objects to be created

10. Using the Move and Rotate tools, reference Figure 2.31 for placement of objects. Leave a gap where the handle goes.

11. Then select all the separate pieces, including the Bell object. It needs to be oriented so it fits on the clock body, which means it needs to be rotated as a whole.

12. From the Main toolbar, select Group ➤ Group, as shown in Figure 2.33, and then name the group **Bell**.

13. Select each object and name it appropriately.

This will allow you to orient the Bell group object to fit with the other clock objects. We are moving on, but don't worry, we will get back to the bell later in the chapter.

FIGURE 2.33
In the Group menu,
choose Group and name
the group Bell.

14. Save the file as c02_Bell_End.max and use it for the next section. To check your progress, open c02_ex8_bell_end.max.

The next step in the process is to make the clock face by creating the hour hand, the minute hand, and the second hand. This could be done by creating an image of a clock face in a graphics program like Photoshop and then applying that image as a surface onto the 3D Clock object. For this exercise, you will be creating the clock face elements—the numbers and hands—as 3D objects, using another set of modifiers, Extrude and Bevel. The Extrude modifier adds depth to a shape—that's it. It's simple and incredibly useful. The Bevel modifier also adds depth to a shape but allows you to add a round bevel to the edges.

Exercise 2.9: Creating the Clock Numbers and Hands

Load c02_ex9_face_start.max from the scenes folder of the Clock project on the companion web page or use the file you have been working with. To create the clock numbers, follow these steps:

1. Start in the Create panel ➢ Shapes ➢ Text. Before you create the text shape, set up the text parameters.

2. Select the typeface down arrow next to the font name in the Parameters rollout.

3. Choose Times New Roman. If you do not have that typeface, just choose whichever font you desire.

4. Change Size to 1.45.

5. In the Text Type-In box, type 12. All parameters should match Figure 2.34.

FIGURE 2.34 Text shape parameters

6. Move the mouse into the viewport over the number 12 on the image of the clock face, and then click.

7. Now open the Modify panel, and in the Modifier List, click Bevel.

8. In the Bevel Values rollout, change Level 1: Height to 0.01 and Outline to 0.01. This will extrude the 12 shape and taper the mesh wider at the top.

9. Check the box next to Level 2 and change Height to 0.01; leave Outline at 0.0.

10. Check the box next to Level 3 and change Height to 0.01; set Outline to -0.01.

11. Match all bevel levels to those in Figure 2.35.

12. Now in the Parameters rollout in the Surface group, select Curved Sides.

13. Change Segments to 2, and check the box next to Smooth Across Levels, as shown in Figure 2.36. This will give the 12 rounded smooth sides.

FIGURE 2.35 Bevel Values rollout showing all of the shape parameters for the number 12

FIGURE 2.36 Parameters rollout for the bevel modifier

14. At the top of the Modify panel, change the name to **12**, click the color swatch next to the Name (text field) Type-In, and choose black. Select OK. Figure 2.37 shows the results of the Bevel modifier. Move the number into place over the number in the image plane.

FIGURE 2.37 Bevel modifier applied to the number

15. To create the remaining numbers, select Create ➢ Shapes ➢ Text and place the cursor over the number 1.

16. Add the Bevel modifier; the same parameters you used for the number 12 will be repeated. This makes it easy to finish off the rest of the clock numbers.

Because you set up the parameters for the number 12, the text shape will repeat the same parameters for the number 1.

17. Repeat steps 15 and 16 for each number on the clock face. Then name each new number, and change the color to black.

18. Select all the numbers by holding Ctrl and clicking each.

19. Then choose Group from the Group menu, as you did with the Bell object.

20. Name the group **Numbers**.

Follow these steps to create the clock hands:

1. Select the Create panel ➣ Shapes ➣ Rectangle. Create a rectangle over the minute-hand image.

2. Back in the Create panel, uncheck the box next to Start New Shape. This will allow you to create a second piece that is connected to the rectangle.

3. Select Circle and create a circle over the circle base of the minute hand.

4. Open the Modify panel, and in the modifier stack, in the Selection rollout, select Vertex mode (█).

5. In the Geometry rollout, select Refine and click each side of the rectangle in the middle, as shown in Figure 2.38.

Create new vertices.

FIGURE 2.38   Use Refine to add two vertices to the right and left sides of the rectangle.

In the Modifier Stack, you will see that the rectangle and circle objects have combined into an editable spline—a 2D object that provides controls for manipulating an object's three sub-object levels: vertex, segment, and spline.

6. Select and move the vertices on the top of the rectangle so they come to a point. Move the vertices on the bottom so they match the image of the minute hand in the viewport.

7. Go to the Modify panel, and from the Modifier List, add the Extrude modifier.

8. Change Amount to 0.025.

9. Change the Name to **Minute hand** and the color to black.

10. Repeat the same steps (1–10) on the hour hand. The second hand is even easier; just create a rectangle, make sure Start New Shape is still unchecked, and then create another rectangle.

11. Move and rotate each clock hand into the position you see on the clock image shown in Figure 2.39.

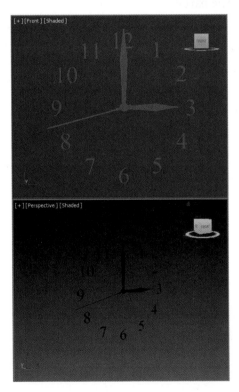

FIGURE 2.39   The clock hands positioned to match the clock face

Of course, you don't have to position the hands exactly as they are shown in the image.

12. When you have finished positioning the hands, save the file as
c02_Face_End.max. To check the progress of your work you can open
c02_ex09_face_end.max.

Bringing It All Together

Most of the pieces are created for the clock. Now you just have to put it all together.
Each piece was created in its own 3ds Max file. To bring them all together, you will
use Merge. Merge allows you to bring into one scene different 3ds Max files. You
can also just build all the parts to your model in a single 3ds Max file; we will look
at that technique in later chapters.

Exercise 2.10: Using Merge

Follow these steps to merge all the parts:

1. To begin, click the Application button and choose Reset. This will clear
any data from previous work and reset the 3ds Max settings. Read the
dialogs carefully; they might prompt you to save your previous file and
to reset.

2. Click the Application button, choose Import, and click Merge, as
shown in Figure 2.40.

FIGURE 2.40 Merge is found in the Application menu under Import.

3. Navigate to the scenes folder of the Clock project, and select c02_ex6_body_end.max. Click Open.

4. From the list in the Merge dialog box, choose the Clock Body object and click OK to close the dialog box. In the new scene, the clock body will appear, located in the same spot as it was in the other 3ds Max file.

5. Repeat the same steps for the handle, face, and bell scenes.

6. Select the Bell group object, and from the Edit menu, choose Clone. This opens a Clone Options dialog box with clone options that are explained in more detail in the sidebar "The Clone Options Dialog Box."

7. Click OK to close the Clone Options dialog box, choose the Select And Move tool (W), and move the new Bell object to the other side of the clock body.

8. Move and rotate the Bell group so it is positioned correctly on the clock body.

9. The objects will need to be adjusted; use the transform tools and your best judgment. To check your progress you can open c02_ex10_merge_end.max.

▶

We prefer to use the Shift+transform technique, which uses Shift+Move/Rotate/Scale to create a clone of the object. Hold Shift and move the Bell group object to the desired location. When you let go of the mouse, the Clone Options dialog box appears.

THE CLONE OPTIONS DIALOG BOX

Making a *copy* creates a completely separate clone from the original. An *instance* is a copy, but it is still connected to the original. If you edit the original or an instance, all of the instances change (including the original). A *reference* is dependent on the original, and the connection goes only one way; change the original, and the reference will change, but change the reference, and only it will be affected, depending on its location in the modifier stack. The changes are for modifiers and not for transforms.

Still something missing? Well, this is where we leave you. With 90 percent done, it's time to use the many tools you learned about in this chapter to finish the clock. All you have left to create are the clock feet and the bell hammer. Take a look at Figure 2.41 for an example of the finished clock to this point.

FIGURE 2.41 The clock so far

Now You Know

In this chapter, you learned how to set up reference images in your scene for more accurate modeling of an existing object, an alarm clock. You saw how to create a primitive and convert it into an editable poly object to add edge loops and edit its shape. You also created 2D shapes and splines to outline your model's initial shapes, and then you used the Graphite Modeling Tools set to flesh out the alarm clock, learning how to use the Lathe, Extrude, and Bevel tools along the way. Finally, in this chapter, you learned how to combine all the pieces of the alarm clock model into a single scene using the Copy and Merge functions.

CHAPTER 3

Modeling in 3ds Max: Architectural Model Part I

Building models in 3D is as simple as building them out of clay, wood, stone, or metal. Using Autodesk® 3ds Max® software to model something may not be as tactile as physically building it, but the same concept applies: You have to identify how the model is shaped and figure out how to break it down into manageable parts that you can piece together into the final form.

Instead of using traditional tools to hammer or chisel or weld a shape into form, you will use the vertices of the geometry to shape the computer-generated (CG) model. As you have seen, the 3ds Max polygon toolset is quite robust.

In this chapter, you will explore the many 3ds Max architectural modeling tools by building components such as walls, doors, and windows. These objects are called *Architecture Engineering and Construction (AEC)* tools, and they are parametric to give them an advantage over imported geometry from CAD programs. There are many ways you can build an interior space—simply put, a couple of boxes and you're done—but to really create a refined and realistic interior, you will need to take time to add details.

In this chapter, you will learn to:

▶ **Set up the scene**

▶ **Build the room**

▶ **Add special details to the room**

Setting Up the Scene

When you open the 3ds Max program, a system of measurement is set up to measure geometry in your scene. By default your file is set to Generic Units, where one unit is defined as 1.000 inch.

You can change the generic units to equal any system of measurement you prefer; you can use US Standard units (feet and inches) or metric units. You should choose your units of measure before you begin creating your scene, not during the modeling process.

Exercise 3.1: Setting Up Units

First, download the c03_ArchModel project folder from the book's web page at www.sybex.com/go/3dsmax2015essentials. Place the files on your hard drive. Open the 3ds Max 2015 program and set a 3ds Max project. Choose the c03_ArchModel folder from your hard drive, flash, or network drive and follow these steps. To start with a new file, go to the Application menu ➤ New.

1. Go to the Customize menu and choose Customization, and then Units Setup, as shown in Figure 3.1.

2. Change the units from the default Generic Units to US Standard.

3. From the US Standard drop-down menu, choose Feet w/Decimal Inches, as shown in Figure 3.2, and click OK.

4. Save the file and use it to continue to the next exercise.

FIGURE 3.1 Accessing the Units Setup options

FIGURE 3.2 From the US Standard drop-down menu, choose Feet w/Decimal Inches.

Exercise 3.2: Importing a CAD Drawing

Using reference materials will help you efficiently create your 3D model and achieve a good likeness in your end result. The temptation to just wing it and start building the objects is strong, especially when time is short and you're raring to go. You should always suppress this temptation in deference to a well-thought-out approach to the task. Sketches, photographs, and drawings can all be used as resources for the modeling process. Not only are references useful for giving you a clear direction in which to head, but you can also use them directly in the 3ds Max software to help you model. Photos, especially those taken from different sides of the intended model, can be added to a scene as background images to help you shape your model.

For this chapter, you will be using an AutoCAD drawing as the reference and as a template to build the walls, doors, and windows. You will be supplied with a CAD drawing that will make it much easier to follow the reference.

Figure 3.3 shows the room that you will create in this chapter. There are a few changes from the original room. The opening that leads to the hallway is going to become a door. We will add decorative elements, such as a fancy baseboard.

In the future, if you don't have a drawing using detailed measurements of a room, you can create your own layout or blueprints because proper measurements and scale are vital when creating a convincing interior space.

FIGURE 3.3 Images of the room to be created

1. Select the Application button (⟩•) ≻ Manage ≻ Set Project Folder and choose the c03_ArchModel project folder, downloaded from the book's web page at www.sybex.com/go/3dsmax2015essentials. For this procedure, either continue with file from previous exercise or use the c03_ex2_import_start.max file.

2. Again, select the Application button and choose Import ≻ Import. Because you have already set your project to the ArchModel project, you will be taken straight to the import folder for that project.

3. Select the Room.dwg file. This is an AutoCAD drawing file that contains no 3D objects; it contains a drawing using 2D lines. Click OK.

The AutoCAD DWG/DXF Import Options dialog box will open, as shown in Figure 3.4.

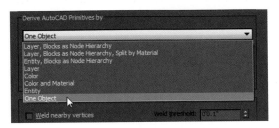

FIGURE 3.4   **The AutoCAD DWG/DXF Import Options dialog box**

4. In the Derive AutoCAD Primitives By drop-down menu, choose One Object and then click OK. The AutoCAD drawing shown in Figure 3.5 will appear.

▶

The viewport should show a 2D collection of lines making up the layout of a room. The drawing has three basic parts: the walls, the window, and the doors. The figure has some colors associated with those three parts. These colors will not be reflected in the imported drawing.

▶

This is a CAD drawing of the living room and dining room of a typical house, which was created for this book by Nastasia Jorgenson, an interior design student from the Art Institute of California – Los Angeles.

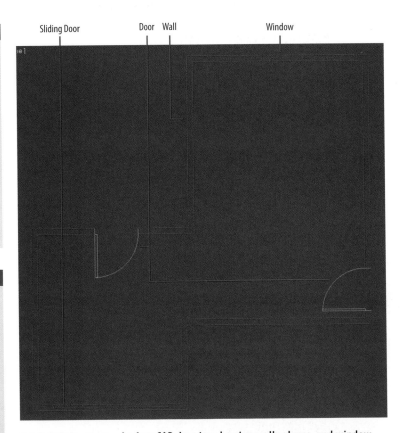

FIGURE 3.5   **An AutoCAD drawing showing walls, doors, and window**

5. Select the imported AutoCAD drawing, and then choose the Move tool in the main toolbar. At the bottom of the interface are the Transform Type-Ins and three type-in boxes labeled X, Y, and Z.

6. Change the X, Y, and Z values in the type-in boxes to X: 0'0.0", Y: 0'0.0", and Z: 0'0.0". This will center the AutoCAD drawing of the floor plan to the center of the environment.

7. In the command panel, go to the Create panel, and in the Name And Color rollout, rename the AutoCAD drawing **Floorplan**.

8. Save the file, and to check your work open c03_ex2_import_end.max.

Building the Room

The Wall objects you will create are a part of the AEC Extended objects and are designed for use in the architectural, engineering, and construction fields.

Exercise 3.3: Creating the Walls

To perform this exercise, you can use your completed file from Exercise 3.2, or you can load c03_ex3_walls_start.max from the Scenes folder of the c03_ArchModel project on the book's companion web page at www.sybex.com/ go/3dsmax2015essentials.

1. Select and maximize the Top viewport (Alt+W).

2. In the main toolbar, click and hold the Snaps Toggle button, and from the tool flyout, choose the 2D Snaps button (⬛).

3. Right-click the Snaps Toggle button to bring up the Grid And Snap Settings dialog box.

4. Uncheck Grid Points and check Vertex, as shown in Figure 3.6.

FIGURE 3.6   The Grid and Snap Settings dialog box

5. Close the dialog box. This will make it possible to snap from the vertices in the AutoCAD drawing.

6. Go to the Create panel, and from the Geometry drop-down menu choose AEC Extended and click the Wall button.

7. You should see the wall parameters:

   a. Set Width to 0'5.0" unless it is already set to this value. This will define the thickness of the wall.

   b. Set Height to 8'0.0" unless it is already set to this value. This will define the height of the wall.

   c. Change Justification to Left, as shown in Figure 3.7.

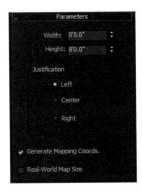

FIGURE 3.7 The Parameters rollout for the Wall object

8. In the Top viewport, click and release an outside corner of the room in the AutoCAD drawing; then move in a clockwise direction to a connected corner, and click to set the position of that corner. This will create a wall 0'5.0" thick and 8'0.0" tall between the two corners you clicked.

9. Continue around the room, clicking the outside wall corners, making sure you snap to the vertex of the lines at each corner. Disregard the doors and windows in the drawing and put your walls right over them.

10. When you have made it all the way around the room, click the corner where you started.

If you mistakenly click something, you can press Backspace, which will undo the last click.

11. A Spline pop-up warning will ask, Weld Point? Click Yes and right-click to release the wall primitive.

12. Press Alt+W to return to the four-viewport layout, and look at the walls in the Perspective viewport. The finished wall is shown in Figure 3.8.

FIGURE 3.8 The finished wall shown in the Perspective viewport

13. With the wall selected, go to the Modify panel and look at the parameters.

14. In the modifier stack, click the black box with the plus sign.

15. To edit the walls—say, to straighten out a wall or extend a wall to make a space bigger—select the Vertex component in the Modify panel.

16. From the Top viewport, at the corners of the room, you should see small plus signs. The plus signs are the wall object vertices, allowing the walls to be edited. Select one of the vertices and move it to adjust the wall sections it is connected to.

17. Click the Segment component, and then click a wall in your scene.

18. You can use the Parameters section at the bottom of the rollout to change the settings for the wall, as shown in Figure 3.9.

FIGURE 3.9 Wall parameters

The wall has three components: Vertex, Segment, and Profile. You can edit a wall primitive in a way that's similar to how you edit splines.

You can also adjust the wall primitive by changing the Height or Width value of the wall in the Modify panel.

19. Save the scene file. To check your work, open `c03_ex3_walls_end`
`.max`. Now that the walls are laid out, we'll move on to the doors.

Exercise 3.4: Creating the Doors

The 3ds Max Door objects that are available allow you to control the look of the door—not just the size but the frame and glass inserts as well. They also let you determine whether the door is open or closed. The types of door are Pivot (which is the most common), BiFold, and Sliding. To perform this exercise, you can use your previous file from the ArchModel project, or you can load `c03_ex4_doors_`
`start.max` from the Scenes folder of the `c03_ArchModel` project on the book's companion web page at www.sybex.com/go/3dsmax2015essentials.

1. Select the Wall object if it isn't already selected.

2. Turn on See-Through mode using Alt+X. This will make the wall appear slightly transparent with a gray cast, but you will be able to see the AutoCAD drawing underneath.

3. Go to the Create panel. From the drop-down menu, choose Doors. Choose Pivot under Object Type.

4. Make sure the Top viewport is active, and zoom in on the door in the horizontal wall on the left in the AutoCAD drawing.

5. The 2D Snaps Toggle button should still be active. If it's not active, go to the main toolbar and click the 3D Snaps Toggle button, hold it down, and choose 2D Snap from the flyout.

6. Starting at the left of the door opening on the outside of the wall, click and drag to the right side of the opening in the AutoCAD drawing underneath until it snaps; then release the mouse button. Then move the cursor and click the opposite side of the wall to set the door thickness.

7. Now move the cursor toward the top of the viewport to adjust the door height.

8. Click again to set any height. Don't try to get the exact height; you will set the correct height in the next step.

9. Go to the Modify panel and enter the correct value for the Height parameter for the door: 6'8.0". Check Flip Hinge, as shown in Figure 3.10. Flip Hinge sets the edge on which the door swings.

You won't be able to see the adjustment in the Top viewport, so you should look in another viewport as you drag to set the height.

FIGURE 3.10 The Door object parameters

When door primitives are created using snaps, you can insert a door in a Wall object, automatically linking the two and creating a cutout for the door. This doesn't always work; many factors can affect the outcome. If the door fails to create the cutout, you can move on to the next step. If it does create the cutout, skip step 10.

10. In the main toolbar, click the Select and Link tool ( ), and click and drag from the door to the wall, as shown in Figure 3.11. This will make a doorway opening in the wall. The next type of door to be added is the sliding glass door, as shown previously in Figure 3.3 (left image).

FIGURE 3.11 Use the Select And Link tool to create an opening in the wall for the door. This is necessary only if autolinking doesn't work.

11. In the Top viewport, zoom into the sliding door in the AutoCAD drawing.

12. In the Create panel, choose Sliding under Object Type.

13. Start by clicking and dragging from the right outside of the door to the left outside of the door, making sure to snap to the vertices where the door lines meet the wall lines. This will establish the width of the sliding door. Release the mouse button.

14. Move your cursor to the inside of the door and click when your cursor snaps to the vertex.

15. Click and drag the cursor to set any height, and click to finish.

16. Don't worry if you can't get the height correct; just type 6'8.0" in the Height Type-In field, as you did for the previous door.

17. Switch to the Perspective viewport and check to see if the sliding door looks correct.

18. Use the Select and Link tool and click and drag from the door to the wall to create the opening in the wall. The finished sliding door is shown in Figure 3.12.

> Because of the Snaps Toggle tool, the width and depth of the door will already be correct.

> The automatic linking should create a cutout for the door. If it fails to work, move on to the next step. If it does create the cutout, skip to step 19.

FIGURE 3.12 The sliding door in the wall

19. Add the remaining door by repeating steps 2–10.

20. This is a good time to save your file. To check your work, open c03_ex4_doors_end.max. You will create the window in the room in the next exercise.

Exercise 3.5: Creating the Window

AEC Window objects work in a way that is similar to the way the Wall and Door objects work. There are six window types: Awning, Fixed, Projected, Casement, Pivoted, and Sliding. You will be using the Fixed window for this section. You can continue with your file from the previous exercise, or you can load c03_ex5_windows_start.max from the Scenes folder of the ArchModel project on the companion web page to continue.

1. Go to the Create panel, and from the drop-down menu, choose Windows. Choose Fixed under Object Type.

2. In the main toolbar, click and hold the Snaps Toggle button. This will bring up the Snaps flyout. Choose the 2D Snaps button.

3. Create the Window object as you did the Door objects: Use the snaps to click/drag from left to right, following the drawing; then drag to create the depth and then the height.

4. In the Modify panel, go to the Fixed Window parameters and change Height to 6'0.0". If the automatic linking failed to work, move on to the next step. If it does create the cutout, skip to step 6.

5. Use the Select and Link tool and click from the window to the wall to create the opening in the wall, just as with the doors.

6. Press S to turn off Snaps.

7. Switch to a Perspective viewport so you can see the newly created window; then select and move the window up so it is centered on the wall, as shown in Figure 3.13.

FIGURE 3.13 The window is centered on the wall.

8. Save the file for use in the next section. To check the finished file, open c03_ex5_window_end.max. The model to this point is shown in Figure 3.14.

FIGURE 3.14   Walls with doors and a window

Exercise 3.6: Adding a Floor and a Ceiling

You can continue with your file from the previous exercise, or you can load c03_ex6_floor_start.max from the Scenes folder of the ArchModel project on the companion web page. What's a room without a floor and ceiling? Not any room we want to walk into. To create the floor and ceiling for your room, you will use the Line tool to create a shape:

1. Go to the Create panel and click the Shapes button (![icon]); then click the Line tool, as shown in Figure 3.15.

2. Press S on your keyboard to turn on the Snaps Toggle tool.

3. In the Top viewport, click the outside corner of the room, then click the other corners around the room in a clockwise direction, and then click again the corner where you started.

4. The Spline dialog box will appear. Click Yes. This closes the line to form a closed shape.

The Snaps Toggle tool should still be set to the 2D Snaps Toggle option. Keep it that way. This will ensure that the line stays at the ground plane of the scene.

5. Choose the Select Object tool (Q), and select the line you just created, if it is not already selected.

6. Go to the Modify panel (⬚), and from the Modifier List drop-down menu, choose Extrude, as shown in Figure 3.16.

FIGURE 3.15
Select the Line tool.

FIGURE 3.16 From the Modifier List drop-down menu, choose Extrude.

7. Now look at the Extrude parameters, and change the Amount value to 0'0.1". You need to give just a little thickness to the floor.

8. Switch to the Front viewport, and move the new Floor object down so the top of the floor lines up with the bottom of the walls. Turn off the Snap tool (S).

9. Rename the new object **Floor**. To create the ceiling, you are going to make a clone of the floor.

10. Select the floor, and while holding the Shift key, move the Floor object up to the top of the Wall object.

11. Let go of the mouse button; a Clone Options dialog box will appear, as shown in Figure 3.17.

FIGURE 3.17 The Clone Options dialog box

For now, you don't need to have the Ceiling object visible; you will be using it in a later chapter. You can hide the Ceiling object.

You can also choose Unhide By Name to bring up a dialog box from which you can choose a specific item from a list to unhide.

12. Choose Copy from the Object section, rename the object **Ceiling**, and click OK.

13. Center your cursor over the Ceiling object and right-click.

14. From the quad menu, choose Hide Selection.

15. When you are ready to have the ceiling back in your scene, you can right-click anywhere in your scene and select Unhide All.

16. Save the file, and to check your progress open c03_ex6_floor_end.max.

Adding Special Details to the Room

In architectural terminology, a *baseboard* is a board covering the area where the wall meets the floor. Baseboards are used to cover the gap between the wall and the floor as well as add a sense of style to a room. An example of the baseboard we will be creating is shown in Figure 3.18.

FIGURE 3.18   **The baseboard molding**

This room has a baseboard but not a very good one, so creating a more stylish one would be a great way to add some pizzazz to the room. Also, feel free to modify the baseboard to meet your skill level with the Line tool.

Exercise 3.7: Creating Baseboard Moldings

You can use your file from the previous exercise, or you can load c03_ex7_ details_start.max from the Scenes folder of the ArchModel project on the book's companion web page. To begin creating the baseboard, you will use a spline that has already been created: the floor:

1. In the Perspective viewport, select the Floor object.

2. Select and maximize the Top viewport (Alt+W), and in the Edit menu, choose Duplicate ➤ Clone.

3. In the Clone Options dialog box, choose Copy and change the name to **Baseboard Path**. Click OK

4. In the Modify panel, remove the Extrude modifier by right-clicking the modifier in the modifier stack and choosing Delete when the context menu appears, as shown in Figure 3.19.

FIGURE 3.19 Deleting the Extrude modifier in the modifier stack

5. In the modifier stack, click the plus sign in the black box to expand the Line entry to display the sub-objects of the line. Select Spline mode.

6. Select the sub-object spline of the baseboard line. It will turn red when selected. You may not be able to see it because the walls are on top of the shape.

7. In the Geometry rollout, scroll down to Outline.

8. In the Outline Type-In, which is to the right of the Outline button, change the amount to –0'6.0", as shown in Figure 3.20.

Outline clones the spline and offsets it on all sides as specified by the amount in the Outline Type-In.

FIGURE 3.20   Change the Outline amount to −0'6.0"
to offset the spline.

9. Select the original spline and delete it. Click Line to exit Spline mode. Because you are using the newly created spline for the baseboards, you don't need the original line. Now you'll create the shape of the molding, shown in Figure 3.21.

7.3″

1.3″

FIGURE 3.21
Profile of the baseboard
molding

10. Switch from the Top viewport to the Front viewport.

11. Click the Application button, and choose Import ➢ Merge. From the Scenes folder of the ArchModel project folder, choose the Baseboard Image Plane.max file. Click Open.

12. Select the Baseboard Image Plane object. Click OK in the Merge dialog box.

You can use the keyboard shortcut (F) to switch from the Top viewport to the Front viewport.

If you don't want to create your own baseboard shape, you can merge in one that is already created. Refer to step 11 and select the Baseboard Path.max file.

13. Switch to the Front viewport and change the viewport shading to Realistic. Enter Isolate Selection mode (🔒) by selecting the icon at the bottom of the interface below the timeline (F3). This will hide everything in the scene except the image plane.

14. Choose Create ➢ Shapes ➢ Line, and at the top-right corner of the baseboard, click and release the left mouse button. This will create a corner point.

15. Move the mouse to the left, where the baseboard begins to curve down, and click and drag to create a Bezier vertex. This is a vertex type that has handles, which allow for greater control over the curve in the line segments.

16. Drag until the curve is following the curve of the baseboard.

17. Now continue around the baseboard cross section until you are back at the first vertex that you created. Click the first vertex and select Yes from the dialog box to close the spline.

18. Right-click to release the Line tool.

19. Rename the shape **Baseboard Shape**. If the line needs to be edited, go to the Modify panel and select Vertex mode. In Vertex mode, you can edit the path to match the image on the image plane.

20. Exit Isolate Selection mode and then select the baseboard path. Go to the Modify panel, and from the Modifier List, choose Sweep.

21. In the Section Type rollout, choose Use Custom Section, and in the Custom Section Types area, select Pick.

22. Pick the baseboard shape to create the baseboard, as shown in Figure 3.22. Some parameters need to be adjusted.

◀

The Sweep modifier extrudes a cross section along a path, creating a 3D version of the baseboard cross section.

FIGURE 3.22   Picking the baseboard shape in the Sweep modifier

23. In the Sweep Parameters rollout, check the box next to Mirror On XZ Plane. This will flip the baseboard shape so it is facing in toward the room. The baseboard molding should run along the floor except at the door openings. Right now, the molding is going straight through the door opening, as shown in Figure 3.23. It isn't difficult to fix; just edit the path.

FIGURE 3.23   The baseboard molding is going through the door opening.

24. Switch to a Perspective viewport (Alt+W) to exit Maximize Viewport and then Ctrl+click the floor plan and the baseboard to select them both.

25. Enter Isolate Selection mode (Alt+Q), and then select just the baseboard.

26. Zoom in on the door on the right of the Top viewport.

27. Go to the Modify panel, and in the modifier stack, choose Vertex mode.

28. Go to the Geometry rollout and click the Refine button.

The Refine button allows you to add vertices without affecting the spline curve.

29. Move to the baseboard spline and click directly on the spline on both sides of the door to add new vertices. Right-click to exit Refine.

30. Switch to Segment mode; select the segment in between the two new vertices and delete it, as shown in Figure 3.24.

FIGURE 3.24 Use Refine to add two new vertices on either side of the door; then delete the segment.

31. Repeat the same process for the remaining pivot door and sliding door.

32. When you finish, select the Sweep modifier in the Modify Stack to exit Edit mode in the Sweep modifier. Exit Isolate Selection mode. The finished results of the Sweep modifier are shown in Figure 3.25.

33. Save the file. You can check your work by opening `c03_ex7_detail_end.max`.

FIGURE 3.25   The baseboard with proper gaps at the doors

Now You Know

In this chapter, you learned how to use some of the 3ds Max architectural modeling tools. Starting with an imported AutoCAD drawing and using it to build up the walls, you then added doors and windows. The walls, doors, and windows are part of the AEC (Architectural, Engineering, and Construction) primitives and make modeling architectural spaces very simple. You then used the 2D spline tools to create the floors and moldings. By adding the Sweep modifier to the spline, you transformed the baseboard moldings into beautiful details that are special additions to the room.

CHAPTER 4

Modeling in 3ds Max: Architectural Model Part II

In this chapter, you will continue working within the interior design subject from the previous chapter by modeling and adding some furniture—specifically, a couch and chair.

In this chapter, you will learn to:

▶ **Model a couch**

▶ **Model a lounge chair**

Model the Couch

When you are starting a modeling project, make sure you have plenty of measurements, like those in the photo of the couch that will be modeled in this chapter, shown in Figure 4.1. Always remember to reference images for your modeling project. Modeling this couch is a straightforward process. If you break it down into separate components, it is just 16 different-sized boxes. The boxes are soft and cushy; they have various details, but nonetheless they are still just boxes, with the exception of the chaise lounge end of the couch, which is the only piece that isn't a box shape.

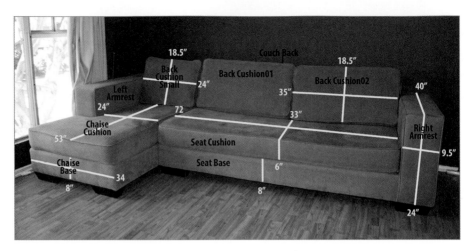

FIGURE 4.1 Couch with measurements

Exercise 4.1: Blocking Out the Couch Model

Certification Objective

Blocking out the model means creating a simpler version of the model starting with whatever primitives fit the bill—in this case, boxes. Using the measurements shown in Figure 4.1, you will create a series of boxes and then orient them to mimic the couch. The first piece you'll create is the bottom (the part between the seat cushions and the feet). It is 8 inches high by 72 inches wide by 33 inches deep. In the previous chapter, you used standard units of measurement (feet and inches), but for this chapter, you will use the default generic units. If your units are still set to feet and inches, refer to Exercise 3.1, "Setting Up Units," in Chapter 3, "Modeling in 3ds Max: Architectural Model Part I," to review how to change the setting to generic units. Then follow these steps:

1. Open a new file in your Autodesk® 3ds Max® software, and select the Perspective viewport. Then go to the command panel and choose Create ➢ Geometry and click Box.

2. In the Keyboard Entry rollout, enter **33** for Length, **72** for Width, and **8** for Height, but don't change the XYZ Type-In boxes.

3. Click the Create button.

4. The box should be in the center of the scene. Rename the box **Seat Base**.

5. Create the cushion above this box: Select the box with the Move tool, and then hold Shift and move the box up in the Z-axis to create a new box so that it is on top of the old box. This is a quick method you can

use to clone an object. The Clone Options dialog box will appear, as shown in Figure 4.2.

FIGURE 4.2 The Clone Options dialog box

6. In the Clone Options dialog, select Copy. Change the name from Box to **Seat Cushion** and click OK.

7. Go to the Modify panel and change the Height of the new cushion box to **6.0**.

8. As in step 1, create another box, but change the parameters to 40 for Length, 9.5 for Width, and 24 for Height. Rename the box **Right Armrest**.

9. Move the box so it sits on the right side of the two stacked boxes.

10. Create a clone for the left side of the couch using the same Shift and Move technique you used in steps 5 and 6.

11. Now for the back piece: this is the part the back cushions rest against. You don't see it in the picture in Figure 4.1, but it is there. Create a box with Length set to 6, Width set to 96, and Height set to 27. Move it behind the seat-cushion boxes to form the backrest, as shown in Figure 4.3 (left).

FIGURE 4.3 The first few pieces to start the couch (left); the blocked-out couch (right)

Creating the chaise part of the couch is a bit more challenging. You'll create a box now, and later you can alter it with the wing on the side.

12. Select the Perspective viewport. Choose the Create panel ➤ Geometry and select Box, and in the Keyboard Entry rollout, input 53 for Length, 24 for Width, and 8 for Height. Click the Create button.

13. Move the new box to the left of the seat cushions: Hold Shift and move the new box up so it is sitting on the old box. Choose Copy from the dialog box, and then change the box's height to 6.0.

14. Create another box with the following measurements: Length = 8, Width = 35, and Height = 18.5. Click the Create button to create a box for the back pillows.

15. Move the box so that it is sitting on top of the seat cushions and against the right armrest.

Colors are assigned to the objects randomly when the primitives are created. You can change the colors by selecting each object and in the Modify panel ➤ Name And Color, select the color swatch and choose a color from the color picker.

16. Make a clone of this box and move it to the left, so it is next to the other pillow.

17. Make one more clone, and move it to the left so it sits on top of the chaise seat cushions. This box is too wide. With the box selected, go to the Modify panel and change Width to 24.0.

18. Create three backrest cushions (two the same size and one that is smaller). As you are creating the couch pieces, name them. Refer to Figure 4.1 for the measurements and names.

19. Once the cushions are created, move them into place on the couch to finish blocking out the couch, as shown in Figure 4.3 (right).

Save the file, and to check your work you can open c04_ex1_block_end.max from the scenes folder of the c04_ArchModel project files from the companion web page at www.sybex.com/go/3dsmax2015essentials.

Exercise 4.2: Using NURMS to Add Softness

Certification Objective

Non-Uniform Rational Mesh Smooth (NURMS) is a subdivision surface technique that allows you to take a low-poly model and smooth the surface into a high-poly model. This isn't a lighting trick; you are actually changing the geometry of the model. When you apply NURMS to your model, you will see a control cage in the shape of the low-poly model; this is the mesh you actually model.

Be cautious: Poly counts rise very quickly and an iteration count that's needlessly high can slow you down.

Subdivision increases the poly count of your model; every level of subdivision increases the number of polygons by a factor of four. At a subdivision level (or iteration) of 1, 1 polygon in the control cage will become 4 polygons in the subdivided model. At an iteration level of 2, that 1 polygon becomes 16 polygons, and so on. When you're working on a model with NURMS, it is best to work with a lower iteration level and then render with a higher level of iterations.

Polygons are flat between the vertices, but when NURMS is turned on, a flat polygon starts to curve and smooth out as it subdivides. When you use NURMS smoothing, the more distance there is between the edges on a mesh, the smoother the result will be. When you want sharp corners, just place the edges close together. When turning on NURMS, those close edges will retain their sharpness better. If you want a smoother, more rounded surface, then place the edges farther apart.

The best way to model with smooth surfaces is to use quad polygons in a grid formation; two edges will cross each vertex—and because each edge flows from vertex to vertex uninterrupted, the edges will continue and the 3D form will be smoothed predictably. If you have a vertex with no more than four edges coming out of it, the splines will end and the mesh may not smooth the way you expect it to.

All of the couch cushions will receive the same treatment, so let's go over the next technique using one of the armrests of the couch and the chaise lounge section. After you're finished with that, you can practice the techniques on the remaining couch boxes yourself. Continue with the file from the previous exercise or open the c04_ex2_NURMS_start.max file from the scenes folder of the c04_ArchModel project folder. Then follow these steps:

1. Select the Right Armrest object. Click the Isolate Selection Toggle button ( ).This turns off the view of the other objects in the scene to allow you to focus on this one piece.

2. In the Ribbon ➤ Modeling tab, select Polygon Modeling ➤ Convert To Poly.

3. Then choose the Edit tab and click Use NURMS (). You will see a box that looks like the air was let out of it, as shown in Figure 4.4.

4. Back in the modeling ribbon, select the Edit panel and click the Use NURMS button again to turn it off.

5. In the Edit tab, click the SwiftLoop tool ( ) and hover your cursor over the box to reveal a loop of edges on the box.

6. Place one of the lines shown in Figure 4.5 by clicking where you want the loop to be added on the box, and then place the other three loops, as shown in Figure 4.5. Right-click with your mouse to release the SwiftLoop tool.

If you want to fully understand how edges flow and end across a 3D surface as a result of subdivision leads, spend some time studying topology, which is key to creating good 3D models that subdivide well when animated.

Editing the box is easier at this stage while it is still in box form.

If you refer to the picture of the couch from Figure 4.1, you'll see that the arm is much more structured and closer to the shape of a box.

FIGURE 4.4   Couch armrest with NURMS applied

FIGURE 4.5   Use the SwiftLoop tool to add edge loops to the box.

7. Turn on Use NURMS again to see the difference after using the SwiftLoop tool. Then turn Use NURMS off again to prepare for the next section.

8. Save the file, and to check your work open c04_ex2_NURMS_end.max from the scenes folder of the c04_ArchModel project.

If you refer to the picture in Figure 4.1, you can see that the couch arm is even more squared off than the current mesh. In the next section, you will learn how to add more detail.

Exercise 4.3: Building Detail on the Couch Model

Certification
Objective

The next step in the process of creating the couch is to add the piping, which is the round decorative trim along the seams of the pillows, as shown in Figure 4.6. Continue with the file from the previous exercise or open the c04_ex3_detail_start.max file from the scenes folder of the c04_ArchModel project.

FIGURE 4.6   Decorative piping runs along the seams of the couch.

1. Start by selecting the Armrest object. In the Edit tab, turn off Use NURMS. Then in the Polygon Modeling tab, enter Edge mode. Ctrl+click to select the edges on the box that are identified in Figure 4.7.

Select these edges on both sides of the box.

FIGURE 4.7 Select the highlighted edges.

2. Go to the Edges tab, and open the Chamfer Settings caddy. Change Edge Chamfer Amount to **0.15**, press Enter on your keyboard, and then click OK.

3. Switch to Polygon mode and select the polygons that were created with the chamfer.

4. In the Graphite Modeling Tools tab, go to the Polygons panel and open the Extrude caddy.

5. Change the extrusion type to Local Normal, as shown in Figure 4.8.

FIGURE 4.8 Set the extrusion type to Local Normal.

6. Set the Height to −0.2, press Enter, and then click the Apply and Continue button (⊕). This will keep the caddy open and allow you to perform another extrusion.

7. Change the Height to 0.3, press Enter, and then click the OK button (✓) in the caddy.

The couch looks pretty good, but if you look closely, you can see that it is still very choppy around the corners. The NURMS iterations need to be turned up.

8. Go to the Edit panel and select Use NURMS. The Use NURMS tab appears in the modeling ribbon (sometimes a floating window will appear instead).

9. Turn up the Iterations to 2. The finished product looks pretty good, as shown in Figure 4.9. Now it is time to perform the same piping detail on the seat and back cushions of the couch.

F I G U R E   4 . 9   The finished couch armrest

10. Exit Isolate Selection mode and exit Polygon mode by selecting the Polygon button in the Polygon Modeling tab.

11. The seat cushion and three back cushions need to have piping just like the couch arm, so repeat steps 1 through 10 for the cushions.

12. The seat base and couch back don't have any piping, so smooth them using NURMS and the SwiftLoop tool to add edges where needed.

13. Select vertices and polygons and move them around to give the surfaces a more random and organic or "lived-in" appearance.

14. Save the file, and to check your work open c04_ex3_detail_end.max from the scenes folder of the c04_ArchModel project.

Now is your chance to practice adding the detail to the remaining pieces on the couch. We finished everything but the chaise lounge part of the couch using NURMS with an Iterations level of 2. In the Name And Color rollout we changed the color so the finished pieces would be a consistent color. This is not required to continue with the exercise.

Exercise 4.4: Creating the Chaise Lounge

The chaise lounge isn't that much different from the rest of the couch. It just has a wing section that comes out from the side, as shown in Figure 4.11. Continue with the file from the previous exercise or open the c04_ex4_chaise_start.max file from the scenes folder of the c04_ArchModel project. Begin by creating the rough chaise cushion.

Certification
Objective

1. Start by choosing Create ➢ Geometry ➢ Standard Primitive and create a box. Set the Parameters to Length = 52.0, Width = 24.0, and Height = 8.0. It should be positioned between the left armrest and the seat cushion. Rename the box **Chaise Base**.

2. Convert the box to a polygon (Ribbon ➢ Modeling tab ➢ Polygon Modeling ➢ Convert To Polygon).

3. Add a new edge, as shown in Figure 4.10. Use the SwiftLoop tool, and then right-click to release it.

4. Enter Polygon mode, and select the polygon on the outside edge of the box.

5. In the Ribbon ➢ Modeling tab ➢ Polygon tab ➢ Extrude ➢ Extrude Settings, enter **10.0** as the Extrude amount, and click OK. Figure 4.11 shows the extruded wing of the chaise.

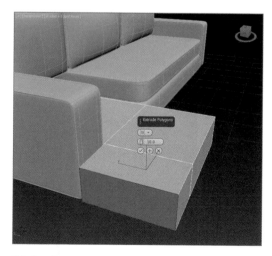

FIGURE 4.10 Add a new loop to the chaise box.

FIGURE 4.11 Use Extrude to create the wing on the chaise.

6. Clone the cushion using the Shift+Move technique, and move the clone upward until it is sitting on top of the cushion. Release the mouse button, in the Clone dialog choose Copy, and rename the clone **Chaise Cushion**.

7. Now that you have completed the chaise lounge section of the couch, you just have to add the finishing touches. Then enter Isolate Selection mode.

8. Add new edges using the SwiftLoop tool, matching Figure 4.12.

FIGURE 4.12   Use SwiftLoop to add an edge loop on the chaise cushion box.

9. Enter Edge mode, and select the outside edges of the chaise cushion on the top and bottom. Ctrl+click to make multiple selections at once.

10. Go to the Edges tab, and open the Chamfer Settings caddy. Change Edge Chamfer Amount to **0.15**, press Enter, and then click OK.

11. Switch to Polygon mode and select the polygons that were created with the chamfer.

12. In the Ribbon ➢ Modeling tab, go to the Polygons panel and open the Extrude caddy.

13. Change the Extrusion type to Local Normal.

14. Set the Height to **–0.2**, press Enter, and then click the Apply and Continue button (⊕). This will keep the caddy open and allow you to perform another extrusion.

15. Change the Height to 0.3, press Enter, and then click OK in the caddy.

16. Go to the Edit panel and select Use NURMS. The Use NURMS tab appears in the modeling ribbon (sometimes a floating window will appear instead).

Repeat the same process on the chaise base, except the base has no piping. Save your file, and to check your work open c04_ex4_chaise_end.max from the scenes folder of the c04_ArchModel project.

Exercise 4.5: Modeling the Couch Feet

The final pieces you need to create for the couch are the feet. The feet are all the same, so you just need to create one foot, copy it, and put it in place under the couch. In Figure 4.13, look at the feet and note that they are a box shape that is thinner on the bottom. Continue with the project from the previous exercise or open the c04_ex5_feet_start.max file from the scenes folder of the c04_ArchModel project.

Certification Objective

FIGURE 4.13 The couch feet with measurements

1. Go to the command panel's Create panel, select Geometry, and click Box.

2. Click and drag in the Perspective viewport to create a box that will be the first foot.

3. Then go to the command panel's Modify panel, and enter 4.0 for Length, 9.5 for Width, and 3.0 for Height.

When the Taper modifier is applied, nothing will happen to your model until you change the Taper parameters.

A *modifier* changes the geometric structure of a model, and a Taper modifier will move the vertices near the top or bottom closer together. Using a Taper modifier is an easy way to make simple changes to your model.

4. In the Modify panel, click the Modifier List to expand and choose Taper.

5. Change Amount to **0.15**, as shown in Figure 4.14. Press Enter on your keyboard to set the amount.

FIGURE 4.14
The Taper parameters

6. Now move the couch foot into place under one of the corners of the couch. Use the clone operation (hold down the Shift key while you move the foot) to make duplicates of the foot and place them around the bottom of the couch at the remaining corners.

7. Take the time to select each couch foot box and rename it; use a simple naming convention such as Couch Foot01, 02, 03, and so on.

8. Save the file, and to check your work open c04_ex5_feet_end.max from the scenes folder of the c04_ArchModel project.

Now that the couch is finished, as shown in Figure 4.15, it should resemble the original couch but perhaps without the lived-in look and feel the real couch has. You can create some of that look by moving vertices and polygons so that it does not appear quite so perfect.

FIGURE 4.15   **The final couch**

Modeling the Lounge Chair

To model the chair, you'll be taking a different approach. You'll use a spline technique that the software is particularly good at. If you are used to Maya CV curves, the Bezier will seem a bit awkward, but if you are used to Photoshop's Pen tool, then the 3ds Max Line tools' way of making lines should be pretty easy. It isn't just the way you make the lines that makes the 3ds Max tools so nice; it's also the tools you use to make the lines into 3D objects.

Figure 4.16 shows the chair that will be modeled in this section. Click the Application button and choose Reset from the list that appears. This will set your interface and file back to a startup state.

FIGURE 4.16   The chair for the spline-modeling exercise

Exercise 4.6: Creating Image Planes

This exercise begins with creating planes and applying reference images to them. Set your project to the c04_ArchModel project downloaded to your system. Open c04_ex6_image_start.max. The image with measurements is shown in Figure 4.17.

FIGURE 4.17   The lounge chair with measurements

1. In a new scene, go to the Left viewport and create a plane.

2. In the Parameters rollout of the command panel, set Length to **23.6** and Width to **64.6**.

3. Rename this box **Lounger_Side** View.

The units are in generic units (inches), which is the 3ds Max default.

4. With the plane still selected, go to the Modify tab, and in the Parameters rollout, set Length Segs and Width Segs to **1**.

5. Then select the Move tool (W) in the main toolbar, and in the Transform Type-In areas at the bottom of the user interface, input **0.0** for X, **0.0** for Y, and **0.0** for Z to place the image at the center of the scene, known as the origin point.

6. Repeat steps 1 through 4 with the Front viewport active. The plane parameters are **23.6** for Length and **22.2** for Width.

7. Move the plane to these coordinates using the Transform Type-In area: X = **–11.0**, Y = **32.3**, Z = **1.5**.

8. Rename the plane **Lounger_Front View**.

9. Save the file, and to check your work open the c04_ex6_image_end.max file from the scenes folder of the c04_ArchModel project.

Exercise 4.7: Adding the Images

While adding the material to the image planes it's critical to ensure that the features of the chair that appear in both reference images (the front and the side) are at the same height. For instance, the top of the chair should be at the same height in both the front and side views to make the modeling process easier. Continue with the file from the previous exercise or open the c04_ex7_image_start.max file from the scenes folder of the c04_ArchModel project folder.

1. Make sure the Front and Left viewports are set to Shaded.

2. Open Windows Explorer and navigate to the ArchModel/sceneassets/images folder on your hard drive from the c04_ArchModel project you downloaded from the book's web page.

3. Drag Lounger_Side View.tif from the Explorer window to the image plane in the Left viewport.

4. Drag Lounger_Front View.tif onto the image plane in the Front viewport.

5. Save the file, and to check your work open the c04_ex7_image_end .max file from the scenes folder of the c04_ArchModel project folder.

The image planes should have the two images mapped on them, as shown in Figure 4.18.

FIGURE 4.18 Mapped image planes in viewports

Exercise 4.8: Building the Splines for the Chair Frame

Now it's time to create the splines for the lounge chair. Continue with your own couch file or load c04_ex8_spline_start.max from the scenes folder of the c04_ArchModel project from the book's web page. The colors added to the images that we used on the planes are to help you build the splines for the lounge chair. To begin, you will build a spline using the green line as a reference.

Certification Objective

1. Select the Left viewport and then maximize the viewport (Alt+W).

2. Go to the command panel and enter Create ➢ Shapes (), and then select the Line tool. You will use the Line tool to create a spline that follows the side view of the chair. Refer to Figure 4.19; it shows where the vertices should go (corresponding to the numbers in parentheses in the following steps).

FIGURE 4.19 Create vertex points by following the numbers.

3. Starting at the bottom left of the green line in Figure 4.19, click and release the mouse button to create a corner vertex (1).

4. Move your mouse up and to the right; click and release for a corner vertex (2).

5. Move to the right; click and release for a corner vertex (3).

6. Continue right; click and release for a corner vertex (4).

7. Continue right; click and release for a corner vertex (5).

8. Drag to make a Bezier curve on the green line (6).

9. Right-click and release to create another corner vertex (7), and then right-click to release the Line tool.

10. In the Modify panel, select Modifier Stack and enter Vertex mode.

11. Select vertex 2 shown in Figure 4.19. In the Geometry rollout, click the Fillet button and drag the vertex until the curve matches the curve in Figure 4.20, an approximate amount of 0.8.

FIGURE 4.20 A vertex fillet creates two vertices from one and curves the segment between them.

12. Repeat the process on vertices 3, 4, and 5. The completed spline is shown in Figure 4.21. Use whatever Fillet value is appropriate for the part of the lounge chair you are working on.

Fillet will split the vertex into two separate vertices and curve the segment in between them.

FIGURE 4.21   The competed spline for the side of the lounge

13. When you've finished, exit Vertex mode.

14. Switch to the Move tool (W) and select the spline.

15. Then, in the Front viewport, Shift+Move and align the spline to the frame of the chair on the left side, as shown in Figure 4.22.

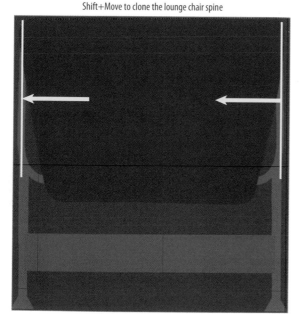

FIGURE 4.22   Use Shift+Move to clone the chair spline so it lines up with the chair frame on the left.

16. When the Clone Options dialog pops up, select Copy and then click OK. Now, these two splines need to be attached to form a single spline. This will allow you to create the bridge piece that runs along the two ends of the frame. Let's get the image planes out of the way.

17. Select both image planes and then right-click to bring up the quad menu. Choose Hide Selection from the Display menu.

18. With either spline selected, go to the Geometry rollout, click the Attach button, and then click the other spline, as shown in Figure 4.23.

FIGURE 4.23   Attach both sides of the chair frame.

19. Enter Vertex mode. In the Geometry rollout, click the Connect button (below the Weld button).

20. Rotate the Perspective viewport so you can see both splines.

21. Click and drag from the vertex on the bottom end of the spline to the vertex on the other side, as shown in Figure 4.24. Do the same for the top end of the spline frame.

FIGURE 4.24 Use Connect to create a segment between the two separate splines.

22. Right-click to exit from Connect.

23. Select the four vertices at the ends of the frame, and in the Geometry rollout, click the Fillet button and move to one of the selected vertices. Drag the vertex until the curve looks appropriate, an amount of about 1.8.

24. With the spline selected, go to the Rendering rollout and check the boxes for Enable In Viewport and Enable In Renderer.

25. Select Radial and change Thickness to 0.8.

26. Click the Render Production button (⬛) in the main toolbar to see the results of the spline rendering, shown in Figure 4.25.

FIGURE 4.25 The finished lounge frame with spline rendering enabled

SPLINE RENDERING

When modeling using splines, there is a very cool function you can use to create a shape along a path. The splines you just created are the paths. In the parameters of the editable spline, there is a rollout called Rendering. The controls let you turn on and off the renderability of the spline and specify its thickness. Once you enable the function, the mesh can be seen in the viewport and will show when rendered. The default 3D mesh that is enabled is a radial mesh, which would make a pipe of sorts, but there is also a rectangular mesh, and both shapes have parameters that can be edited.

You can create the remaining parts of the frame, the arc shape, using the same technique. Continue with your chair file or load c04_ex8_spline_end.max from the scenes folder of the c04_ArchModel project from the book's web page. This file has the completed seat/back frame, as shown in Figure 4.26.

FIGURE 4.26 The arc frames are attached and connected at the base and top.

Exercise 4.9: Building the Chair Cushion

For the lounge chair cushion, you can't use the same spline technique you used on the frame. To create it, you have to return to the technique you used for the couch: Create a simple box representation and then use NURMS to soften it. Continue with your own lounge chair file or load c04_ex9_cushion_start.max from the scenes folder of the c04_ArchModel project from the book's web page.

1. Go to the command panel, select Create ➢ Geometry, and click Box.

2. In the Perspective viewport, create a box, and then in the Modify panel, change Length to **64.0**, Width to **22.0**, and Height to **3.0**. Change Length Segs to **4**. Move the box so it is over the lounge chair frame.

3. In the Ribbon ➢ Modeling tab, select Polygon Modeling ➢ Convert To Poly.

4. In the Ribbon ➢ Modeling tab, choose Edit ➢ SwiftLoop, and add two edge loops close to the ends. These will help you rough out the shape of the lounge cushion.

5. Switch to Vertex mode (1); select and move the vertices where the segments are and line them up to follow the chair frame, as shown in Figure 4.27.

FIGURE 4.27 Arrange the vertices on the box so they follow the lounge chair frame.

6. Use SwiftLoop again, and place edge loops along the left and right edges as well as along the sides. This will keep the outer edges from curving in too much to keep the box shape.

7. Go to the Ribbon ➢ Modeling tab ➢ Edit ➢ Use NURMS. In the Use NURMS panel, set Iterations to **2**, as shown in Figure 4.29. NURMS has smoothed out the model and molded the lounge-chair cushion to the frame, but it still needs some work.

8. Use SwiftLoop to add edge loops, as shown in Figure 4.28. This will help to mold the cushion to the frame.

Turn off Use NURMS if you need to see the model more clearly.

Set
Iterations to 2

Use SwiftLoop to add edges
in these specific areas.

FIGURE 4.28   Turning up NURMS iterations and using SwiftLoop to smooth out the model

9. Save your file; to check your work open `c04_ex9_cushion_end.max` from the `scenes` folder of the `c04_ArchModel` project from the book's web page.

To finish the cushion, continue adjusting the edges/vertices to create the perfect shape. Also, look at the original reference image in Figure 4.16. There are straps that connect the cushion to the frame. Using the same spline techniques, create the straps to add realism to the overall look. Use the Line tool to create an oval shape that surrounds the frame, and in the Rendering rollout, choose Rectangular (see Figure 4.29).

FIGURE 4.29   Create straps using splines and the Rendering rollout.

Exercise 4.10: Creating the Chair's Base

The base is made up of the objects on which the frame of the lounge chair sits. There are nine different objects: the four legs, four blocks that sit between the legs, and a block that connects the legs together, as shown in Figure 4.30.

Certification Objective

F I G U R E   4 . 3 0   The lounge base

Follow these steps to create the lounge base:

1. Continue with your chair file or load c04_ex10_base_start.max from the scenes folder of the c04_ArchModel project on the companion web page.

2. Start by un-hiding the side image plane. Maximize the Left viewport and zoom in so you can see one of the base legs, which are the yellow box shapes.

3. Create a box that is the general size of the base leg. The parameters are as follows: Length = 13.2, Width = 4.0, Height = 0.35, Length Segs = 1, Width Segs = 1, and Height Segs = 1.

4. Activate See-Through mode (Alt+X) so you can see the image plane through the box primitive, and move the box so it is aligned with the lounge chair frame, as shown in Figure 4.31.

FIGURE 4.31 Create a box the size of the base leg in the image plane.

5. Choose the Ribbon ➢ Modeling tab ➢ Polygon Modeling ➢ Convert To Poly, and enter Vertex mode.

6. In the Left viewport, move the vertices so they line up with the yellow box in the image plane, as shown in Figure 4.32.

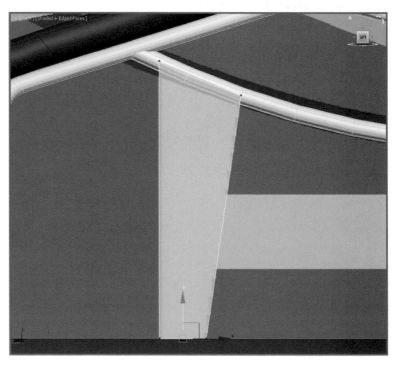

FIGURE 4.32 Move the vertices so they line up with the image plane.

7. Choose the Ribbon ➢ Modeling tab ➢ Edit ➢ SwiftLoop, and add a loop at the bottom. This will set up for adding the foot. Right-click to exit SwiftLoop.

8. Switch to a Perspective viewport and rotate the viewport so you can see an angled view.

9. Enter Polygon mode, and select the polygons between the new edge loop and the bottom of the Leg object. Exit See-Through mode (Alt+X).

10. Choose the Ribbon ➢ Modeling tab ➢ Polygons ➢ Extrude ➢ Extrude Settings. In the caddy, change the extrusion type to Local Normal and change the Height to 1.6. Press Enter to set the input; then click the OK button in the caddy, as shown in Figure 4.33.

FIGURE 4.33   Use Extrude to begin the creation of the foot.

11. Choose the Ribbon ➢ Modeling tab ➢ Edit ➢ SwiftLoop, and add edge loops, as shown in Figure 4.34, with edged faces turned on for better visibility.

FIGURE 4.34   Add edge loops using SwiftLoop in designated areas.

12. Choose the Ribbon ➢ Modeling tab ➢ Edit and turn on Use NURMS.

13. This looks very good, but you'll need to move vertices and/or edges to refine the shape of the object to match the leg shown in Figure 4.30.

14. When the leg is finished, copy it three times and position the copies so they are aligned with the frame (use Figure 4.16 as a reference for the position of the legs).

15. Create the remaining pieces using the same techniques you used to create the leg.

16. Save the file. To check your work open c04_ex10_base_end.max from the scenes folder of the c04_ArchModel project on the companion web page.

The final result is shown with appropriate colors applied (default colors) in Figure 4.35.

FIGURE 4.35   The final base shown with frame and cushion

Bringing It All Together

Now that the furniture is built, it's time to furnish the room you built in Chapter 3. You can do this by merging the furniture 3ds Max files into the room file. Merge allows you to load objects from one 3ds Max file into your current file. Open the c03_room_final.max file from the c03_ArchModel project folder. Or use the file that you completed in Chapter 3. Then follow these steps:

1. In the c03_room_final.max project file, click the Application button () and select Import ➢ Merge.

2. When the Merge File dialog box opens, navigate to the c04_ArchModel project folder, select the c04_Couch_Final.max file or use your own file, and click Open. The Merge dialog box will open, and you will see a list of objects available to merge from that file.

3. At the bottom of the dialog box, select All, as shown in Figure 4.36, and click OK. If you use your own files, the names may be different than those in the figure.

> Merged objects come into a scene already selected. They always merge into a scene at the same X, Y, Z coordinates as in their original file.

FIGURE 4.36　In the Merge dialog box, select the All button at the bottom of the dialog.

4. Click the Zoom Extends All Selected button located at the lower-right corner of the interface; it is a flyout, which means there are more buttons under Zoom Extends All; this will zoom in on the already selected Couch objects.

5. Go to the Group menu and select Group. Name the group **Couch** and click OK.

6. Position the couch in the room.

7. Check the images of the room for couch location (see reference Figure 4.1 from the beginning of the chapter). Check the Front and Left viewports to make sure the couch is level with the floor.

8. Repeat steps 1 through 7 to merge in and place the spline chair using the file c04_LoungeChair_Final.max.

Groups can also be nested, meaning you can have a group within a group.

GROUPING

Grouping lets you combine objects into a group. A group uses something like an invisible carrying case, called a *dummy object*, to hold your objects. Select the group and move it around, and the objects will move along with it. A group has its own pivot point. You can transform and modify a group as if it were a single object. If you want to modify an individual object in the group, do the following:

1. Select the group and then go to the Edit ➣ Group menu and choose Open. A pink bracket will appear. The objects can be individually selected.

2. Select and modify an individual object inside the group, as needed.

3. When you have finished and want to close the group, choose Edit ➣ Group ➣ Close.

4. When you want to dissolve a group, just select the group, and in the Edit ➣ Group menu, choose Ungroup.

These two pieces of furniture look great, but they don't fill up the room. To help furnish your newly built room, you can merge some prebuilt items into the space. Repeat steps 1 through 7 for the extra furniture pieces, which can be found in the Chapter 04 Extra Furniture folder in the scenes folder of the c04_ArchModel project. The room will look better after you merge the objects. The next phase for you may be to create some of your own objects to populate the room.

Now You Know

In this chapter, you learned how to make use of the Graphite Modeling tools to build a couch and chair. You started by blocking out the couch and then added NURMS to create smoothness before moving on to detailing and finishing the couch model. Then, using reference images, you created splines with the Line tool to draw out the shape of a chair before moving on to the cushions and the frame. From there we looked at how groups work to bring objects together.

CHAPTER 5

Introduction to Animation

Animation is the process of changing values of an object over time by setting keyframes and controlling those values. *Keyframing* is the process—borrowed from traditional animation—of setting positions and values at particular frames of the animation. The computer interpolates between these keyframes to fill in the other frames to complete a smooth animation.

Animation puts your scene into action and adds life to your characters. It is change over time. Anything in a scene that needs to change from one second to another will need to be animated to do so.

Everyone has their own reflexive sense of how things move. This knowledge is gleaned through years of perception and observation. Therefore, your audience can be more critical of a CG scene's motion than its lighting, coloring, or anything else. You know when something doesn't look right. So will your audience.

It's thrilling to see your hard work on a scene come to life with animation. On the flip side, it can be extremely aggravating to see your creation working improperly. Making mistakes is how you learn things, and your frustrations will ease over time. The results of your first several attempts at animating a scene will not look like Pixar films, but that should not dissuade you from working on more animations and scenes. You will get better with more practice.

The best way to learn how to animate is to jump right in and start animating. By doing so, you'll get a good look at the Autodesk® 3ds Max® software animation tools so you can start editing animation and developing your timing skills.

In this chapter, you will learn to:

▶ **Animate the ball**

▶ **Read animation curves**

▶ **Refine the animation**

Animating the Ball

Certification
Objective

A classic exercise for all animators is to create a bouncing ball. It is a straight-forward exercise, but there is much you can do with a bouncing ball to show character. Animating a bouncing ball is a good exercise in physics as well as cartoon movement. You'll first create a rubber ball, and then you'll add cartoonish movement to accentuate some principles of the animation. Aspiring animators can use this exercise for years and always find something new to learn about bouncing a ball.

Exercise 5.1: Setting Keyframes

In preparation, download the c05_IntroAnimation project from the companion web page at www.sybex.com/go/3dsmax2015essentials to your hard drive. Set your current project by clicking the Application button, choosing Manage ➤ Set Project Folder, and navigating to the c05_IntroAnimation project that you downloaded.

Open the c05_ex1_ball_start.max scene file from the scenes folder of the c05_IntroAnimation project folder you downloaded. If you receive a Gamma & LUT Settings Mismatch warning, click OK.

Start with the *gross animation,* or the overall movements. This is also called *blocking.* First, move the ball up and down to begin its choreography.

Follow these steps to animate the ball:

1. Select the ball, and then go to the Hierarchy panel (![icon]).

2. Choose Pivot, and under the Adjust Pivot rollout, click the Affect Pivot Only button.

3. Zoom in on the ball in the Front viewport, and with the Move tool drag on the Y-axis of the pivot to move to the bottom of the ball.

4. Click the Affect Pivot Only button again to deactivate.

5. Move the time slider to frame 10. The time slider is at the bottom of the screen below the viewports, as shown in Figure 5.1. It's used to change your position in time, counted in *frames.*

FIGURE 5.1 The time slider is used to change your position in time, counted in frames.

6. Click the Auto Key button below the time slider. The Auto Key button, the currently selected viewport, and the time slider all turn red, as shown in Figure 5.2. This means that any movement in the objects in your scene will be recorded as animation.

FIGURE 5.2 The Auto Key button records your animations.

7. Using the Camera viewport, select the ball and move it down along the Z-axis to the ground plane, so it is 0 units in the Z-axis Transform Type-In box at the bottom of the interface. You can also just enter the value in the Z-axis Transform Type-In box and press Enter. This will work the same as using the Move tool to transform.

8. Save the file, and to check your work you can open file c05_ex1_ball_end.max from the scenes folder of the c05_IntroAnimation project folder from companion web page at www.sybex.com/go/3dsmax2015essentials.

SCRUBBING THE TIME SLIDER

You can click and drag the horizontal time slider bar to change the frame in your animation on the fly; this is called *scrubbing*. The bar displays the current frame/end frame. By default, your 3ds Max window shows a start frame of 0 and an end frame of 100. When you move the time slider, the movement is reflected in the viewports.

This exercise has created two keyframes, one at frame 0 for the original position of the ball and one at frame 10 for the position to which you just moved the ball.

Exercise 5.2: Copying Keyframes

Now you want to move the ball up to the same position in the air as it was at frame 0. Instead of trying to estimate where that was, you can just copy the keyframe at frame 0 to frame 20.

You can see the keyframes you created in the timeline; they appear as red boxes. Red keys represent Position keyframes, green keys represent Rotation, and blue keys represent Scale. When a keyframe in the timeline is selected, it turns white. Now let's copy a keyframe:

1. Continue with the project from the previous exercise or open the c05_ex2_ball_start.max scene file from the scenes folder of the c05_Intro to Animation project folder you downloaded. If you start with the file from the scenes folder you will need to turn on the Auto Key button.

2. Select the keyframe at frame 0; it should turn white when it is selected.

3. Hold down the Shift key (this is a shortcut for the Clone tool), and click and drag the selected keyframe to copy it to frame 20. This will create a keyframe with the same animation parameters as the keyframe at frame 0, as shown in Figure 5.3.

FIGURE 5.3 Press Shift and drag the keyframe to copy it to frame 20.

4. Click and drag the time slider to scrub through the keyframes. You should see the ball start in the up position and then move down and then back up.

5. Turn off Auto Key.

6. Save the file, and to check your work you can open file c05_ex2_ball_end.max from the scenes folder of the c05_IntroAnimation project folder.

Exercise 5.3: Using the Track View - Curve Editor

Certification
Objective

Right now the ball is going down and then back up. To continue the animation for the length of the timeline, you could continue to copy and paste keyframes as you did earlier—but that would be very time-consuming, and you still need to do your other homework and clean your room. A better way is to loop, or *cycle,* through the keyframes you already have. An *animation cycle* is a segment of animation that is repeatable in a loop. The end state of the animation matches up to the beginning state, so there is no hiccup at the loop point.

In 3ds Max, you use the Parameter Curve Out-of-Range Types feature to cycle animation. This is a fancy way to create loops and cycles with your animations and specify how your object will behave outside the range of the keys you have created. This brings us to Track View, which is an animator's best friend. You will learn the underlying concepts of the Curve Editor as well as its basic interface throughout this exercise.

Track View is a function of two animation editors, the Curve Editor and the Dope Sheet. The Curve Editor allows you to work with animation depicted as curves on a graph that sets the value of a parameter against time. The Dope Sheet displays keyframes over time on a horizontal graph, without any curves. This graphical display simplifies the process of adjusting animation timing because you can see all the keys at once in a spreadsheet-like format. The Dope Sheet is similar to traditional animation exposure sheets, or X-sheets.

You will use the Track View - Curve Editor (or Curve Editor for short) to loop your animation in the following steps:

Navigation inside the Track View - Curve Editor is pretty much the same as navigation in a viewport; the same keyboard/mouse combinations work for panning and zooming.

1. Continue with the project from the previous exercise or open the c05_ex3_ball_start.max scene file from the scenes folder of the c05_IntroAnimation project folder you downloaded.

2. With the ball selected, in the menu bar choose Graph Editors ➤ Track View - Curve Editor. In Figure 5.4, the Curve Editor displays the animation curves of the ball so far.

FIGURE 5.4   The Curve Editor shows the animation curves of the ball.

3. A menu bar runs across the top of the Curve Editor. In the Edit menu, choose Controller ➤ Out Of Range Types, as shown in Figure 5.5. Doing so opens the Param Curve Out-of-Range Types dialog box, shown in Figure 5.6.

FIGURE 5.5   Selecting Out Of Range Types

FIGURE 5.6   Choosing to loop your animation

4. Select Loop in this dialog box by clicking its thumbnail. The two little boxes with arrows beneath it will highlight, as shown in Figure 5.6. Click OK. Once you set the curve to Loop, the Curve Editor displays your animation, as shown in Figure 5.7. The out-of-range animation is shown as a dashed line.

FIGURE 5.7   The Curve Editor now shows the looped animation curve.

5. Scrub your animation in a viewport and see how the ball bounces up and down throughout the timeline range.

6. Save the file, and to check your work you can open file c05_ex3_ ball_end.max from the scenes folder of the c05_IntroAnimation project folder.

Reading Animation Curves

As you can see, the Curve Editor gives you control over the animation in a graph setting. The Curve Editor's graph is a representation of an object's parameters, such as Position (values shown vertically) over time (time shown horizontally). Curves allow you to visualize the interpolation of the motion. Once you are used to reading animation curves, you can judge an object's direction, speed, acceleration, and timing at a mere glance.

Certification Objective

Here is a quick primer on how to read a curve in the Curve Editor.

In Figure 5.8, an object's Z Position parameter is being animated. At the beginning, the curve quickly begins to move positively (that is, to the right) on the Z-axis. The object shoots up and comes to an *ease-in*, where it decelerates to a stop, reaching its top height. The ease-in stop is signified by the curving beginning to flatten out at around frame 95.

F I G U R E   5 . 8   The object quickly accelerates to an ease-in stop.

In Figure 5.9, the object slowly accelerates in an *ease-out* in the positive Z direction until it hits frame 100, where it suddenly stops.

FIGURE 5.9   The object eases out to acceleration and suddenly stops at its fastest velocity.

In Figure 5.10, the object eases out and travels to an ease-in where it decelerates, starting at around frame 69, to where it slowly stops, at frame 100.

FIGURE 5.10   Ease-out and ease-in

Finally, in Figure 5.11, to showcase another tangent type, step interpolation holds its position from frame 0 to frame 20 and then makes the object jump from its Z position in frame 20 to its new position in frame 21.

FIGURE 5.11   Step interpolation makes the object "jump" suddenly from one value to the next.

Figure 5.12 shows the Curve Editor, with its major aspects called out for your information.

Navigation   Key Tangents toolbar   Tangent actions   Key entry

Menu bar
Key controls
Toolbar
Controller window
Key Editing Window

FIGURE 5.12   The Curve Editor

Refining the Animation

Let's play the animation now. In the bottom right of the interface, you will see an animation player with the sideways triangle to signify Play Animation. Select the Camera01 viewport and click the Play Animation button. The framework of the movement is getting there. Notice how the speed of the ball is moving in a consistent way. If this were a real ball, it would be dealing with gravity; the ball would speed up as it got closer to the ground and there would be "hang time" when the ball was in the air on its way up as gravity took over to pull it back down.

This means you have to edit the movement that happens between the keyframes. This is done by adjusting *how* the keyframes shape the curve itself, using tangents. When you select a keyframe, a handle will appear in the user interface (UI), as shown in Figure 5.13.

Certification Objective

FIGURE 5.13   **The keyframe handle**

This handle adjusts the tangency of the keyframe to change the curvature of the animation curve, which in turn changes the animation. There are various types of tangents, depending on how you want to edit the motion. By default the Auto tangent is applied to all new keyframes. This is not what you want for the ball, although it is a perfect default tangent type to have.

ANIMATION CONTROLLERS

Anything you animate is handled by a controller. Controllers store animation and interpolate between values. There are three default controllers:

Position: Position XYZ

Rotation: Euler XYZ

Scale: Bezier Scale

Exercise 5.4: Editing Animation Curves

Certification Objective

Let's edit some tangents to better suit your animation. The intent is to speed up the curve as it hits the floor and slow it down as it crests its apex. Instead of opening the Curve Editor through the menu bar, this time you are going to use the shortcut:

1. Continue with the project from the previous exercise or open the c05_ex4_ball_start.max scene file from the scenes folder of the c05_IntroAnimation project folder you downloaded.

2. Close the large Curve Editor dialog box, unless it is already closed.

3. At the bottom-left corner of the interface, click the Open Mini Curve Editor button shown in Figure 5.14.

> The Mini Curve Editor is the same as the one you launch through the main menu. A few tools are not included in the Mini Curve Editor toolbar, but you can find them in the menu bar.

FIGURE 5.14 Click the Open Mini Curve Editor button.

4. With the ball selected, scroll down the Controller window on the left of the Mini Curve Editor by dragging the Pan tool (the hand cursor) to find the Ball object's position tracks.

5. Click the Z Position track. This will bring to the Key Editing window only the curves that you want to edit. The Z Position curve is blue, as is almost everything relating to the Z-axis. The little gray boxes on the curves are keyframes.

6. Select the keyframe at frame 10. The key will turn white when selected. You will change this key's tangency to make the ball fall faster as it hits and bounces off the ground.

7. In the Mini Curve Editor toolbar, change the tangent type for the selected keyframe from the Auto default to Fast by clicking the Set Tangents to Fast icon ().When you do this, you will see the animation curve change shape, as shown in Figure 5.15.

FIGURE 5.15   The effect of the new tangent type

8. Select the Camera01 viewport and play the animation. You can easily correlate how the animation works with the curve's shape when you watch the time slider travel through the Mini Curve Editor as the animation plays.

9. Save the file, and to check your work you can open file c05_ex4_ball_end.max from the scenes folder of the c05_IntroAnimation project folder.

You may need to scrub the time slider, which in the Curve Editor appears as double yellow vertical lines, out of the way if you are on frame 10.

If you need to zoom or pan in the Curve Editor's Key Editing window, you can use the same shortcuts you would use to navigate in the viewports.

FINESSING THE ANIMATIONS

Although the animation has improved, the ball has a distinct lack of weight. It still seems too simple and without any character. In situations such as this, animators can go wild and try several different things as they see fit. Here is where creativity helps hone your animation skills, whether you are new to animation or have been doing it for 50 years.

Animation shows change over time. Good animation conveys the *intent,* the motivation for that change between the frames.

Exercise 5.5: Squash and Stretch

The concept of *squash and stretch* has been an animation staple for as long as there has been animation. It is a way to convey the weight of an object by deforming it to react (usually in an exaggerated way) to gravity, impact, and motion.

You can give your ball a lot of flair by adding squash and stretch to give the object some personality. Follow along with these steps:

1. Continue with the project from the previous exercise or open the c05_ex5_ball_start.max scene file from the scenes folder of the c05_IntroAnimation project folder you downloaded.

2. Press the N key to activate Auto Key.

3. Open the Mini Curve Editor if it isn't already open, and drag the yellow double-line track bar time slider to frame 10.

4. Click and hold the Scale tool to access the flyout.

5. Choose the Select And Squash tool (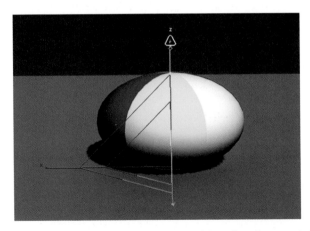).

6. Select the ball if it isn't already selected, and center the cursor over the Z-axis of the Scale Transform gizmo in the Camera viewport.

7. Click and drag down to squash about 20 percent. Doing so will scale down on the Z-axis and scale up on the X- and Y-axes to compensate and maintain a constant volume, as shown in Figure 5.16.

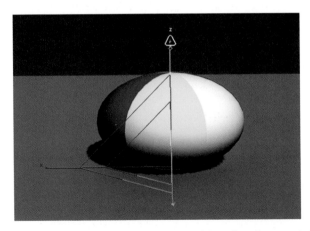

FIGURE 5.16   Use the Select And Squash tool to squash the ball on impact.

8. Move to frame 0, and click and drag up to stretch the ball up about 20 percent, so that the ball's scale in Z is about 120. When you scrub

through the animation, you will see that the ball is stretched at frame 0; then the ball squashes and stays squashed for the rest of the time. You'll fix that in the next step.

9. In the Mini Curve Editor, scroll in the Controller window until you find the Scale track for the ball.

10. Highlight it to see the keyframes and animation curves.

11. Click and hold the Move Keys tool in the Mini Curve Editor toolbar to roll out and access the Move Keys Horizontal tool ()

12. Click and drag a selection marquee around the two keyframes at frame 0 in the Scale track to select them.

13. Hold the Shift key and then click and drag the keyframes at frame 0 to frame 20.

14. In the Mini Curve Editor's menu bar, choose Edit ➢ Controller ➢ Out Of Range Types. Choose Loop, and then click OK.

15. Play the animation. The curves are shown in Figure 5.17.

16. Save the file, and to check your work you can open file c05_ex5_ball_end.max from the scenes folder of the c05_IntroAnimation project folder.

FIGURE 5.17 **The final curves**

Exercise 5.6: Setting the Timing

Well, you squashed and stretched the ball, but it still doesn't look right. That is because the ball should not squash before it hits the ground. It needs to return to 100 percent scale and stay there for a few frames. Immediately before the ball hits the ground, it can squash into the ground plane to heighten the sense of impact. The following steps are easier to perform in the regular Curve Editor than in the Mini Curve Editor. So close the Mini Curve Editor by clicking the Close button on the left side of its toolbar.

1. Continue with the project from the previous exercise or open the `c05_ex6_ball_start.max` scene file from the `scenes` folder of the `c05_IntroAnimation` project folder you downloaded.

2. Move the time slider to frame 8; turn on Auto Key if it is not still active.

3. Select the ball and open the Curve Editor; in the Controller window, select the ball's Scale track so that only the scale curves appear in the Editing window.

4. In the Curve Editor's toolbar, click the Add Keys icon ( ). Your cursor will change to an arrow with a white circle at its lower right.

5. Click directly on the Scale curve to add a keyframe on all the Scale curves at frame 8. Because scales X and Y are the same value, you will see only two curves instead of three.

6. The keys are white when selected. In the Key Entry toolbar, you will find two text type-in boxes. The box on the left is the frame number, and the box on the right is the selected key's (or keys') value. Because more than one key with a different value is selected, there is no number in that type-in box.

7. Enter **100** (for 100 percent scale) in the right type-in box, for the scale in X, Y, and Z for the ball at frame 8, as shown in Figure 5.18.

FIGURE 5.18 Enter a value of 100.

8. Move the time slider to frame 12, and do the same thing in the Curve Editor. These settings are bracketing the squash so that it squashes only a couple frames before and a couple frames after the ball hits the ground.

9. Press the N key to deactivate Auto Key.

10. Save the file, and to check your work you can open file `c05_ex6_ball_end.max` from the `scenes` folder of the `c05_IntroAnimation` project folder.

Once you play back the animation, the ball will begin to look a lot more like a nice cartoonish one, with a little character. Experiment by changing some of the scale amounts to have the ball squash a little more or less, or stretch it more or less to see how that affects the animation. See if it adds a different personality to the ball. If you can master a bouncing ball and evoke all sorts of emotions from your audience, you will be a great animator indeed.

Exercise 5.7: Moving the Ball Forward

Now that you have worked out the bounce, it's time to add movement to the ball so that it moves across the screen as it bounces. Layering animation in this fashion, where you settle on one movement before moving on to another, is common. That's not to say you won't need to go back and forth and make adjustments through the whole process, but it's generally nicer to work out one layer of the animation before adding another. The following steps will show you how:

1. Continue with the project from the previous exercise or open the c05_ex7_ball_start.max scene file from the scenes folder of the c05_IntroAnimation project folder you downloaded.

2. Press the N key to activate Auto Key again. Move the time slider to frame 0.

3. With the Select And Move tool, and move the ball in the Camera01 viewport to the left so it is still within the camera's view. That's about −30 units on the X-axis.

4. Move the time slider to frame 100.

5. Move the ball to the right about 60 units so that the ball's X Position value is about 30. Don't play the animation yet; it isn't going to look right.

6. Go to the Curve Editor, scroll down in the Controller window, and select the X Position track for the ball, as shown in Figure 5.19. There is no keyframe at frame 100; this is because of the loop that you set on the ball earlier; it will be addressed in the following steps.

FIGURE 5.19   The X Position track of the ball does not look right.

4. Also expand the XForm track, and then go to the Gizmo track and select the Y Rotation track. You will see the curve in the Key Editing window.

5. Select the keyframe at frame 0; it has a value of 0 and the keyframe at frame 100 has a value of 360.

6. Select both keyframes and change the tangents to Linear, as shown in Figure 5.23.

FIGURE 5.23 The Gizmo track's Y-axis rotation is selected in the Controller window and Linear tangents are set.

7. Close the Curve Editor and play the animation.

8. Save the file, and to check your work you can open file c05_ex10_ball_end.max from the scenes folder of the c05_Intro to Animation project folder.

9. Play the c05_BallRender.avi movie file located in the renderoutput folder of the Intro to Animation project to see a render of the animation.

Now You Know

In this chapter, you began your adventure into animation by learning how to set and manipulate keyframes by animating a ball. Using the Track View - Curve Editor, we looked into how to read and edit animation curves to help you refine motion on the animated ball. This chapter also showed you the animation principle of squash and stretch to give weight to an animated object. Finally, you finished the animation using the XForm modifier as a tool to add an additional pivot point with which to animate.

CHAPTER 6

Animation Principles

This chapter is a continuation of the animation work you began in Chapter 5, "Introduction to Animation." It introduces you to some new animation fundamentals. We will look at using some animation principles by completing a knife-throwing project.

In this chapter, you will learn to:

▶ **Create anticipation and momentum to make knife throwing appear realistic**

Anticipation and Momentum in Knife Throwing

This exercise will give you more experience with Autodesk® 3ds Max® software animation techniques. You will edit more in the Curve Editor and be introduced to some animation principles and concepts, anticipation, momentum, and secondary movement. First, download the project files for this chapter from this book's companion web page (www.sybex.com/go/3dsmax2015essentials). Set your project folder by choosing Application ➢ Manage ➢ Set Project Folder and selecting the c06_Animation Principles project that you downloaded.

Exercise 6.1: Blocking Out the Animation

To begin this exercise, open the c06_ex1_blocking_start.max file in the c06_Animation Principles project folder. When you open the file, you might see a Gamma & LUT Settings Mismatch error dialog; click OK, and then follow these steps.

1. Move the time slider to frame 30 and activate the Auto Key button.

2. Move the knife to the TARGET object, as shown in Figure 6.1.

FIGURE 6.1   Move the knife to the target at frame 30.

3. Move the time slider to frame 15, where the knife is halfway between its start and the target, and in the Camera001 viewport, move the knife slightly up on the Z-axis, as shown in Figure 6.2, so that the knife moves with a slight arc.

FIGURE 6.2   Move the knife up slightly at frame 15.

4. Click the Time Configuration icon at the bottom of the UI next to the navigation controls. Figure 6.3 shows the Time Configuration dialog box.

FIGURE 6.3   Change the frame range in the Time Configuration dialog box.

5. In the Animation section, change End Time to 30 from 100 and click OK. The time slider will reflect this change immediately.

6. Play your animation, and you should see the knife move with a slight ease-out and ease-in toward the target, with a slight arc up in the middle. You are going to move the keyframes from frame 0 to frame 10 so there is a pause before the knife moves toward the target.

7. Open the Curve Editor and scroll down in the Controller window until you see the Knife X, Y, and Z Position tracks.

8. Hold the Ctrl key and select all three tracks to display their curves (if they are not already selected), as shown in Figure 6.4.

FIGURE 6.4 The initial curves for the knife

9. Drag a selection marquee around the three keyframes at frame 0.

10. In the Key Controls toolbar, select and hold the Move Keys tool ( ) to access the flyout icons, and select the Move Keys Horizontal tool in the flyout ( ). Use this tool to move the keyframes to frame 10.

11. This will compact the curve, so you need to move the keyframes at frame 15 to the new middle, frame 20.

12. Now you can turn off the Auto Key button (N). The finished curve is shown in Figure 6.5.

FIGURE 6.5 Finished curves with the position of the knife starting at frame 10

That's it for the gross animation (or *blocking*) of the shot. To check your work, open the c06_ex1_blocking_end.max file in the c06_Animation Principles project folder.

Exercise 6.2: Trajectories

When it comes to animation, it is very helpful to be able to see an object's *trajectory* (the path the object is taking over time). To begin this exercise, open the c06_ex2_trajectories_start.max file in the c06_Animation Principles project folder:

1. Select the THROW KNIFE object.

2. In the command panel, click the Motion icon ().

3. Click Trajectories, as shown in Figure 6.6. The viewports will display a red curve to show you the path of the knife's motion as it arcs toward the target, as shown in Figure 6.7.

FIGURE 6.6 Turning on Trajectories for the knife

The large, hollow, square points on the trajectory curve represent the keyframes set on the knife so far.

FIGURE 6.7 The curve shows the trajectory for the knife's motion.

4. Select the Sub-Object button at the top of the Motion panel. Keys is your only sub-object choice in the pull-down menu to the right of the button.

5. Select the middle keyframe and move it up or down to suit your tastes.

6. Once you settle on a nice arc for the path of the knife, turn off Trajectories mode by clicking the Parameters button in the Motion panel.

As you can imagine, the Trajectories option can be useful in many situations. It not only gives you a view of your object's path; it also allows you to edit that path easily and in a visual context, which can be very important. To check your work, open the c06_ex2_trajectories_end.max file in the c06_Animation Principles project folder.

Exercise 6.3: Adding Rotation

Throwing knives in real life is usually a bad idea, but you can throw something else at a target (the inanimate kind) to see how to animate your knife. You'll find that the object will rotate once or twice before it hits its target. To begin this exercise, open the c06_ex3_rotation_start.max file in the c06_Animation Principles project folder. To add rotation to your knife, follow these steps:

1. Select the knife and then press N to activate Auto Key (if it isn't already active). Move to frame 30, and press E for the Select and Rotate tool.

2. In the Camera001 viewport, rotate on the Y-axis about 443 degrees.

3. With the knife selected, open the Curve Editor.

4. Scroll down to locate the X, Y, and Z Rotation tracks.

5. Select the keys at frame 0, and then use the Move Keys Horizontal tool to move the keyframes to frame 10. Figure 6.8 shows the Curve Editor graph for the rotation on the knife.

FIGURE 6.8 The Curve Editor graph for the rotation on the knife

6. Press N to deactivate Auto Key.

7. Play the animation, and you will see that the knife's position and rotation ease in and out. Stop animation (/ is the shortcut key).

8. Go back to the Curve Editor; change Move Keys Horizontal back to Move Keys.

9. Then select X Position track; then select both keyframes and change them to Linear.

10. Now select the Z Position track; you'll need to finesse this one a bit more than you did the X Position track. You are going to use the handles on the tangents that appear when you select a key. These handles can be adjusted.

11. Select the keyframe at frame 10; then center your cursor over the end on the tangent handle and drag using the Move Keys tool. Pull it up so it is even with the curve. Then repeat the same with the keyframe at frame 30. Figure 6.9 illustrates how you want the Z Position animation curve to look. This will give the trajectory a nice arc and a good rate of travel. Now it is time to edit the Rotation keys.

The rotations or movement would not ease in or out with a real knife. Its speed would be roughly consistent throughout the animation.

If the total value of the rotation is more than 360 degrees, it will increase the speed of the rotation. This will add one full revolution to the animation and some more excitement to the action.

FIGURE 6.9   Adjust the curve for the knife's arc through the air.

12. The first thing you can do is add a bit of drama to the knife to make the action more exciting. To this end, you can see that the rotation of the knife is too slow.

13. Choose the X Rotation track and select its key at frame 30.

14. In the Key Entry Type-In, change the value to about **−660**.

15. Adjust the tangent handles to resemble the curve shown in Figure 6.10. The knife will speed up just a bit as it leaves the first rotation keyframe. The speed will be even as it goes into the last keyframe.

FIGURE 6.10   Match your curve to this one.

With just a little bit of fast rotation as the knife leaves frame 10, you give the animation more spice. The knife should now have a slightly weightier look than before, when it rotated with an ease-in and ease-out. To check your work, open the c06_ex3_rotation_end.max file in the c06_Animation Principles project folder.

Exercise 6.4: Adding Anticipation

Now let's animate the knife to create *anticipation,* as if an invisible hand holding the knife pulled back just before throwing it to get more strength in the throw. This anticipation, although it's a small detail, adds a level of nuance to the animation that enhances the total effect. To begin this exercise, open the c06_ex4_anticipation_start.max file in the c06_Animation Principles project folder. Follow these steps:

1. Move the time slider to frame 0.

2. Select the knife, go to the Curve Editor, scroll in the Controller window, and then select the X Rotation track for the knife.

3. In the Curve Editor toolbar, click the Add Keys icon ( ), bring your cursor to frame 0 of the curve, and click to create a keyframe. Doing so creates a key at frame 0 with the same parameters as the next key, as shown in Figure 6.11.

FIGURE 6.11   Add a key to the beginning to create anticipation for the knife throw.

4. Select the Move Keys tool, and select the keyframe at frame 10.

5. In the Key Entry Type-In box, change the value of the key at frame 10 to 240. If you play back the animation, it will look weird. The knife will cock back really fast and spin a bit. This is due to the big hump between frames 0 and 10.

It's common to try something and rely on Undo—even several times—to get back to the starting point. You can also save multiple versions of your file to revert to an earlier one.

▶

6. Keep the tangent at frame 0 set to the default, but change the tangent on the key at frame 10 to Linear ( ). Play the animation. You'll have a slight bit of anticipation, but the spice will be lost and the knife will look less active and too mechanical.

7. To regain the weight you had in the knife, press Ctrl+Z to undo your change to the tangency on frame 10 and set it back to what you had. You may have to undo more than once.

8. Now, select the Move Keys Vertical tool ( ), which is under the Move Keys tool. Select the keyframe at frame 10, and then select the In tangent handle. This is the tangent handle on the left of the key.

▶

By pressing Shift as you dragged the tangent handle, you broke the continuity between the In and Out handles so that only the In handle was affected.

9. Press Shift and drag the tangent handle down to create a curve that is similar to the one shown in Figure 6.12.

FIGURE 6.12   To create a believable anticipation for the knife throw, set your curve to resemble this one.

10. Play back the animation. It should look much better now.

To check your work, open the c06_ex4_anticipation_end.max file in the c06_Animation Principles project folder.

Exercise 6.5: Following Through

The knife needs more weight. A great way to show that in animation is by adding follow-through; have the knife sink into the target a bit. To begin this exercise, open the c06_ex5_followthrough_start.max file in the c06_Animation Principles project folder.

To add follow-through to your animation, use these steps:

1. Click the Time Configuration icon and change End Time to 45 to add 15 frames to your frame range.

2. Click OK. Doing so will not affect the animation; it will merely append 15 frames to the current frame range.

3. Select the knife and go to frame 30, where it completes its hit on the target.

4. In the Curve Editor, select the X Position track of the knife.

5. Add a keyframe with the Add Keys tool at frame 35. Select the Move Keys tool, and then select the keyframe at frame 35.

6. Note the value of the key in the type-in boxes at the top right of the Curve Editor (*not* the type-in boxes at the bottom of the main UI). You will want to set the value for the key at frame 35 to about 1330 to sink it farther into the target.

7. With these relative values, scrub the animation between frames 30 and 35. You should see the knife's slight move into the target. The end of your curve should look like the curve in Figure 6.13. You still need to add a little bit of follow-through to the rotation of the knife to make it sink into the target better.

◀

If your values are different, adjust accordingly so you don't add too much movement. Also make sure the movement flows *into* the target and not back out of the target as if the knife were bouncing out.

FIGURE 6.13   Your animation should end like this.

8. In the Curve Editor, select the X Rotation track to display its curve.

9. Add a key to the curve at frame 35. The value of the key at frame 30 should already be about –660.

10. Set the value of the keyframe at frame 35 to about **–655**. Keep the tangent set at Auto.

11. If your values are different, adjust according to what works best in your scene.

Be careful about how much the knife sinks into the target. Although it is important to show the weight of the knife, it is also important to show the weight of the target; you do not want the target to look insubstantial. To check your work, open the c06_ex5_followthrough_end.max file in the c06_Animation Principles project folder.

Exercise 6.6: Transferring Momentum to the Target

To make the momentum work even better for the knife animation, you will have to push back the target as the knife hits it. The trouble is, if you animate the target moving back, the knife will stay in place, floating in the air. You have to animate the knife *with* the target.

Parent and Child Objects

Certification Objective

To animate the knife and target together, the knife has to be linked to the target so that when the target is animated to push back upon impact, the knife will follow precisely because it is stuck in the target. Doing this won't mess up the existing animation of the knife because the knife will be the child in the hierarchy and will retain its own animation separate from the target. To begin this exercise, open the c06_ex6_momentum_start.max file in the c06_Animation Principles project folder. Just follow these steps:

1. Go to frame 35, about when the knife impacts.

2. On the far left of the main toolbar, choose the Select and Link tool ().

3. Select the knife and drag it to the target, as shown in Figure 6.14 (left image). Nothing should change until you animate the target object.

4. Move the time slider to frame 34 and press the N key to activate the Auto Key tool.

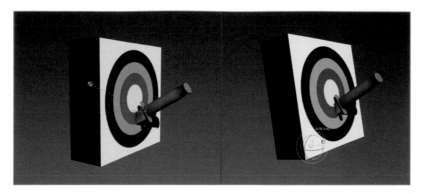

FIGURE 6.14   Link the knife to the target (left), and then rotate the target in the X-axis (right).

5. With the Select and Rotate tool, select the TARGET object and rotate it back about 5 degrees, as shown in Figure 6.14 (right image).

The pivot of the target has already been placed properly, at the bottom back edge.

6. Go to the Curve Editor, scroll to find the Y Rotation track for the TARGET object, select the keyframe at frame 0, and move it to frame 30.

7. Then hold the Shift key, and click and drag the keyframe (which will make a copy of it) to frame 37.

8. Change the tangent for the key at frame 30 to Fast and leave the other key tangents alone.

9. Add a little wobble to the target to make the animation even more interesting. This can be done easily in the Curve Editor. Use Add Keys to add keys at frames 40 and 44.

10. Using the Move Keys Vertical tool, give the key at frame 40 a value of about 1.7. Your curve should resemble the one in Figure 6.15.

FIGURE 6.15   The target animation curve

11. Finally, add a little slide to the target. Using the Select And Move tool, move the time slider to frame 37, and move the target just a bit along the X-axis.

12. Go to the Curve Editor, scroll to the X position of the TARGET object, select the keyframe at frame 0, and move it to frame 30 so the move starts when the knife hits the target.

13. Change the tangent for frame 30 to Fast and leave the other tangent at Auto. Deactivate Auto Key.

Done! Play your animation. Experiment and change some of the final timings and values of the target's reaction to the impact to see different weights of the knife and target and how the weight looks to the viewer. To check your work, open the c06_ex6_momentum_end.max file in the c06_Animation Principles project folder.

You can see a sample render of the scene in the c06_knife_animation.mov QuickTime file in the renderoutput folder of the c06_Animation Principles project.

Now You Know

In this chapter, you learned some new animation fundamentals: anticipation and momentum. Anticipation is used to show the knife preparing for action and makes the action appear more realistic. By adding rotation to the beginning of the animation it is as if an invisible hand is holding the knife and pulling it back just before throwing. This gives the throw more strength. Momentum describes how heavy the knife is while moving through space, so it pushes the target as the knife hits.

CHAPTER 7

Character Modeling Part I

In games, characters are cleverly designed and created to achieve the best look with the least amount of mesh detail to keep the polygon count low. Drawing on this knowledge, the film industry has taken many game-modeling techniques and modified them for film, creating low-poly efficient models and then adding detail (or polygons) when needed. With that in mind, this chapter and the next introduce you to character modeling, using the Editable Poly toolset to create a cute alien suitable for character animation. The alien character used in this book was designed by Andrew Montemayor, a graduate of the Art Institute of California - Los Angeles, who specializes in storyboarding, character design, and background design.

This chapter begins with the basic form of the character.

In this chapter, you will learn to:

▶ **Set up the scene**

▶ **Block out the alien body**

▶ **Refine the alien body**

Setting Up the Scene

You can import and use sketches of the character's front and side as background images as you create the character using the Autodesk® 3ds Max® software toolset. You can use additional sketches of your character from several points of view as quick references to help you reach your goal.

HIGH- AND LOW-POLY MODELING

High-polygon-count models are used when a model's level of detail needs to be impeccable, such as when the model is used in close-ups. High-polygon models are also used to generate displacement and normal maps to use on lower-resolution models. This technique is used to add needed detail without the issues that come with high-resolution models.

Low-polygon-count modeling, also called *low-poly modeling,* refers to a style of modeling that sacrifices some detail in favor of efficient geometry and places a very low load on the system on which it is being created or rendered. The number of triangles needed to consider something low-poly is based on the rendering platform and increases as the technology improves.

Exercise 7.1: Creating the Image Planes

The 3ds Max default system of measurement is generic units. One generic unit equals one inch.

▶

▶

When you apply the image to the plane, it is important to keep it proportional, maintaining its width and length with no stretching or squeezing of the images.

You'll begin this exercise by creating crossed boxes and applying reference images to them. Set your project to the c07_CharacterModel project you downloaded from the book's web page at www.sybex.com/go/3dsmax2015essentials.

1. In a new scene, select the Front viewport.

2. In the Create panel ➢ Geometry, select Plane. Select the Keyboard Entry rollout and set Y: to 30. This will move the bottom of the plane in line with the 0 axis within the front view. Set Length to 60 and Width to 42. Click the Create button.

3. Rename the plane Image Plane Front.

4. With the plane still selected, choose the Modify tab, and in the Parameters rollout, set Length Segs and Width Segs to 1.

5. Click in a blank space in the user interface (UI), and then press Ctrl+Shift+Z on your keyboard to initiate the shortcut for Zoom Extents All.

6. In the main toolbar, turn on Angle Snap Toggle () or press A on your keyboard. Doing so will snap your rotation to every 5 degrees.

7. Select the Select and Rotate tool (E) and select the Image Plane Front object. Hold down the Shift key on the keyboard and, in the Front viewport, rotate the image plane by dragging along the Y-axis 90 degrees.

8. Using the Shift key and a Transform tool activates the Clone Options dialog box, shown in Figure 7.1.

FIGURE 7.1 The Clone Options dialog box

9. In the Clone Options dialog box, under Object, select Copy; name the copy **Image Plane Side** and click OK.

This is a good time to save your file. To check your work, open the c07_ex1_setup_end.max file in the c07_CharacterModel project folder.

Exercise 7.2: Adding the Images to the Planes

At this point, you add the reference materials onto the planes to provide a reference inside the scene itself while you model the character. Therefore, it's critical to ensure that the features of the character that appear in both reference images (the front and the side) are at the same height. For instance, the top of the head and the shoulders should be at the same height in both the front and side views to make the modeling process easier. Either continue the exercise using your previously saved file or open c07_ex2_image_start.max.

1. Change the shading in the Front and Left viewports to Shaded if it isn't already set to Shaded. Turn off the grid in both viewports by selecting the viewport and using the keyboard shortcut G.

2. Open a Windows Explorer window and navigate to the c07_CharacterModel/sceneassets/images folder on your hard drive.

3. Drag Alien_Front.jpg from the Explorer window to the Image Plane Front object in the Front viewport.

4. Drag Alien_Side.jpg onto the Image Plane Side object in the Left viewport.

5. Turn on Edged Faces; you can use the keyboard shortcut F4. The image planes should have the two images mapped on them, as shown in Figure 7.2.

FIGURE 7.2   Mapped image planes in viewports

To check your work, open the c07_ex2_image_end.max file in the c07_CharacterModel project folder.

Blocking Out the Alien Model

When starting a model a good practice is to block out the basic form of the character and focus on the size and crucial shapes of the major elements; and then add detail for the finer features. The following exercises describe the steps required to block out the alien's major features.

Exercise 7.3: Forming the Torso

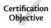

Certification Objective

The basic structure for the torso begins with a simple box primitive. After converting the box into an editable poly, you will use the Symmetry modifier on the object so that any manipulations performed on one side are also performed on the other. You will begin forming the basic shape of the torso by moving the editable poly's vertices and extruding its polygons in the following steps.

Continue with the previous exercise's scene file, or open the c07_ex3_torso_
start.max scene file in the scenes folder of the c07_CharacterModel project
folder downloaded from this book's web page. Then follow these steps:

1. In the Perspective viewport, select the Shading viewport label menu
   and choose Shaded, and then press F4. This will turn on Edged Faces;
   do this if it isn't already set that way.

2. Start by creating a box primitive in the Perspective viewport with
   these parameters: Length: **9**, Width: **10**, Height: **19**, Length Segs: **3**,
   Width Segs: at **2**, and Height Segs: **4**, as shown in Figure 7.3.

The box primitive is a
starting point for the
detail needed to create
the body form.

3. Press Alt+X to make the box see-through.

**FIGURE 7.3   Box
parameters**

4. Change the box's name to **Alien Body**.

5. Position the box at X: 0, Y: 0.0, Z: 22.0 so it is aligned with the Alien's
   torso, as shown in Figure 7.4.

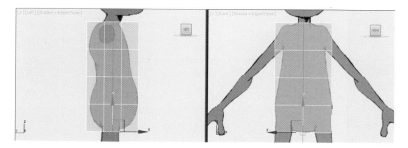

FIGURE 7.4   Box position from the front and side views

6. In the Ribbon ➢ Modeling tab ➢ Polygon Modeling panel, click
   Convert To Poly.

7. In the Polygon Modeling panel, enter the Vertex sub-object level.

8. In the Left viewport, select and move the vertices to match the outline of the character on the image plane, as shown in Figure 7.5. Use a selection box to select the vertices from the Left viewport. This will ensure that you are selecting both the back vertex and the vertex that can be seen in the viewport.

FIGURE 7.5 Move the vertices to match the alien's image in the Left viewport.

9. In the Polygon Modeling panel, enter Polygon sub-object level.

10. In the Front viewport, drag a selection marquee around the right half of the box and delete it. The reason for doing this is to cut your work in half. You will build half of the body and then copy it to the other side.

11. In the Polygon Modeling panel, enter Vertex sub-object level.

12. Move the vertices to match the outline of the character from the Front view, as shown in Figure 7.6.

FIGURE 7.6 Move the vertices to match the alien's image in the Front viewport.

13. From the Front viewport, select the vertices on the front outside edge and move them closer to the center, as shown in Figure 7.7. Click the Vertex button again to exit Vertex mode.

FIGURE 7.7   Select and move vertices towards the center of the model.

14. In the Ribbon ➢ Modeling tab ➢ Edit ➢ SwiftLoop, place a new loop on the inside, as shown in Figure 7.8. You will use this loop when you build the alien's leg.

FIGURE 7.8   Use SwiftLoop to place an edge on the model.

In this section you are just building the torso and setting things up for the following exercises. Save the file; to check your work against ours, open the `c07_ex3_torso_end.max` file in the `c07_CharacterModel` project folder.

Exercise 7.4: Creating Symmetry

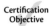
Certification
Objective

So far, you've modeled only one half of the torso; you will use a modifier to copy the half torso and mirror it to create the rest of the torso. Continue with the previous exercise's scene file, or open the `c07_ex4_symmetry_start.max` scene file in the `scenes` folder of the `c07_CharacterModel` project downloaded from this book's web page.

1. Select the alien torso, and in the Modify panel choose Symmetry from the Modifier list. When the modifier is applied, the model will disappear; this is because of the default parameters in the modifier.

2. In the Parameters section check the Flip box in the Mirror Axis area, as shown in Figure 7.9.

> Any edits you make to the original half of the mesh from the Symmetry modifier in the stack will also occur on the other half when the Symmetry modifier is applied to the mesh.

FIGURE 7.9   The Symmetry modifier creates a full torso.

3. Go to the Modify panel, and in the modifier stack select Editable Poly.

4. In the Ribbon ≻ Modeling tab ≻ Edit, select Use NURMS. This will show the model with smoothing, but because the Symmetry modifier is still active, the end result is not shown, so you see only half the model smoothed.

5. From the modifier stack on the toolbar select the Show End Result On/Off Toggle button (), to show the effect of the entire stack. Now the whole model is visible, as shown in Figure 7.10.

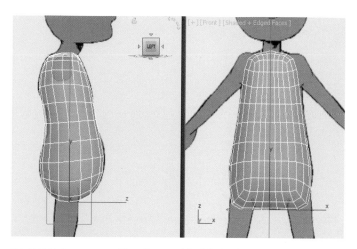

FIGURE 7.10   The alien model with the Symmetry modifier and Use NURMS applied

The model with Use NURMS applied reveals some problems. In the next exercises you will begin blocking out the arms and refining the torso. Save the file; to check your work, open the c07_ex4_symmetry_end.max file in the c07_ CharacterModel project folder.

Exercise 7.5: Blocking Out the Arms

The arms for the alien are skinny and slightly longer than a human's arms, but other than that they are similar, with hands, wrists, elbows, and so on. Thus the alien arms will have three sections: upper arm, lower arm, and hand. Continue with the previous exercise's scene file, or open the c07_ex5_arm_start.max scene file in the scenes folder of the c07_CharacterModel project folder.

Certification
Objective

1. Start by removing the Symmetry modifier by right-clicking the modifier and choosing Delete from the menu. Then from the Ribbon ➤ Modeling tab ➤ Edit, turn off Use NURMS.

2. Move the Image Plane Front object back along the Y axis to 20.0.

3. On the Ribbon ➤ Modeling tab ➤ Polygon Modeling panel, enter Polygon mode.

4. From the Left viewport select the polygon where the armhole is, as shown in Figure 7.11.

FIGURE 7.11 Select the polygon in the armhole location.

5. Switch to the Front viewport, and in the Ribbon ➢ Modeling tab ➢ Polygons panel choose Bevel ➢ Bevel Settings. Use the default setting, which is Bevel Height: 10.0 and Bevel Outline: -1.0, as shown in Figure 7.12. Click OK.

FIGURE 7.12 Position the arm with the image plane.

6. Use the Move tool to position the new extruded arm to line up with the front view image.

7. Select the Rotate tool and rotate the selected polygon 65 degrees on the Z axis, as shown in Figure 7.13.

FIGURE 7.13   Rotate the polygon 65 degrees.

8. The polygon at the end of the arm should still be selected, so select the Ribbon ➢ Modeling tab ➢Polygons panel ➢ Bevel ➢ Bevel Settings. Change the settings on this first bevel to Bevel Height: 1.0 and Bevel Outline: 0.5. Click Apply and Continue. Then set the second bevel to Bevel Height: 6.5 and Bevel Outline: -0.5, as shown in Figure 7.14. Click OK.

FIGURE 7.14   Bevel settings for completing the arm to the wrist

9. Use the Move tool to line up the arm with the front view image at the wrist.

10. In the Ribbon ➤ Modeling tab ➤ Edit, select Use NURMS; now the problems with arms are more evident, as shown in Figure 7.15. Turn off Use NURMS, because it is easier to fix these issues on the rough model.

11. Enter Vertex mode, select the vertex at the armpit, and move it down to line up more accurately with the image plane, as shown in Figure 7.15.

FIGURE 7.15 Problems with the model are more evident with Use NURMS active.

12. Repeat the process on vertex at the shoulder and lower arm. Turn on Use NURMS again and adjust further. Some parts of the model will not look correct even with the changes. More subdivisions need to be added.

13. Select the Ribbon ➤ Modeling tab ➤ Edit ➤ SwiftLoop, and add a loop below where the shoulder begins and another a bit below that. You should still be in Vertex mode, so move the vertices again to

better match the image plane, as shown in Figure 7.16. Do all this with Use NURMS turned on. When you have finished, turn off Use NURMS.

FIGURE 7.16   Use SwiftLoop to add edges to fix problems with the model.

The orange cage surrounding the model is the Use NURMS cage, which shows the model before the sub-divisions have been added. Turn on Use NURMS to see cage.

Now you are starting to see some shape in the torso and arm. Save the file. To check your work, open the c07_ex5_arm_end.max file in the c07_CharacterModel project folder.

Exercise 7.6: Blocking Out the Leg

The legs for the alien are exactly like a human's legs with three sections: upper thigh, knee, and calf. For the leg modeling you will use a different technique than you used for the arm. The method has no official name, so for this chapter it will be called the Shift+Move Extrude method. This method is similar to using the Extrude or Bevel tools and works only with Border and open-ended Edges modes. For this chapter you will use the Border mode. Continue with the previous exercise's scene file, or open the c07_ex6_leg_start.max scene file in the scenes folder of the c07_CharacterModel project folder.

Certification
Objective

1. In the Perspective viewport, select the model. Enter Polygon mode and select the polygon at the bottom of the model, as shown in Figure 7.17.

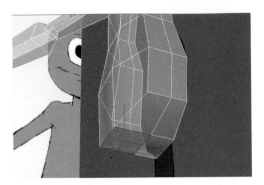

FIGURE 7.17 Select the polygon at the bottom of the alien model to begin blocking out the leg.

2. Delete the polygon.

3. Enter Border mode (⟲).

4. Enter Border mode (3 is the keyboard shortcut) of the deleted polygon if it is not already selected.

5. Press W on the keyboard to access the Move tool.

6. While looking through the Front viewport, hold Shift on the keyboard and move the border down until it sits at the center of the alien's thigh.

7. Switch to the Scale tool (R) and scale the border down so it matches the width of the thigh in the image plane, as shown in Figure 7.18.

> Border mode can be described as the edges surrounding a hole in a model. Border mode has all the traditional modeling tools like Extrude and Bevel.

FIGURE 7.18 Use Scale to change the width of thigh, and then use the Shift+Move Extrude method to extrude the thigh.

8. Switch to the Left viewport and adjust the model to match the image plane.

9. Repeat the Shift+Move Extrude method to extrude down to just above the knee.

10. Use the Scale and Move tools to adjust the position and size of that section of the leg to match the Front and Left viewports, as shown in Figure 7.19.

FIGURE 7.19 The left side image shows the leg from the Front viewport, and the right side image shows the leg from the Left viewport.

11. Use the Shift+Move method again and extrude the leg a small amount in the middle of the knee area, and then repeat to extrude just below the knee.

12. Use the Scale and Move tools to adjust the position and size of that section of the leg to match the Front and Left viewports.

13. Repeat the Shift+Move method and extrude to the center of the calf; repeat to extrude to above the ankle.

14. Switch to Vertex mode, and move vertices to further adjust the model to match the image planes from the front and left views, as shown in Figure 7.20. Exit Vertex mode by clicking the Vertex button in the Ribbon ➢ Modeling tab ➢ Polygon Modeling.

FIGURE 7.20   Front view of the completed leg (left image); left view of the completed leg (right image)

Notice how at the bottom of the leg Use NURMS is working, but at the end of the arm it is not. This is because of the deleted polygon. Use NURMS ignores areas where the geometry is deleted.

15. Go to the Ribbon ➤ Modeling tab ➤Edit ➤ Use NURMS.

16. In the Modify panel ➤ Modifier List, choose the Symmetry modifier. Check the Flip box to see the whole model.

17. Press Alt+X to exit See-Through mode.

18. At the bottom of the interface, select the Isolate Selection Toggle button ( ).

19. Exit Edged Faces mode by selecting a viewport and pressing F4 on the keyboard. Repeat this in all viewports.

20. Enter Polygon mode, select the polygon at the end of the arm, and delete it. This will create the same look as at the bottom of the leg. The completed model is shown in Figure 7.21.

FIGURE 7.21   The completed model shown from the Left and Front viewports

The completed model looks pretty good. The body itself isn't all that exciting. The alien has a soft and blobby body—too much junk food and not enough exercise. There are a few details that need to be refined. The area where the arm and chest meet is too squared off; this transition needs to be smoothed out. The chest needs some simple breast detail. The knees need more definition. The alien has no backside; it looks just like the front. So adding some shoulder blades and some backside definition will help, like a butt crack—sorry to have to be blunt! Save the file. To check your work, open the c07_ex6_leg_end.max file in the c07_CharacterModel project folder.

Exercise 7.7: Refining the Body

Some of the areas to refine are the knees, groin, chest, shoulders (front and back), and backside, as shown in Figure 7.22. Continue with the previous exercise's scene file, or open the c07_ex7_body_start.max scene file in the scenes folder of the c07_CharacterModel project folder. This file has the alien model isolated. The Symmetry modifier has been removed and Use NURMS is turned off. If you are using your own file, exit Isolate mode, remove the Symmetry modifier, and turn off Use NURMS.

Certification
Objective

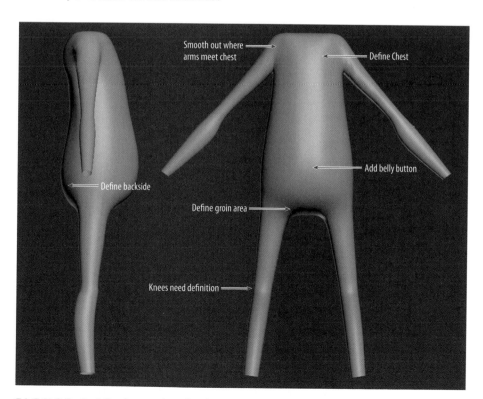

FIGURE 7.22   Areas to be refined on the model

Adding Detail to the Knee

The knee doesn't need anything too complicated, just a few extra edges to add some detail.

1. Select the model and enter Edge mode.

2. Select the edge at the front of the knee.

3. In the Ribbon ➢ Modeling tab ➢Edges ➢ Chamfer ➢ Chamfer Settings caddy, change Edge Chamfer Amount to **0.6**, and click OK.

4. In the Ribbon ➢ Modeling tab ➢Edit. At the bottom of the tab under Constraints, select Constrain to Edge ().

5. Switch to Vertex mode and from the Left viewport move the vertices at the back of the knee closer together, as shown in Figure 7.23. Make sure you drag a selection box around the vertices because from the Left viewport you see only the vertex facing the camera, but there is another vertex. You can also turn on See-Through mode so you can see both front and back vertices.

6. Now move the vertices at the front of the knee to the right (from the Left viewport). You want the edges sticking out more, as shown in Figure 7.23. Click the Constrain to None (⬛) button to exit Constraints.

Double-clicking on an edge is a shortcut to the Ribbon ➢ modeling tab ➢ Modify Selection ➢ Loop tool.

An easy way to move the sub-object selections is to use Constraints. Constraints allow you to move a sub-object selection along adjacent edges, faces, or normals. A *normal* is a vector that points directly away from and is perpendicular to the face.

FIGURE 7.23   The knee vertices moved to add more detail

Refining the Groin Area

The alien doesn't have any sex organs; the area just needs to be smoothed out and a crease needs to be added where the leg meets the body.

1. Add an edge to the top of the thigh using SwiftLoop.

2. Add another edge loop on the torso between the thigh and the center of the body. Refer to Figure 7.24 to see where it needs to be placed.

3. Switch to Vertex mode and move the vertices (use the Constrain to Edge tool), as shown in Figure 7.24. These simple edges will add a very subtle crease at this area. To exit Constraints click the Constrain to None button.

4. To see what the model looks like now, turn on Use NURMS. In the Use NURMS tab in the Ribbon ➢ Modeling tab (Use NURMS can also be a floating menu) change Iterations to 2, as shown in Figure 7.25.

5. Exit Vertex mode by selecting the Vertex icon in the Ribbon ➢ Modeling tab ➢ Polygon Modeling.

    Did you think we were going to add something X-rated? Sorry! The alien is strictly G-rated.

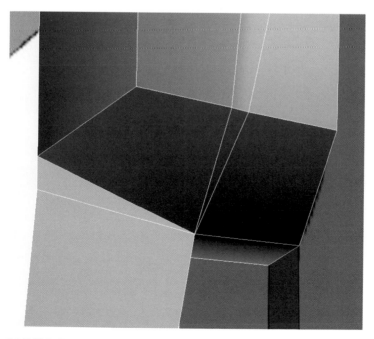

FIGURE 7.24   With vertices added, the groin area is more refined.

F I G U R E   7.25   Groin area with Use NURMS active

Refining the Backside

The backside (or *behiny* as my seven-year-old says) looks very similar to the front, so to give it some distinction you will add a backside "crack," a crease to set it apart from the front. Turn off Use NURMS to continue.

1. Select the alien body and enter Isolate Selection mode.

2. Using the ViewCube®, rotate the Perspective view so the backside can be seen.

3. In the Modify panel ➢ Modifier List, select the Symmetry modifier. Check the Flip box, and in the modifier stack select the Show End Results On/Off Toggle (▮), which sits directly below the modifier stack. This will allow you to work on the model and see the other side of the model updating.

4. Enter Vertex mode.

5. Select the vertex at the intersection of the backside and leg. Zoom in very close because the vertices are very close together. You will need to select the left side vertex closest to the model center, as shown in Figure 7.26.

FIGURE 7.26 The left image shows the zoomed-out area; the right image shows the zoomed-in area where you need to select the vertex.

6. In the Ribbon ➢ Modeling tab ➢ Edit ➢ Constraints, select Constrain to Edge.

7. Move the selected vertex toward the center of the model.

8. Repeat the move on the two vertices directly above the vertex moved in step 7, as shown in Figure 7.27.

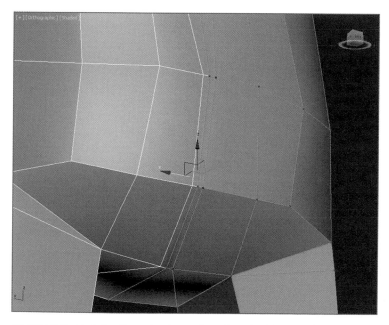

FIGURE 7.27 Move the three selected vertices closer to the center of the model.

9. Select the three vertices at the center of the model.

10. In the Ribbon ≻ Modeling tab ≻ Edit ≻ Constraints, select Constrain to Normal. This will isolate the movement perpendicular to the model.

11. Move the select vertices in toward the inside of the model.

12. Turn on Use NURMS, and exit Vertex mode. Turn off Edged Faces in the Rendering Type menu, or use the keyboard shortcut F4. Click away from the model to deselect it; the completed backside is shown in Figure 7.28.

FIGURE 7.28 The completed backside of the alien

Remaining Refinements

At this point most of the things that need to be refined have been refined. There are a few things you can add using the same techniques used in the previous section. For example, you could add a few extra loops in the elbow area, as shown in Figure 7.29.

Some of the changes can't be done to the model in separate halves with the Symmetry modifier active. This will be remedied in the following chapter. Save your file. To check your final results against ours, open the c07_ex7_body_end .max file in the c07_CharacterModel project folder. The final alien body is shown in Figure 7.30.

FIGURE 7.29 The left image shows the elbow with the loops added; the right image shows the changes with Use NURMS turned on.

FIGURE 7.30 The final alien body; the left image is the front and the right image is the back.

Exercise 7.8: Building the Neck

Before building the head you have to build up the neck. Either continue with the exercise scene file from the previous section, or open the c07_ex8_neck_ start.max scene file in the scenes folder of the c07_CharacterModel project folder on the book's web page at www.sybex.com/go/3dsmax2015essentials. If you are continuing with your file, exit Isolate Selection mode.

1. Select the alien body, go to the Modify panel, and in the modifier stack right-click the Symmetry modifier and choose Delete from the menu.

2. In the Edit tab of the modeling ribbon, turn off Use NURMS.

3. Enter See-Through mode (Alt+X).

4. In the Polygon Modeling tab, enter Polygon mode. Select the two polygons where the neck would be placed and delete the polygons using the Delete key on the keyboard.

5. In the Polygon Modeling tab, enter Edge mode.

6. Select the edges where the polygons were deleted, as shown in Figure 7.31.

FIGURE 7.31 Select the edges around the neck hole.

7. Switch to the Move tool (W) if it isn't already selected.

8. In the Left viewport, hold down Shift, and with the Move tool move the edges halfway up the neck and slightly forward, following the image plane (the Shift+Move Extrude method). Release the Shift key.

9. Shift+Move again to extrude the edges to the top of the neck, as shown in Figure 7.32. Exit See-Through mode (Alt+X).

FIGURE 7.32   Use the Shift+Move Extrude method to create two more sets of polygons for the alien's neck.

10. The neck is too square. To round it out you will add another edge to the top of the arm and the side of the neck. In the Ribbon ➤ Modeling tab ➤ Edit tab ➤ SwiftLoop, add a loop on the middle top of the arm, as shown in Figure 7.33.

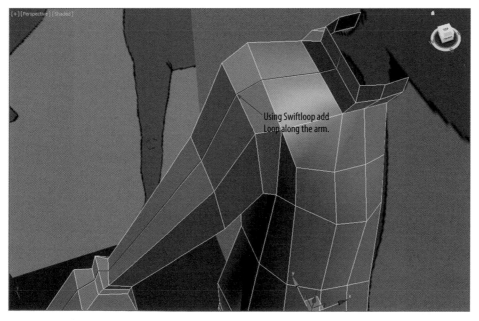

FIGURE 7.33   Using SwiftLoop, add a new edge to the top of the arm and neck to help in rounding out the neck.

11. Enter Vertex mode; select and move the vertices at the neck to round out the neck, as shown in Figure 7.34.

FIGURE 7.34 The adjusted shape of the neck

12. Switch to the Front viewport, and enter See-Through mode.

13. The area of the neck where it meets the shoulder needs more definition. In the Ribbon ➢ Modeling tab ➢ Edit tab, select SwiftLoop and add a loop between the lower loop at the neck and the loop at the shoulder. You can do this while still in Vertex mode. Exit SwiftLoop by right-clicking in the selected viewport.

14. From the Front viewport move the vertices to better follow the neck and shoulder in the image plane, as shown in Figure 7.35. Exit See-Through mode.

FIGURE 7.35 Adjust the vertices to match the neck of the alien in the image plane.

15. The arm needs to be adjusted. The new loop that runs down the arm will flatten it out when NURMS is applied. So, select the vertices running down the outside of the arm and move them up so that the inside edge is higher than the outside edges, as shown in Figure 7.36.

FIGURE 7.36 Move up the vertices on the outside of the arm to round out the top of the arm.

16. Exit Vertex mode. Check the model by turning on Use NURMS. The final neck and arm are shown in Figure 7.37.

FIGURE 7.37 Final neck and arm

Save the file you are working with. To check your work open the c07_ex8_neck_end.max scene file in the scenes folder of the c08_CharacterModel project folder.

Now You Know

In this chapter, you learned how to begin creating the basic form of the alien character. First, you used reference planes of the alien, and then from a simple box, you formed a torso to match the general shapes shown in the reference images. You extruded and shaped the arms and legs to match as well. As you can see, the more you model, the easier the process becomes and the more detailed and finessed your models turn out. In the next chapter you'll create the alien hands, feet, and head, and then add the remaining body refinements.

CHAPTER 8

Character Modeling Part II

Realistic computer-generated (CG) characters are common in television and films; they appear as stunt doubles, as members of vast crowds, and as primary characters. Sometimes using a CG character works better than using a real person. Using a CG stunt double is safer and sometimes cheaper than using a live stunt person, and weird creatures can be created with better clarity by using CG rather than puppetry or special makeup effects.

In this chapter, you will continue with the model of the alien, focusing on using the Editable Poly toolset to create an alien model suitable for character animation and for use in a game engine.

This chapter includes the following topics:

▶ **Creating the alien head**

▶ **Creating the alien hands**

▶ **Creating the alien feet**

▶ **Completing the alien**

Creating the Alien Head

The alien's head will consist of three parts: the neck, the head shape, and the eye and mouth. The easiest way to create these is to start with the head shape.

Exercise 8.1: Blocking Out the Head

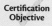
Certification
Objective

The head is the most important part of the alien, or any humanoid/anthropomorphic (human characteristics) character. Its most important feature is the face, which communicates expressions and moods and allows people to relate to this character. The head itself is easy, but the face is another story. The face is more complex and needs more detail than any other part of the alien. Either continue with the previous file from Chapter 7 or open the c08_ex1_head_start .max scene file in the Scenes folder of the c08_CharacterModel project. This process starts with a simple primitive box.

1. In the Create panel ➤ Geometry ➤ Standard Primitives, select Box. In the Perspective viewport, create a box with Length = 9.0, Width = 9.0, Height = 13.5, Length Segs = 3, Width Segs = 3, and Height = 3. Enter See-Through mode (Alt+X), and then move the box so it is aligned with the alien head in the Left and Front viewports, as shown in Figure 8.1.

FIGURE 8.1   Align the box with the alien head.

From this point forward the Graphite Modeling Tools tab will be called the Ribbon ➤ Modeling tab or just the Modeling tab.

2. In the Ribbon ➤ Modeling tab ➤ Polygon Modeling choose Convert To Poly.

3. The edges that are running around the eyes need to be moved so that they surround the eyes. Enter Edge mode, and from the Front viewport select the top horizontal edge (make sure the entire edge loop is selected by double-clicking) and move it above the eye. Repeat for all the edges around the eye so it looks like Figure 8.2.

FIGURE 8.2   Move the edges so they surround the eye.

4. Now it's time to make this box more spherical. Enter Vertex mode and from the Front viewport select the four vertices at the corners.

5. Switch to the Scale tool (R), make sure the Transform gizmo is in the center of the box, and scale by centering the cursor inside the scale transform triangle and dragging until the corners are aligned with the image plane.

6. Change to the Left viewport and repeat the process. Then repeat the process from the Top viewport. When finished, the box will look like Figure 8.3. Exit Vertex mode.

Double-clicking an edge is a shortcut to select the edge loop.

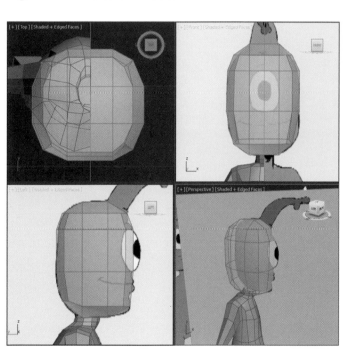

FIGURE 8.3 By selecting the corners and scaling them inward, you make the head more spherical.

Save the file you are working with. To check your work open the c08_ex1_head_end.max scene file in the scenes folder of the c08_CharacterModel project folder.

Exercise 8.2: Building the Nose

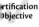

rtification Objective

It's time to build the alien's "nose," which is coming out of his forehead. Either continue with the previous file or open the c08_ex2_nose_start.max scene file in the scenes folder of the c08_CharacterModel project folder.

1. Enter Polygon mode, and select the polygon at the top of the head where the forehead is.

2. In the Ribbon ≻ Modeling tab ≻ Polygons ≻ Bevel ≻ Bevel Settings, set the Bevel Height to 2.5 and the Bevel Outline to -0.15, and then click OK.

3. Repeat the process from step 2 by selecting the Bevel Setting, set the Bevel Height to 2.5 and the Bevel Outline to -0.5, and click OK.

4. Repeat the bevel again on the nose using the settings from the previous step.

5. Switch to Vertex mode and adjust the vertices to follow the alien's nose in the image plane, as shown in Figure 8.4. Exit Vertex mode when finished.

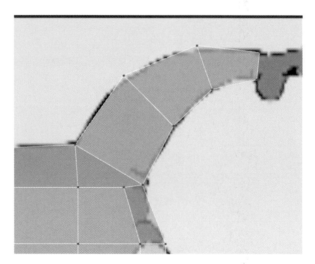

FIGURE 8.4   In Vertex mode edit the alien's nose to match the image plane.

6. Enter Polygon mode and select the polygon at the eye.

7. To create the eye socket go to the Ribbon ≻ Modeling tab ≻ Polygons ≻ Bevel ≻ Bevel Settings. You will be creating three bevels:

   Bevel 1:

   ▶ Bevel Height: 0.0

   ▶ Bevel Outline: -0.1

   ▶ Click the Apply And Continue button ().

Bevel 2:

► Bevel Height: **-0.1**

► Bevel Outline: **0.0**

► Click Apply And Continue.

Bevel 3:

► Bevel Height: **-1.5**

► Bevel Outline: **0.0**

► Click OK.

8. To add a bit of a ridge around the eye you will move around some of the edges that you created in the previous step. Enter Edge mode and double-click the edge on the inside of the eye socket.

9. Select the Move tool and move the edge about halfway to the inside of the eye socket.

10. Select the edge on the top inside of the eye socket, and move this edge toward the outside of the eye socket. The eye socket will now resemble Figure 8.5.

FIGURE 8.5 Move the new edges to create a small ridge around the eye socket.

11. The nose needs more definition, so at the base add another edge loop using SwiftLoop (select the Ribbon ➢ Modeling tab ➢ Edit ➢ SwiftLoop).

12. To finish the alien's nose enter Edge mode on the Ribbon ➤ Modeling tab ➤ Polygon Modeling tab, and at the end of the nose select the top and bottom edges. Make sure the Scale gizmo is in the center of the selected edges. If it isn't in the center, change the Use Center flyout to Use Selection Center, as shown in Figure 8.6.

FIGURE 8.6 To make sure the Scale gizmo is at the center of the selected edges, select Use Selection Center from the Use Center flyout on the main toolbar.

13. Switch to Polygon mode and from the Modeling tab ➤ Polygons ➤ Bevel ➤ Bevel Settings, you will be creating four bevels for the nose:

     Bevel 1:

     ▶ Bevel Height: 0.0

     ▶ Bevel Outline: 0.2

     ▶ Click Apply And Continue.

     Bevel 2:

     ▶ Bevel Height: 0.3

     ▶ Bevel Outline: 0.0

     ▶ Click Apply And Continue.

     Bevel 3:

     ▶ Bevel Height: 0.0

     ▶ Bevel Outline: -0.2

     ▶ Click Apply And Continue.

Bevel 4:

▶ Bevel Height: -0.2

▶ Bevel Outline: -0.15

▶ Click OK.

14. The head started out as a box, and even with all the changes it still has a hint of the box about it. Deleting a few edges will give the head a more rounded look. Select the edges where the corners of the box were, as shown in Figure 8.7.

FIGURE 8.7 Select the edges on the head that were once the corners of the original box.

15. To delete the edges hold down the Ctrl key and press the Backspace key on your keyboard. This is a shortcut for choosing the Ribbon ➢ Modeling tab ➢ Edges ➢ Remove. It is very important to hold down Ctrl while using this tool so that it will remove the associated vertices where edges cross the remaining edges.

16. This makes the head thinner than before, so switch to Vertex mode, change to the Front viewport, and turn on See-Through mode (Alt+X). Move vertices out to match Figure 8.8. Repeat the process for the Left viewport. Exit See-Through mode.

F I G U R E   8 . 8   From the Front viewport, in Vertex mode, move the vertices so they match the alien's jaw line in the image plane (right). Repeat from the Left viewport (left).

17. To test the head so far, turn on Use NURMS; in the Use NURMS tab set the iterations to **2**. This will show the head smoothed out so you will be able to see any flaws so far. At this point, you can edit the head to refine and more closely match the image plane, as shown in Figure 8.9.

F I G U R E   8 . 9   The refined head

The head is not complete; the nose tip needs to be refined and the alien's mouth has not been started. These parts will be addressed later in the chapter. Save the file you are working with. To check your work open the c08_ex2_nose_end.max scene file in the scenes folder of the c08_CharacterModel project.

Building the Alien Hand

The alien hand is simple and cartoonish, with just three fingers and a thumb. You won't be adding details such as lines on the palm or nails. In this section, you will create three simple fingers for the alien.

Exercise 8.3: Building the Palm of the Hand

Continue with the previous exercise's scene file, or open the c08_ex3_palm_start.max scene file in the scenes folder of the c08_CharacterModel project folder. The first thing to do is to merge in the image plane containing the hand.

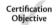
Certification Objective

1. In the Applications menu choose Import ➢ Merge.

2. Navigate to the scenes folder of the c08_CharacterModel project folder. Open c08_ex3_hand_image plane.max.

3. In the Merge dialog box, select Hand Image Plane and click OK. The image plane will land in the correct spot, below the arm. If it is not in the correct position, move the image plane so it is beneath the end of the arm, as shown in Figure 8.10.

FIGURE 8.10 The hand image plane positioned at the end of the wrist

When you create a box its color is randomly assigned. So don't be concerned if the color you see is different than the color in the images in this book.

4. In the Create panel ➤ Geometry ➤ Standard Primitives, in the Top viewport, create a box with the parameters shown in Figure 8.11. Name the box **Alien Hand**.

FIGURE 8.11 The parameters for the box that will create the hand

5. In the Ribbon ➤ Modeling tab choose Polygon Modeling ➤ Convert to Poly.

6. Turn on See-Through mode (Alt+X).

Save the file you are working with. To check your work you can open the c08_ex3_palm_end.max scene file in the scenes folder of the c08_CharacterModel project folder.

Exercise 8.4: Beveling the Fingers

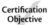

Certification Objective

Using Bevel to create the fingers allows you to extrude and scale the shape of the fingers with a single tool. Continue with the previous exercise's scene file, or open the c08_ex4_fingers_start.max scene file in the scenes folder of the c08_CharacterModel project folder.

1. Select the Alien Hand object. Enter Vertex mode if you are not already in it. Use the Move tool to rearrange the vertices to match what is shown in Figure 8.12.

2. In Polygon mode, select the three polygons on the front of the hand, where the fingers will be, as shown in Figure 8.13.

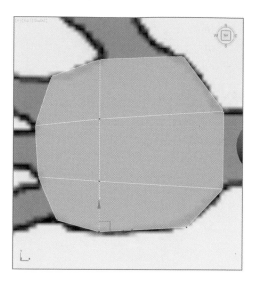

FIGURE 8.12 Rearrange the vertices to match the palm in the image plane.

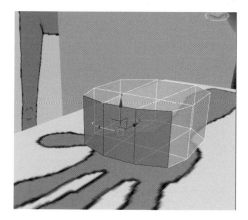

FIGURE 8.13 Select the three polygons to prepare for beveling the fingers.

3. From the Ribbon choose the Modeling tab ➢ Polygons ➢ Bevel ➢ Bevel Settings, set Extrusion Type to By Polygon, enter a Height value of **1.2**, and press Enter. Set the Outline amount to **-0.2** and press Enter. Click the Apply And Continue button. Now enter a

Height value of **1.2** and press Enter. Set Outline to **0.3**, press Enter, and click Apply And Continue. Now enter a Height value of **1.2** and press Enter. Set Outline to **-0.3**, press Enter, and click OK.

4. Select the polygon on the side of the palm close to the wrist where the thumb will be. In the Modeling tab of the Ribbon choose Polygons ➢ Bevel ➢ Bevel Settings, set Extrusion Type to By Polygon, enter a Height value of **0.6**, and press Enter. Set Outline to **-0.3**, press Enter, and click OK.

5. Switch to Vertex mode; arrange the vertices of the new thumb extrude to follow the image plane, as shown in Figure 8.14.

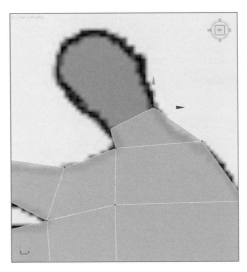

FIGURE 8.14 Rearrange the thumb vertices to follow the thumb in the image plane.

6. Create a new bevel, set Height to **0.9** and Outline to **0.25**, and press Enter. Then click Apply And Continue. Set Height to **0.9** and Outline to **0.25**, press Enter, and click OK.

7. In the Ribbon select the Modeling tab ➢ Edit ➢ Use NURMS. In the Use NURMS tab, set Iterations to **2**.

8. Enter Vertex mode, and select and move the vertices to better fit the hand in the image plane shown in the Top viewport, as shown in Figure 8.15. Then switch to the Front viewport (F).

You can edit an object's sub-objects (vertices, edges, polygons) while NURMS is turned on.

FIGURE 8.15   The hand from the Top viewport

If you continued with the file from the previous exercise, continue with steps 9–11. If you started with the c08_ex4_fingers_start.max scene file, skip to step 12.

9. In the Application menu choose Import ➤ Merge.

10. Navigate to the scenes folder of the c08_CharacterModel project. Open c08_ex4_hand_image plane side.max.

11. In the Merge dialog box, select Hand Image Plane Side and click OK. The image plane will land in the correct spot, under the arm. If it is not in the correct position, move the image plane so it is under the end of the arm and lines up with the hand.

12. Enter Vertex mode and continue to edit the hand to match the hand image plane side. The tops of the fingers need to be flattened out. You can also make whatever other changes you think appropriate.

13. The thumb needs to be angled down. Enter Polygon mode, and select the polygon at the end of the thumb.

14. In the Modeling tab of the Ribbon, choose Modify Selection ➤ Grow, and click Grow twice to select the remaining thumb polygons.

◄

In the command panel, look for the type-in area where you can change the name of the object. Next to that is a small color swatch; click it. This will bring up the Object Color dialog box, which will allow you to change the color of the hand. Materials always override object colors.

15. Switch to the Rotate tool, and in the main toolbar select Local from the Reference Coordinate System drop-down menu, as shown in Figure 8.16.

FIGURE 8.16
Select Local from the
Reference Coordinate
System drop-down menu.

16. Rotate the polygons 60 degrees along the Y axis (use the green control handle on the gizmo).

17. Switch to the Move tool and move the thumb polygons down into a more realistic position. Don't worry if they don't line up perfectly with the thumb in the image plane.

18. Select the polygon at the wrist and delete it. Exit Polygon mode by clicking the Polygon icon button.

19. From the Top viewport and in the main toolbar, select the Mirror tool (▶◀). In the dialog box change Mirror Axis to Y and click OK. The completed hand is shown in Figure 8.17. Exit See-Through mode (Alt+X).

Oops! The hand was modeled correctly, but the thumb was created on the wrong side. No problem—use the Mirror tool.

FIGURE 8.17 The final alien hand shown and isolated

Our alien has very simple hands: no nails, hair, wrinkles, or creases. It is not within the scope of this book to cover the tools to create these details. Use the tools you have been learning, and experiment with adding various details to the hands. Perhaps you can start by adding fingernails; you can do this by beveling polygons at the tip of the fingers. Save the file you are working with; to check your work open the c08_ex4_fingers_end.max scene file in the scenes folder of the c08_CharacterModel project.

Building the Foot

In this section, you will create a simple three-toed foot for the alien. The techniques are very similar to modeling the hand. You'll start with a box to block out the foot, and then use Bevel to extrude the toes. Then you'll refine the shape and add NURMS to smooth out the foot.

Exercise 8.5: Blocking Out the Foot

Continue with the previous exercise's scene file, or open the c08_ex5_foot_ start.max scene file in the scenes folder of the c08_CharacterModel project.

Certification Objective

In the Application menu choose Import ➣ Merge, and then navigate to the scenes folder of the c08_CharacterModel project. Open the file c08_ex5_foot_ image plane.max. In the Merge dialog box, select Foot Image Plane and click OK. The image plane will land in the correct spot, under the leg. If it is not in the correct position, move the image plane so it is under the end of the leg.

1. Select the alien body, head, hand, and the Hand Image Plane object, right-click to access the quad menu, and choose Hide Selected.

2. From the Top viewport, go to the Create Panel ➣ Geometry ➣ Standard Primitives, and create a box with parameters of Length = 8.0, Width = 5.0, Height =3.0, Length Segs = 3, Width Segs = 3, and Height = 2.

3. Turn on See-Through mode. From the Left viewport, switch to the Move tool, and move the box so it is aligned with the foot in the image plane. Line up the back of the box with the heel in the image plane.

4. Convert the box to an editable polygon (from the Modeling tab of the Ribbon choose Polygon Modeling ➣ Convert to Poly). Enter Vertex mode; from the Top viewport select the top two rows of vertices, change to the Scale tool, and scale the vertices together until they sit on the sides of the heel, as shown in Figure 8.18 (left images).

5. Now select the second row of vertices from the top and move it down below the heel, as also shown in Figure 8.18 (right images).

FIGURE 8.18   Select and scale the vertices together to form the heel; then select the second row from the top and move it down below the heel.

6. Switch to the Left viewport. Select and rearrange the middle and top rows of vertices to match the image in Figure 8.19.

FIGURE 8.19   Edit the middle and top rows of vertices to further refine the foot.

7. Switch back to the Top viewport, and arrange the line of vertices at the base of the toes to match the image in Figure 8.20. This will help correctly align the toes for the bevel.

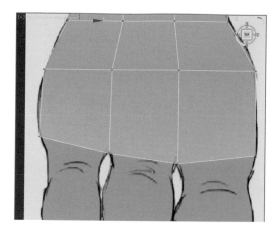

FIGURE 8.20 Edit the line of vertices at the base of the toes.

Save the file you are working with. To check your work open the c08_ex5_foot_end.max scene file in the scenes folder of the c08_CharacterModel project.

Exercise 8.6: Beveling the Toes

Like modeling the fingers, you'll use Bevel, but instead of beveling all the toes at the same time, you will do one at a time, using different settings for each toe. Continue with the previous exercise's scene file, or open the c08_ex6_toes_start.max scene file in the scenes folder of the c08_CharacterModel project.

Certification Objective

1. Switch to Polygon mode, and select the polygons at the front of the foot where the smallest toe is.

2. From the Modeling tab of the ribbon choose Polygons ➢ Bevel ➢ Bevel Settings. In the Bevel caddy apply these settings:

Setting	Bevel Type	Height	Outline
Bevel 1	Local Normal	0.5	-0.3
Bevel 2	Local Normal	0.9	0.3
Bevel 3	Local Normal	0.9	-0.3

This will build the first toe; use the same technique to build the remaining toes. Don't worry if the geometry overlaps; the geometry smoothing that the NURMS creates will fix it. The finalized toes are shown in Figure 8.21.

FIGURE 8.21   Toes extruded using Bevel

3. Now select the three polygons on the top back of the foot and delete them.

4. Enter Border mode ( ). Border mode allows you to select a hole in a mesh so you can modify it with various tools. Select the border of the hole you made when you deleted the polygons in the previous step. This technique allows you to create the ankle.

5. Use the Shift+Move method you used on edges in the previous chapter. From the Left viewport, hold down Shift and move the border up along the Y axis.

6. Switch to Vertex mode. Select and move the vertices at the top of the ankle in toward the ankle in the image plane.

7. Switch to the Front viewport and repeat the process. When you have finished, exit Vertex mode. Exit See-Through mode and select Use NURMS; the results are shown in Figure 8.22.

FIGURE 8.22   The finished foot with the ankle

Save the file. To check your work open the c08_ex6_toes_end.max scene file in the scenes folder of the c08_CharacterModel project.

Completing the Alien

Now that all the parts to the alien are complete, you need to bring them all together. Once the alien is whole you can further refine the model if desired. To begin this process, you need to attach the head, hand, and foot to the main alien body.

Exercise 8.7: Attaching to the Body

Attaching in itself is easy, just a button click, but there are some issues that need to be addressed first. To attach objects correctly you need the objects to have holes or borders where the objects attach to each other. It is recommended to have an equal number of edges on both objects going into the border, as shown in Figure 8.23.

Certification
Objective

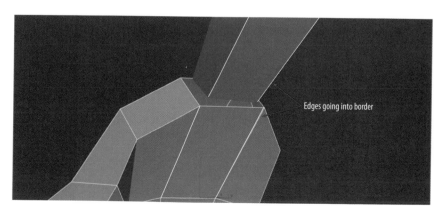

FIGURE 8.23   Hand and lower arm showing the borders meeting and the edges

Figure 8.23 shows the underside of the palm of the hand and the wrist of the alien body. It shows that an equal number of edges are present. Figure 8.24 shows the top side of the same palm and wrist. Notice how the wrist has an extra edge but the palm has two edges, the same as the underside.

FIGURE 8.24   The top of the wrist has an extra edge.

In order to properly attach they have to have an equal number of edges, so you need to add one edge on the top side of the palm. You could use the SwiftLoop tool, but that would add a loop from the top side of the palm to the bottom side. That won't do, so you'll use the Cut tool. Continue with the previous exercise's scene file, or open the c08_ex7_attach_start.max scene file in the scenes folder of the c08_CharacterModel project. If you continue with the file from the previous exercise, you will need to unhide the alien's body, head, and hand. You can either delete the image planes or just keep them hidden. Turn off Use NURMS for the hand and foot.

> Typically having an edge dead end in this way is not desirable; it is preferable to have edges loop around an object. On the hand only one side needed the extra edge.

1. In the Modeling tab of the Ribbon choose Edit ➢ Cut. Cut by clicking from the base of the finger to the border opening, as shown in Figure 8.25. Right-click in the viewport to exit the Cut tool.

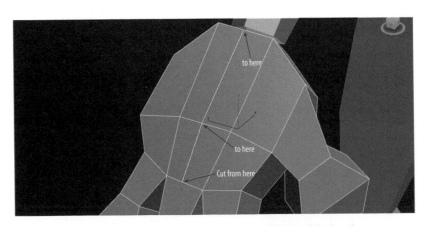

FIGURE 8.25   Use Cut to create new edges on the top of the hand.

2. Select the Alien Body object, and in the Modeling tab choose ➢ Geometry (All), click the Attach button, and then click on the hand. Now both the hand and body can be controlled with the same editable polygon parameters.

3. Enter Border mode, and select the border of the wrist and palm (Ctrl+click to add both borders).

4. In the Modeling tab choose Borders ➢ Bridge. There's no need to use the Bridge settings or caddy. Just click the Bridge button. You will see the new polygon bridge appear.

5. Enter Edge mode, and double-click on the edge at the wrist.

6. Select the Move tool and move the edge higher on the arm. In the main toolbar change the reference coordinate system to Local, and select Constrain To Edge in the ribbon Edit tab. When you have finished, select Constrain To None (). Exit Edge mode by selecting the Edge mode icon.

7. Time for the foot—it requires a different strategy. Select the foot, enter Vertex mode, and select the vertices shown in Figure 8.26 (left).

The wrist and hand may be attached but they are still separate elements within the editable polygon. These separate elements need to be connected. For this you will use Bridge.

Moving just the edges can be difficult, so in the ribbon ➢ Modeling tab ➢ Edit tab, there is a row of buttons at the bottom. These are constraints; they let you use existing geometry to constrain sub-object transformations.

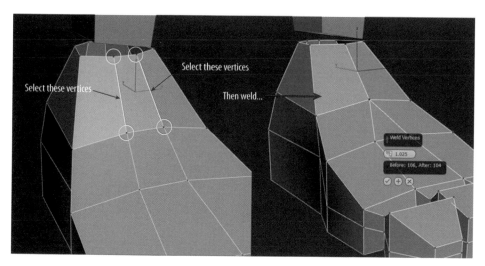

FIGURE 8.26   Select the four vertices on the top front of the foot (left). Use Weld to combine the edges (right).

8. In the ribbon ➣ Modeling tab ➣ Vertices ➣ Weld ➣ Weld Setting caddy, set the Weld threshold to **1.025** (or use whatever value welds the vertices to match the right image in Figure 8.26). This will combine the horizontal vertices, as shown in Figure 8.26 (right). Repeat the process on the back of the foot. Exit Vertex mode.

9. Using the Cut tool, cut an edge on the front of the lower leg to the bottom of the knee, as shown in Figure 8.27. Repeat for the back of the leg.

FIGURE 8.27 Use Cut to create an edge from the bottom of the lower leg to the bottom of the knee.

10. Adding the edges to the leg will make the leg less square. Round out the leg by selecting and moving the vertices on the outer edge of the leg, as shown in Figure 8.28.

FIGURE 8.28 Select vertices on the outer edge of the leg and move them so the leg is more rounded.

11. Now the foot is ready to be attached to the leg. In the Modeling tab choose Geometry (All) ➢ Attach, and then click on the foot.

12. Now you need to bring the two elements together. For the hand you used Bridge; this time you'll use something different. In the Modeling tab choose Vertices ➢ Target Weld (⊙ Target). This tool allows you to select a vertex and weld it to a neighboring target vertex. Click on a vertex on the end of the leg and then on the neighboring vertex on the foot border, as shown in Figure 8.29.

FIGURE 8.29   Attach the foot to the leg using Target Weld.

Save the file. To check your work open the c08_ex7_attach_end.max scene file in the scenes folder of the c08_CharacterModel project.

Exercise 8.8: Using Symmetry

This part is easy because you have done it before. Continue with the previous exercise's scene file, or open the c08_ex8_symmetry_start.max scene file in the scenes folder of the c08_CharacterModel project.

1. Select the Alien Body model.

2. Choose the Modify panel ➤ Modifier List ➤ Symmetry.

3. In the Symmetry modifier, Mirror Axis group, check the Flip box.

4. You need to combine the two sides of the model, so from the ribbon choose the Modeling tab ➤ Polygon Modeling ➤ Collapse Stack.

Save the file you are working with. To check your work open the c08_ex8_symmetry_end.max scene file in the scenes folder of the c08_CharacterModel project.

Collapse Stack collapses the selected object's entire stack into an editable object and preserves the modifiers on the object.

Certification Objective

Exercise 8.9: Finishing the Head

The head will require some of the same steps as the hand and foot. First, the edges at the base of the head have to be rearranged, and then some of the edges coming up to the neck need to be merged so that you have an equal number of edges on both objects. You need to do this before the attach can occur. Continue with the previous exercise's scene file, or open the c08_ex9_head_start.max scene file in the scenes folder of the c08_CharacterModel project.

1. In the Perspective viewport, zoom close into the underside of the head at the hole in the neck. Make sure you are looking at the front of the face.

2. In the Modeling tab choose Edit ➢ Cut. Then use the Cut tool to cut from the corner at the chin of the model down to the neck opening. It is important to start the cut from the vertex at the corner but finish in the middle of the edge at the neck, as shown in Figure 8.30.

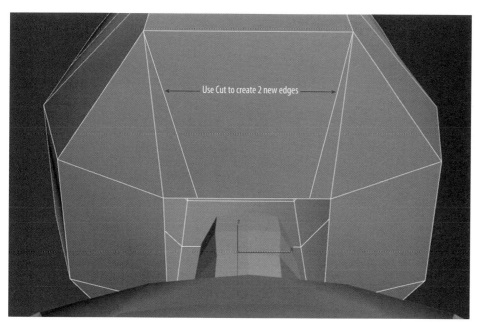

←——— Use Cut to create 2 new edges ———→

FIGURE 8.30   Use the Cut tool to add new edges.

3. Enter Edge mode, and select the edges on either side of the new edges created in the previous step. Ctrl+click on the edges to select both.

4. You cannot just delete the edges; you must remove them. In the Modeling tab choose Edges ➢ Remove (the Backspace key is the keyboard shortcut), as shown in Figure 8.31. This is a simple way to rearrange edges. Repeat the process on the back of the head.

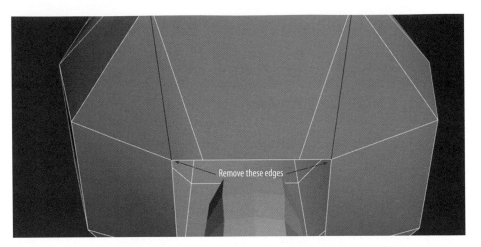

F I G U R E   8 . 3 1   Select the old edges and use the Remove tool to properly delete them.

The opening for the neck is square, so you can switch to Vertex mode and just move them around until the opening is round, or…

5. Switch to Border mode, select the neck border, and in the Modeling tab choose Geometry (All) ➢ Cap Poly. This adds a polygon in the hole.

6. Switch to Polygon mode and select the new cap polygon.

7. In the Modeling tab choose Polygons ➢ GeoPoly. This will rearrange the poly into a more rounded shape, as shown in Figure 8.32.

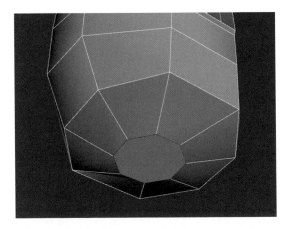

F I G U R E   8 . 3 2   Use GeoPoly to rearrange the polygon into a circular shape.

8. Now delete the selected polygon. Exit Polygon mode.

9. As you did with the foot, you will use the Weld tool to combine certain edges on the body. On the front of the neck, select the top-middle vertex and hold down Ctrl; then click on the two vertices on either side, as shown in Figure 8.33 (left).

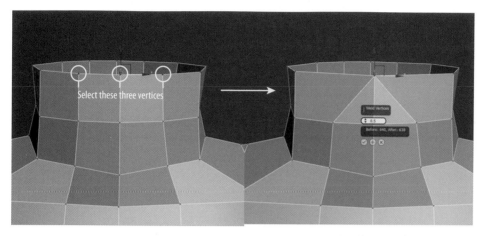

F I G U R E 8 . 3 3   Select the three vertices at the top of the neck (left). Use the Merge tool to combine the vertices (right).

10. Repeat the process on the row below the top row. Then repeat on the row below that until you get to the fourth row down, as shown in Figure 8.34.

F I G U R E 8 . 3 4   The merged vertices on the front of the neck

11. Repeat the process for the back of the neck.

12. Choose Geometry (All) ➤ Attach; then select the head.

13. Switch to Border mode, and select the border of the head and neck (hold down Ctrl to select both).

14. In the Modeling tab ➤ Borders ➤ Bridge ➤ Bridge Settings, keep most of the settings at the default but set Twist 1 to 1.

15. There is still some twisting, so switch back to Vertex mode, and in the Edit tab of the modeling ribbon, use Constrain To Edge to help in moving the vertices, as shown in Figure 8.35.

FIGURE 8.35 Move the vertices at the neck to eliminate the twisting.

There is one more thing that you can do; hidden in the file is an eyeball. Just right-click in the viewport and from the context menu choose Unhide All. If you are using your own file, just merge the c08_ex9_eye.max file from the c08_ CharacterModeling project folder. Save the file you are working with. To check your work open the c08_ex9_head_end.max scene file in the scenes folder of the c08_CharacterModel project. Turn on Use NURMS to see the final model at its smoothed-out best, as shown in Figure 8.36.

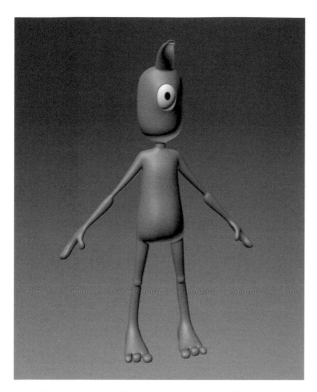

FIGURE 8.36   The completed alien model

Now You Know

In this chapter, you learned how use more advanced modeling tools in completing the modeling of the alien from Chapter 7. The first half of the chapter focused on building the head, hand, and foot for the alien, using many of the same tools from the previous chapter. The last half of the chapter showed how to put the model together using the Symmetry modifier and the Attach feature.

CHAPTER 9

Introduction to Materials

A material defines an object's look—its color, tactile texture, transparency, luminescence, glow, and so on. *Mapping* is the term used to describe how the materials are wrapped or projected onto the geometry (for example, adding wood grain to a wooden object). After you create your objects, the Autodesk® 3ds Max® program assigns a simple color to them, as you've already seen. You define a material by setting values for its parameters or by applying textures or maps. These parameters define the way an object will look when rendered. Much of an object's appearance when rendered also depends on the lighting. In this chapter and in Chapter 13, "Introduction to Lighting: Interior Lighting," you will discover that materials and lights work closely together.

In this chapter, you will learn to:

▶ **Navigate the Slate Material Editor**

▶ **Identify the Standard material**

▶ **Identify the mental ray material**

▶ **Identify shaders**

▶ **Build materials for the couch**

▶ **Build materials for the lounge chair**

▶ **Build materials for the windows**

Navigate the Slate Material Editor

The Material Editor is the central place where you do all of your material creation and editing. You can assign materials to any number of objects as well as have multiple materials assigned to different parts of the same object.

There are two interfaces to the Material Editor: the Slate Material Editor (or Slate) and the Compact Material Editor.

The Slate Material Editor is the interface you will use in this book: it is far superior to the Compact Material Editor and is especially nice when you are first learning mapping, because you can see the material structure, as shown in Figure 9.1.

FIGURE 9.1   The Slate Material Editor

The Slate Material Editor is the default Material Editor, but if it opens as the Compact Material Editor, you can switch it in the menu bar at the top of the Material Editor by selecting Modes ➤ Slate Material Editor.

You can access the Slate Material Editor by choosing from the menu bar Rendering ➤ Material Editor ➤ Slate Material Editor. There is also an icon for it on the main toolbar (🔲), and the keyboard shortcut to open the Slate Material Editor is the M key.

The Slate Material Editor has an interface that uses nodes and wiring to display the structure of materials. It has a simple and elegant layout with the Material/Map Browser on the left for choosing material and map types. The center area is the Active View area, where you build materials by connecting maps or controllers to material components. The area on the right is the Material Parameter Editor; within that area is a Navigator for moving within the Active View area.

Identify the Standard Material

Different materials have different uses. The Standard material is fine for most uses. However, when you require a more complex material, you can change the material type to one that will fit your needs. To change a material type in the Slate Material Editor, just choose from the list under Materials in the Material/ Map Browser. You should see the rollout for Standard. If you are using the mental ray renderer, you will also see a rollout for mental ray and MetaSL. As you can see, the list is extensive; there are not enough pages in this book to cover the multitude of material types, so we will touch on some of the best for an introduction. You will also see some examples using the Slate Material Editor.

Standard Materials

Standard materials typically use a four-color model to simulate a surface of a single color reflecting many colors. The four colors are known as the material's color components. Ambient color appears where the surface is in shadow, diffuse color appears where light falls directly on the surface, specular color appears in highlights, and filter color appears as light shining through an object. Along with the color components, there are parameters that control highlights, transparency, and self-illumination. Some of these parameters are different depending on the shader you are using. With the Standard material, as shown in Figure 9.2, you can imitate just about any surface type you can imagine.

FIGURE 9.2   The Standard material type shown in the Slate Material Editor

Identify the mental ray Material

The 3ds Max comes with several materials created specifically for use with the mental ray renderer. These materials are visible in the Material/Map Browser when mental ray is the active renderer. For the sake of time and space, we are going to cover only one here, Arch & Design.

The mental ray Arch & Design material improves the image quality of architectural renderings. It improves workflow and performance in general and performance for glossy surfaces (such as floors) in particular.

Special features of the Arch & Design material include advanced options for reflectivity and transparency, ambient occlusion settings, and the ability to round off sharp corners and edges as a rendering effect. These material types will be explored further in Chapter 15, "mental ray."

Identifying Shaders

The way light reflects from a surface defines that surface to your eye. With the 3ds Max program, you can control what kind of surface you work with by changing the shader type for a material. In either the Compact or Slate Material Editor, you will find the shader type in the material parameters in the Shader Basic Parameters rollout. This option will let you mimic different types of surfaces, such as dull wood, shiny paint, or metal. The following descriptions outline some of the shaders and the differences in how the shader types react to light, as shown in Figure 9.3.

Blinn   Metal   Anisotropic

FIGURE 9.3   Shader types shown on rendered spheres

Anisotropic   Most of the surface types that you will see typically create rounded specular highlights that spread evenly across a surface. By contrast, *anisotropic* surfaces have properties that differ according to direction. This creates a specular highlight that is elliptical in shape and uneven across the surface, changing according to the direction you specify on the surface. The

Anisotropic shader is good for surfaces such as foil wrappers or hair. There are extra controls for how the specular highlights will fall across the surface.

Blinn   This is the default shader because it is a general-purpose, flexible shader. The Blinn shader creates a smooth surface with some shininess. If you set the specular color to black, however, this shader will not display a specular highlight and will lose its shininess, making it perfect for regular dull surfaces, such as paper or an interior wall.

Metal   The Metal shader is not too different from the Blinn shader. Metal creates a lustrous metallic effect, with much the same controls as a Blinn shader but without the effect of any specular highlights.

When you are first starting, it's best to create most of your material looks with the Blinn shader until you're at a point where Blinn simply cannot do what you need.

Build Materials for the Couch

Now let's dive into creating material for the couch you modeled in Chapter 4, "Modeling in 3ds Max: Architectural Model Part II," to get it ready for lighting and rendering in later chapters.

Study the full-color image of the couch shown in Chapter 4 in Figure 4.1. That will give you an idea of how the couch is to be textured. The couch's material is basically all the same; once you create the material, it can be added to all the couch pieces.

Exercise 9.1: Creating a Standard Material

To begin, set the project to the c9_ArchMaterial project folder, and then open the c9_ex1_standard_start.max file from the scenes folder of the c9_ArchMaterial project folder downloaded from the book's web page at www.sybex.com/go/ 3dsmax2015essentials. This file has the room with the lounge chair and couch set up. When you open this file, the couch is the only furniture visible; the other models have been hidden. Follow these steps:

1. Open the Slate Material Editor (M). In the Material/Map Browser, open the Materials ➤ Standard rollout, and double-click Standard. This will add the Standard material to the Active View area.

2. Double-click the thumbnail with the sphere showing. This enlarges it and makes your material easier to view.

> The black areas of the shader may throw you off at first, but keep in mind that a metallic surface is ideally black when it has nothing to reflect. Metals are best seen when they reflect the environment. The Metal shader requires a lot of reflection work to make the metal look just right.

NAVIGATION IN ACTIVE VIEW

The Active View area uses the same navigation tools as the viewports. At the lower right of the Slate interface are the navigation tools. Keyboard shortcuts and the middle mouse button and wheel also work the same as in the viewports. The Navigator is another way to navigate in the Active View area. The Navigator panel changes the view of your material nodes; the colored box called the Proxy View area corresponds to the currently viewable area in the Active View area.

> It is always best to name your materials precisely. Calling the material Couch might be confusing if you want to use the same material on the curtains or a chair.

3. Double-click again on the node title bar; this adds the node parameters to the Material Parameter Editor.

4. In the Material Parameter Editor, at the top of the rollout, change the name to **Gray/Green Woven Fabric**.

5. In the Blinn Basic Parameters rollout, select the color swatch next to Diffuse. This brings up the color selector.

6. Set Red to 35, Green to 25, and Blue to 15. Click OK. In the material node, the sphere in the thumbnail will change color.

Save your file and move onto the next exercise. To check your work, open the c9_ex1_standard_end.max file from the scenes folder of the c9_ArchMaterial project folder.

Exercise 9.2: Applying the Material to the Couch

Continue with the file you are working on or open the c9_ex2_apply_start.max file from the scenes folder of the c9_ArchMaterial project folder. In the scene, select the couch. In Chapter 4, after the couch was merged into the room file, it was grouped. You can add materials to objects that are grouped; it can save time by applying the materials to all the pieces at the same time. You don't want to do that, so with the Couch selected, follow these steps:

1. On the menu bar, choose Group ➢ Ungroup. Hold Alt on the keyboard and click on the couch feet to deselect them.

2. Select the Gray/Green Woven Fabric material in the Material Editor; a white highlight appears around the material when it is selected. In the Slate Material Editor toolbar, click the Assign Material To

Selection icon (). When you compare the material in the viewport to the material on the couch, you should not see a difference, as shown in Figure 9.4, but the best way to view the material is by rendering the viewport.

FIGURE 9.4   Material in the Material Editor and on the couch in the viewport

3. In the Perspective viewport, use the keyboard shortcut Z to fit the couch model into the viewport. In the main toolbar, click the Render Production button ( ), or press F9 for Render Last. The result is shown in Figure 9.5.

FIGURE 9.5   The render of the couch with a Standard material applied

It is best to judge your material using the render.

Save your file and move on to the next exercise. To check your work, open the c9_ex2_apply_end.max file from the scenes folder of the c9_ArchMaterial project folder.

Exercise 9.3: Adding a Bitmap

The couch material needs some refinement. It looks flat and too perfect, which in this instance isn't a good thing. A material with just color is not enough; what is needed is a map. Two map types are available, 2D and 3D:

▶ 2D maps are two-dimensional images that are mapped onto the surface of 3D objects; the simplest 2D maps are bitmaps (aka image files).

▶ 3D maps are patterns generated procedurally in three dimensions using the 3ds Max software.

Using a map to replace the diffuse color is a way to create a more realistic material because you are using actual images. Using maps in other material components can have various effects, such as making a material look bumpy and controlling its transparency. Continue with the file you are working on or open the c9_ex3_bitmap_start.max file from the scenes folder of the c9_ArchMaterial project folder.

1. In the Slate Material Editor, open the Blinn Basic Parameters rollout and click the small gray box next to the Diffuse color swatch, as shown in Figure 9.6. This is a shortcut to the Diffuse Color Map in the Maps rollout, which you can find if you look lower in the Material Parameter Editor.

FIGURE 9.6 The shortcut button to add an image or bitmap to your material

2. This brings up a separate Material/Map Browser; in the Maps ➤ Standard rollout, choose Bitmap and click OK, as shown in Figure 9.7.

FIGURE 9.7 Choose Bitmap in the Material/Map Browser ➤ Maps ➤ Standard rollout to add an image to your material.

3. In the Select Bitmap Image File dialog box, navigate to the sceneassets\images folder in the c9_ArchMaterial project folder, select the GrayGreenWovenFabric.tif image file, and click Open.

4. Select the bitmap node and then in the Slate Material Editor's toolbar, click the Show Shaded Material in Viewport icon (). In the viewport, the couch shows the fabric image applied, as shown in Figure 9.8. This improves the color and adds some color variations.

If you don't see this map, make sure the Files of Type field is set to TIF Image File or All Formats.

In the Active view area, an additional node has been added to the main material node. The green node is the Bitmap node, which holds the fabric image.

FIGURE 9.8 The couch with the fabric image applied

The image is projected onto the surface of the couch model. How the image looks on the model depends on what are known as mapping coordinates. Right now the bitmap doesn't know how to lay on the surface, so it doesn't look right. Save your file and move on to the next exercise. To check your work, open the c9_ex3_bitmap_end.max file from the scenes folder of the c9_ArchMaterial project folder.

Exercise 9.4: Mapping Coordinates

An image map is two-dimensional; it has length and width but no depth. 3ds Max geometry, however, extends in all three axes. Mapping coordinates define how and where image maps are projected onto an object's surfaces and whether the maps are repeated across those surfaces.

Mapping coordinates can be applied to objects in several ways. When primitive objects are created and the Generate Mapping Coords option is checked at the bottom of the Parameters rollout, the appropriate mapping coordinates are created automatically. The next way is by applying a UVW Map modifier, which is commonly used to apply and control mapping coordinates. You select the type of mapping projection, regardless of the shape of the object, and then set the amount of tiling in the modifier's parameters. The mapping coordinates applied through the UVW Map modifier override any other mapping coordinates applied to an object, and the Tiling values set for the modifier are multiplied by the Tiling value set in the assigned material.

You are going to use a modifier to replace those coordinates on the geometry. The UVW Map modifier allows you to change the bitmap by transforming the UVW Map modifier gizmo. Continue with the file you are working on or open the c9_ex4_mapping_start.max file from the scenes folder of the c9_ArchMaterial project folder.

You can also access Isolate Selection by right-clicking the selected object and choosing Isolate Selection from the quad menu ➤ Display.

1. Select the main seat cushion on the couch, and enter Isolate Selection mode (🔑); the icon is under the timeline at the bottom of the interface (or press Alt+Q).

2. In the Modify panel, select UVW Map from the Modifier List drop-down.

3. Go to the UVW Map modifier parameters, and in the Mapping section, select Box for the projection type.

In the modifier stack, you can see the UVW Map modifier stacked on top of the editable poly. You will also see a flat orange gizmo running through the seat cushion.

4. In the Alignment section, click the Bitmap Fit button, as shown in Figure 9.9. This will take you to the Select Image dialog box.

FIGURE 9.9   The Alignment section for the UVW Map modifier parameters

5. Navigate to the sceneassets\images folder in the c9_ArchMaterial project folder and select the GrayGreenWovenFabric.tif file. Click Open. This will change the size of the UVW Map gizmo to the size and aspect of the image rather than the geometry.

6. In the modifier stack, click the plus sign in the black box next to the UVW Map modifier and select Gizmo.

7. The box gizmo will turn yellow when in sub-object gizmo mode. You will now be able to transform the gizmo to the correct size.

8. Switch to the Uniform Scale tool (⬛) or press R, and scale down the gizmo to 60 percent.

9. In the modifier stack, click the UVW Map modifier again to exit. Now that the couch fabric is where it should be, it is time to add the UVW Map modifier to the remaining pieces of the couch.

10. Exit Isolate Selection mode.

11. Switch to the Move tool, select one of the back couch cushions, and in the Modifier List, choose UVW Map modifier.

12. In the Alignment section, click the Acquire button. Then click on the previous couch seat cushion. The Acquire UVW Mapping dialog will appear. Select Acquire Relative and click OK.

13. Repeat the process on the remaining cushions.

The final results are shown in Figure 9.10.

> The UVW Map modifier has also changed the image on the couch. The size is more consistent throughout the couch, but the size of the fabric texture is too big.

> Acquire takes the UVW mapping information from the seat cushion and copies it onto the back cushion. This is a great time-saver.

FIGURE 9.10   The final results of the couch mapping

Save your file and move on to the next exercise. To check your work, open the c9_ex4_mapping_end.max file from the scenes folder of the c9_ArchMaterial project folder.

Exercise 9.5: Adding Materials to the Feet

The couch is not finished just yet; look closely at the couch feet. If you compare the current scene couch to the image of the real couch, you'll see that the feet should be a dark wood, not the default material on them now. Continue with the file you are working on or open the c9_ex5_feet_start.max file from the scenes folder of the c9_ArchMaterial project folder. Then follow these steps:

1. Open the Slate Material Editor if it isn't already open.

2. In the Material/Map Browser, choose Materials, select a Standard material, and drag it into the Active View area.

3. Double-click the title bar of the material to add the material parameters to the Material Parameter Editor.

4. Change the name to **Dark Red Wood**.

5. Expand the Maps rollout and click the None button across from Diffuse Color. This brings up a separate Material/Map Browser.

6. Choose Bitmap, and in the Select Bitmap Image File dialog box, navigate to the sceneassets\images folder in the c9_ArchMaterial project folder and select the DarkRedWood.jpg image file.

7. Apply the material by clicking and dragging from the node's output socket to the couch foot, as shown in Figure 9.11.

FIGURE 9.11 Apply the Dark Red Wood material by clicking and dragging from the node's output socket to the couch foot.

8. In the Material Editor, click the Show Shaded Material in Viewport icon. The material shows now, but the image has no detail. This is because it needs to have UVW Mapping applied.

9. Select the foot; then, in the Modify panel's Modifier List, add a UVW Map modifier to the couch foot.

10. Change the mapping type to Box, and select Bitmap Fit under Alignment.

11. Navigate to the DarkWood_Grain.jpg image file. Select the image and then click OK in the dialog box. The material now looks correct on the couch foot.

12. Apply the Dark Red Wood material to the remaining couch feet.

Save your file and move on to the next exercise. To check your work, open the c9_ex5_feet_end.max file from the scenes folder of the c9_ArchMaterial project folder.

Exercise 9.6: Applying a Bump Map

You are almost finished with the couch. One important feature of the couch is the bumpiness on the surface of the fabric, as shown in Figure 9.12. This bumpiness changes all the specular and reflective properties on a surface.

FIGURE 9.12 The couch fabric showing the subtle surface bumpiness

Bump mapping is very common in computer graphics (CG). It adds a level of detail to an object fairly easily by creating bumps and grooves in the surface and giving the object a tactile element.

Bump mapping uses the intensity values (the brightness values) of an image or procedural map to simulate bumpiness on the surface of the model without changing the actual topology of the model itself. You can create some surface texture with a bump map; however, you will not be able to create extreme depth in the model. For that, you may want to model the surface depth manually or use displacement mapping instead. Continue with the file you are working on or open the c9_ex6_bump_start.max file from the scenes folder of the c9_ArchMaterial project folder. To add a bump map to the couch, follow these steps:

1. In the Slate Material Editor's Active View area, locate the Gray/Green Woven Fabric material. Double-click the title bar to load the material into the Material Parameter Editor.

2. In the Maps rollout, click the None button next to the Bump map, and in the Material/Map Browser, choose Bitmap.

3. Navigate to the sceneassets\images folder in the c9_ArchMaterial project folder and select the GrayGreenWovenFabric_bmp.tif image file.

4. In the Maps rollout, increase Bump Amount from 30 (the default) to **60**.

5. Render to see the results. You should now see a texture on the couch that resembles the real bumpiness, as shown in Figure 9.13.

No bump map   Bump Map Amount set to 60

FIGURE 9.13 The couch fabric without the bump map (left) and with the bump map (right)

Save your file and move on to the next exercise. To check your work, open the c9_ex6_bump_end.max file from the scenes folder of the c9_ArchMaterial project folder.

Build Materials for the Lounge Chair

In this section, you will be adding materials to the lounge chair. Mapping the lounge chair is in some ways very much like mapping the couch. Figure 9.14 shows the lounge chair that was modeled in Chapter 4.

FIGURE 9.14   The lounge chair

Exercise 9.7: Creating a Leather Material for the Chair Cushion

The file has the lounge chair centered in the viewports, and the chair group is open so you can select the individual pieces. Continue with the file you are working on or open the c9_ex7_chair_start.max file from the scenes folder of the c9_ArchMaterial project folder. You will create the Cushion material using the techniques discussed in the previous section. Then follow these steps:

1. In the Slate Material Editor, add a Standard material to the Active View area. Double-click the material title to add it to the Material Parameter Editor.

2. In the Maps rollout, click the None button next to the Diffuse map, and in the Material/Map Browser, choose Bitmap.

3. Navigate to the sceneassets\images folder in the c9_ArchMaterial project folder, select the Leather.tif file, and rename the material Leather.

4. Select the lounge chair cushion, and apply the Leather material by clicking the Assign Material To Selection button in the toolbar.

5. On the Material Editor toolbar, click the Show Shaded Material in Viewport icon.

6. In the Specular Highlights group, change Specular Level to **20** and Glossiness to **9**. This will give the leather material a bit of gloss.

7. Repeat steps 1 through 6, but add the bitmap to the Bump map channel.

> If you double-click the input socket of the Diffuse Color map on the Standard Material node, the Material/Map Browser will open.

8. When the Select Bitmap Image File dialog box opens, choose `Leather_Bmp.tif`.

9. In the Modify panel's Modifier List, add a UVW Map modifier.

10. Change the Mapping type to Box, and in Alignment, select Bitmap Fit. Navigate to the `Leather.tif` bitmap, select the image, and then click OK. This will change the size of the UVW Map gizmo. The size of the map is now the proper height-to-width ratio, but it is too large.

11. In the modifier stack, click the plus sign in the black box and select Gizmo.

12. Using the Scale tool, scale the gizmo until the material looks correct, as shown in Figure 9.15.

FIGURE 9.15   **The Leather texture is applied to the chair cushion.**

Save your file and move on to the next exercise. To check your work, open the `c9_ex7_chair_end.max` file from the `scenes` folder of the `c9_ArchMaterial` project folder.

Exercise 9.8: Creating a Reflective Material

Reflection occurs when light changes direction as a result of "bouncing off" a surface like a mirror. In the following steps, you will create reflections on the lounge chair frame; what you are going to create is a chrome material that has

100 percent reflections. Continue with the file you are working on or open the c9_ex8_reflect_start.max file from the scenes folder of the c9_ArchMaterial project folder.

1. In the Material Editor, drag a Standard material from the Material/ Map Browser to the Active View area.

2. Double-click the title bar of the material to add it to the Material Parameter Editor.

3. Rename the material **Chrome**, and change the diffuse color to black (R: 0, G: 0, B: 0).

4. In the Specular Highlights group, change Specular Level to **90** and Glossiness to **80**. This will give the chrome material a bit of gloss.

5. In the Material/Map Browser rollout, go to the Maps rollout ➤ Standard, choose Raytrace from the list, and drag the Raytrace map to the Reflection input socket.

6. Apply the Chrome material to the lounge chair frame (which is grouped together in this scene). You won't be able to see the mirror effect of the chrome in the viewport; you will have to render.

7. Click the Render Production button. The result of the render is shown in Figure 9.16. In the figure, the chrome doesn't look smooth. It has a noisy, broken-up look to it. You can correct this by controlling the anti-aliasing.

A reflection creates the illusion of chrome, glass, or metal by applying a map to the geometry so the image looks like a reflection on the surface. A Raytrace map provides reflections on a material. Raytrace reflects the actual surroundings in the scene.

Anti-aliasing smoothes the jagged edges that occur along the edges of diagonal and curved lines when a scene is rendered. SuperSampling performs an additional anti-aliasing pass on the material and can improve the image quality.

FIGURE 9.16   The Chrome material applied to the lounge chair frame

8. In the Chrome material, select the SuperSampling rollout. Uncheck Use Global Settings and check Enable Local Supersampler.

9. Choose Max 2.5 Star from the drop-down menu, and then render. You should see the difference in the reflections, as shown in Figure 9.17.

FIGURE 9.17   Final reflections on the chair frame

SuperSampling Filters

SuperSampling Filters is an anti-aliasing technique, the process of eliminating jagged and pixelated edges (aliasing). It is a method of smoothing images rendered in imagery. There are four SuperSampling filters:

Adaptive Halton   Samples along both the X- and Y-axes according to a random pattern.

Adaptive Uniform   Samples regularly, from a minimum quality of four samples to a maximum of 36.

Hammersley   Samples regularly along the X-axis, but along the Y-axis it spaces them according to a random pattern.

Max 2.5 Star   The sample at the center of the pixel is averaged with four samples surrounding it.

The last material is the material that is on the base of the chair. This should be a very simple material to create, a matte black material. Follow the steps learned throughout this chapter. Use a Standard material, and make the diffuse color black. Set Specular Level to **20** and Glossiness to **15**. Name the material **Base** and apply this material to all the objects from the base, as shown in Figure 9.18.

FIGURE 9.18 The final materials applied to the lounge chair

Save your file and move on to the next exercise. To check your work, open the c9_ex8_reflect_end.max file from the scenes folder of the c9_ArchMaterial project folder.

Build Materials for the Window

The window and doors are special 3D primitive objects. They are a collection of multiple objects attached together: a frame, mullions, and glass. You can edit those objects within the Architecture Engineering and Construction (AEC) object's parameters. You also have the ability to add materials to the individual pieces within the attached whole.

Exercise 9.9: Creating a Multi/Sub-Object Material

The Multi/Sub-Object material (MSOM), which is in the Compound Materials category, lets you assign different materials at the sub-object level of your geometry. In the case of the AEC window, it is already divided into separate sub-object levels, so you just have to apply the material and identify the different parts. Continue with the file you are working on or open the c9_ex9_MSOM_start.max file from the scenes folder of the c9_ArchMaterial project folder. Then follow these steps:

Multi/Sub-Object is just a material that gathers other materials together.

1. In the Slate Material Editor, drag a Multi/Sub-Object material from the Material/Map Browser into the Active View area.

2. Double-click the title bar to add the material to the Material Parameter Editor. Click the Set Number button and change Number of Materials to 5, as shown in Figure 9.19. Change the name to **Window/Door**.

The Set Number parameter allows you to control how many materials can be plugged into the Multi/Sub-Object material.

FIGURE 9.19   Multi/Sub-Object material and parameters

3. Drag a Standard material from the Material/Map Browser to the Active View area, and then from the output socket of the Standard material, drag it to the input socket of the MSOM, as shown in Figure 9.20.

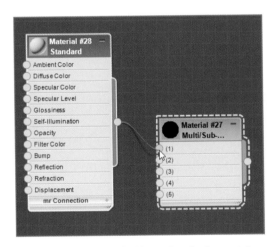

FIGURE 9.20   Adding a Standard material to the Multi/Sub-Object Material node

4. Double-click the new Standard material's title bar to add it to the Material Parameter Editor. Click the Diffuse color swatch to open the color selector; create a red color, and click OK.

5. Repeat the process until you have five Standard materials with five different diffuse colors plugged into the 1 through 5 input sockets of

the MSOM. The finished node is shown in Figure 9.21. The Standard material nodes have been minimized for the figure. The numbers in the MSOM parameters are material IDs.

Geometric primitives have default material identification number assignments. The default material ID assignment depends on the type of geometry. AEC objects like the window and doors already have them assigned; they just have to be identified.

FIGURE 9.21   Finished MSOM with five Standard materials added

6. Apply the MSOM to the window in the living room area, as shown in Figure 9.22. The colors show clearly which section of the window corresponds to which ID number.

FIGURE 9.22   The Multi/Sub-Object material applied to the window object shows the different colors applied to the different parts of the window.

7. The colored materials that were just created are not needed. Select and delete them.

8. Starting with the window glass; select the material bar for ID #3 in the MSOM parameter. This opens the Material/Map Browser, and Select Standard material. Click the material bar for ID #3 in the MSOM parameters. This loads that material's parameters. Rename the material **Window Glass**.

9. In the Blinn Basic Parameters rollout, change Opacity to 0. If you render, you will see a black hole where the green used to be. That is because you are seeing the default color applied to the background in a render. That means the glass is see-through now.

10. In the Maps rollout, click the Reflection Map button.

11. From the Material/Map Browser, choose Raytrace, and then change Reflection Amount to **9**.

12. In the main menu go to the Rendering menu. Choose Environment and then click the color swatch under Background, and change it to a light gray.

13. Render the Perspective viewport. Now the reflection looks more appropriate. Eventually, an image of an outdoor scene will be placed behind the glass. For now, let's continue with the MSOM for the window. Window frames and mullions come in many colors and textures, but for this example you are going to use a shiny white plastic.

14. Double-click the MSOM title bar to load the material into the Material Parameter Editor, and then select any of the material IDs (other than #3).

15. Repeat the same process as in step 8 to load the material in the MSOM.

16. Change the diffuse color to White, and then in the Maps rollout add a Raytrace node to the Reflection map, and change the Amount to **10**, as you did in step 11.

17. Drag from the output socket of the Shiny White Plastic material to the input of the remaining Multi/Sub-Object material's IDs, as shown in Figure 9.23.

This places a clone of the Shiny White Plastic material into the three remaining material slots and completes the window material, as shown in a render in Figure 9.24.

When the scene renders, the Reflection amount will appear to be very high; this is a bit of an illusion because of the black in the background.

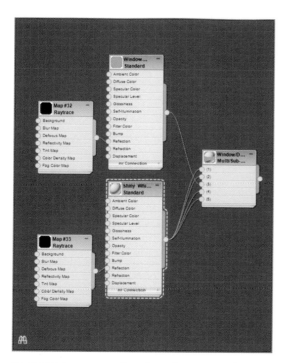

FIGURE 9.23 Drag from the output socket of the Shiny White Plastic material into the input socket of the remaining ID slots of the Multi/Sub-Object material.

FIGURE 9.24 The completed window

The same technique used for the window can be used for the doors, but if you want the doors to be just a plain solid color or simple wood, you can apply a Standard material to the entire Door object. We'll return to this room in Chapter 14 when we look at lighting. Meanwhile, finish assigning materials to the rest of the scene.

Now You Know

In this chapter, you learned how to build materials using the Material Editor. The Slate Material Editor is the center for material creation in 3ds Max. It begins with identifying the different material types and shaders available. You can apply this information to build materials for the couch, lounge chair, window. This chapter provided the information to allow you to move forward with other types of material creation to complete the room.

CHAPTER 10

Textures and UV Workflow: The Alien

Autodesk® 3ds Max® materials simulate the natural physics of how you see things by regulating how objects reflect and/or transmit light. You define a material by setting values for its parameters or by applying textures or maps. These parameters define the way an object will look when rendered. In this chapter and in Chapter 13, "Introduction to Lighting: Interior Lighting," you will discover that materials and lights work closely together.

In this chapter, you will apply material and maps to the alien model from Chapters 7 and 8. You will first set up the model to accept textures properly through a process called UV-unwrap. In contrast to x, y, and z Cartesian coordinates, which are the coordinates for the original 3D object, another set of (2D) coordinates is required to describe the surface of the mesh, so the letters *u* and *v* are used to designate those coordinates. This allows you to lay out the colors and patterns for the alien's body and general look. This process essentially creates a flat map that can be used to paint the textures in a program such as Photoshop. The textures (i.e., the maps) you'll use for the alien have already been created in Photoshop. We will show you how to prepare the model for proper UVs and how to apply the maps you have already painted. We will not demonstrate the actual painting process in Photoshop because that discussion goes beyond the scope of this book.

In this chapter, you'll learn to:

▶ Define UVs on the alien's body

▶ Unwrap UVs on the alien's body

▶ Build the material and apply it to the alien

Define UVs on the Alien's Body

▶

When you open the file, a Gamma & LUT Settings Mismatch dialog might appear. You want to adopt the file's gamma and LUT settings, which is the default option, so you only have to click OK.

Set your project to the c10_UnwrapUV project downloaded from the companion web page at www.sybex.com/go/3dsmax2015essentials. Open the scene file c10_ex1_seam_start.max from the scenes folder of the c10_UnwrapUV project folder.

Keep in mind that any design changes you made to your own alien model may cause discrepancies in the UV unwrapping and mapping steps in the following sections.

You will begin by creating seams to define the shapes of the arms so you'll know where to paint the sleeves of the uniform in an image-editing program like Adobe Photoshop. If you use the c10_ex1_seam_start.max file, you'll see that the alien has been given a new color. Remember that to change the color of any model, you need to use the Name and Color rollout, which appears at the top of all the command panels (other than the Create panel). The new color was added because the unwrap seams that will be added are blue and another color will highlight the seams much better.

Exercise 10.1: Seaming the Alien's Body

1. Change the viewport rendering type to Shaded with Edged Faces (F4) in all the viewports.

2. With your model selected, go to the Modify panel, and from the Modifier List, choose Unwrap UVW.

3. Expand the Unwrap UVW modifier in the modifier stack by clicking the plus sign in the black box next to the Unwrap UVW title. Enter Polygon mode.

4. At the bottom of the Configure rollout, uncheck Map Seams, as shown in Figure 10.1.

5. In the Peel rollout, click the Point-To-Point Seams button, as shown in Figure 10.2. This tool lets you reroute the seams to where you want them.

▶

Unchecking Map Seams turns off the green highlight on the edges; it is generated by default and is not useful in its current state.

FIGURE 10.1 Uncheck Map Seams in the Configure rollout.

FIGURE 10.2 Click the Point-To-Point Seams button.

6. With Point-To-Point Seams enabled, click on the center of a pair of intersecting edges about where you want to define the left shoulder, as shown in Figure 10.3 (left image).

A dashed-line "rubber band" appears next to your cursor, letting you know that the tool is waiting for the next point to be selected.

While Point-To-Point Seams is active, you can navigate using all the viewport navigation tools to look around the model. 3ds Max remembers the last intersection you clicked and draws an accurate seam at the next click.

FIGURE 10.3 Pick this edge intersection to begin defining the seam (left). Choose the next point at the upper shoulder (middle).

7. Select the next intersecting edges in the loop around the shoulder. This creates a blue highlight across the edges, as shown in Figure 10.3 (middle image).

8. Continue around the shoulder until you have a complete loop, ending with the intersection you started with in step 6, as shown in Figure 10.3 (right image).

9. Select the bottommost edge intersection on the underarm and continue selecting edge intersections all the way to the middle point of the wrist, as shown in Figure 10.4.

Also, you can right-click and then start or continue the picks without overlapping them.

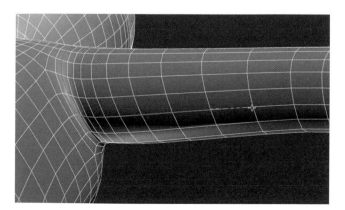

FIGURE 10.4 Select the intersections under the arm.

10. Continue selecting edge interactions around the wrist, as shown in Figure 10.5, until you get back to where you began at the wrist.

FIGURE 10.5   Select edge intersections around the wrist to complete the forearm/wrist seam.

11. Right-click to deactivate the Point-To-Point Seams tool's rubber banding but keep the button active; then continue cutting a new set of UVs for the right arm, just as you did for the left arm.

12. Again right-click and then continue cutting around the torso area; go around the arms at the shoulder and also around the top of the legs, as shown in Figure 10.6.

13. Using the Point-To-Point Seams tool, cut seams for the hands lengthwise down the middle from wrist to wrist. Begin at the wrist on the side of the thumb and work your way around the fingers to the opposite side of the wrist. You can see this progression for the left-hand start in Figure 10.7.

14. Cut another seam from the inside of the left leg down to the ankle. Then continue the seam around the ankle; right-click to complete. The seam is just on the inside of the leg, except where it wraps around the ankle.

FIGURE 10.6   Add these seams to define the torso area.

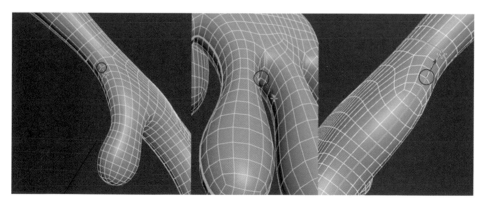

FIGURE 10.7   Cut a new seam around the hand, starting as shown in the left image. Cut a seam around the fingers, as shown in the middle image, finishing at the opposite side of the wrist, as shown in the right image.

15. Create the seam for the right leg in the same way; the seams for both legs are shown in Figure 10.8.

FIGURE 10.8 Using the Point-To-Point Seams tool to cut the seams for the left and right legs.

16. Continue creating seams for the left foot, using the Point-To-Point Seams tool. Start at the back of the foot and create a seam encircling the foot, as shown in Figure 10.9.

FIGURE 10.9 Cut a seam around the foot.

17. Repeat the same seam on the right foot.

18. Now for the head, start at the base of the back of the neck. Cut a seam up to the base of the nose, shown in Figure 10.10 (right image).

19. Cut the seam around the base of the nose. The completed head seam is shown in Figure 10.10 (left image).

FIGURE 10.10 Cut seams for the head. Right image shows seams on the back of the head; left image shown seam that runs around the base of the nose.

20. For the nose, start at the base located at the top of the head. Cut a seam up to the base of the nostril. Cut a seam around the base of the nostril, as shown in Figure 10.11.

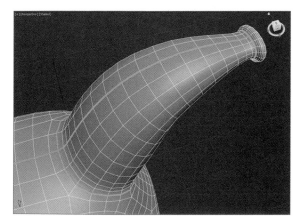

FIGURE 10.11 Cut seams for the nose.

21. Cut a seam from the top of the nostril into the center of the nostril.

22. Save your work before continuing with the next section. To check your work open the c10_ex1_seam_end.max file.

Unwrap UVs on the Alien's Body

Now that the alien's body has seams cut it's time to Unwrap the seamed parts. When sewing clothing you cut the fabric from patterns. Similarly, in this next section you will spread out the patterns so you can paint them to create the texture for the alien surface.

Exercise 10.2: Unwrapping the Alien's Arm

Continue with the scene file from the previous section or open the c10_ex2_unwrap_start.max from the scenes folder of the c10_UnwrapUV project folder.

1. Select the alien, go to the Modify panel, and in the Unwrap UVW modifier in the Edit UVs rollout, select the Open UV Editor button.

2. In the top right of the window, from the drop-down menu choose CheckerPattern (Checker). This will apply a low-contrast checker map to the alien, as shown in Figure 10.12.

The checker pattern applied to the alien will show only if the Edit UVWs dialog box is open. The low-contrast checker will appear only when you select CheckerPattern (Checker) again.

FIGURE 10.12   A low-contrast checker pattern is added to the alien model.

3. With Polygon mode selected in your Unwrap UVW modifier and Point-to-Point Seams toggled off, click on a polygon on the left forearm of your model, and then in the Peel rollout, click the Expand Polygon Selection To Seams icon (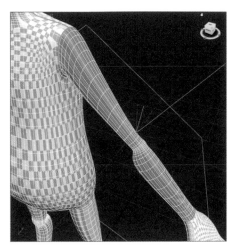). This will select all the polygons that were included when creating seams for the arm, as shown in Figure 10.13.

FIGURE 10.13 The arm's polygons are selected.

4. To unfold the UVs into a usable pattern, click the Pelt Map icon ( ) in the Peel rollout. The Pelt Map dialog box opens.

5. In the Edit UVWs dialog box, click the View menu and toggle off Show Grid and Show Map to simplify the UV view. Before moving on, take a look at the checkerboard pattern on the arm of the alien to recognize how it changes once you pelt, as shown in Figure 10.14.

FIGURE 10.14 The Edit UVWs and Pelt Map dialog boxes showing the left arm UVs

6. To unfold the map, click the Start Pelt button in the Pelt Map dialog box. Doing so moves the UVs in the Edit UVWs dialog box in real time, as shown in Figure 10.15.

FIGURE 10.15 In the Pelt Map dialog box, use Start Pelt to unfold the UVs of the alien's arm.

7. This procedure keeps unfolding the UVs until you stop it, so wait a couple of seconds for the UVs to stop moving and then click Stop Pelt. You're almost finished with the arm; however, if you look at the checkerboard texture in your viewport, you can see that some of the checks are bigger than others. To fix this, complete the remaining steps.

8. Click the Settings box next to the Start Relax button in the Pelt Map dialog box. The Relax Tool dialog box opens. Change the drop-down option to Relax By Polygon Angles.

9. Now, click the Start Relax button in the Relax Tool dialog box. Let Relax run for a good bit until the image matches Figure 10.16.

10. Wait until the UVs stop moving and then click Stop Relax. If it still doesn't match the figure, click Start Relax; then click Apply.

11. Close the Relax Tool dialog box.

12. Check your texture in the viewport; it now shows the checkerboard the way you want it.

FIGURE 10.16 Use the Start Relax button to relax the UVs.

13. Click the Commit button at the bottom of the Pelt Map dialog box, or your changes won't take effect.

14. Close the Edit UVWs dialog box.

15. Repeat steps 1 through 12 for the right arm. You can see in Figure 10.17 that both arms are now laid out—pelted and relaxed.

FIGURE 10.17 Both arms are pelted and relaxed.

16. Save your work before continuing with the next section. To check your work open c10_ex2_unwrap_end.max.

Exercise 10.3: Unwrapping the Alien's Body

Now that you have the arms finished, you have an idea what needs to be done. It's time to unwrap the remaining parts of the body, starting with the alien's torso. Continue with the scene file from the previous section or open `c10_ex3_unwrap_start.max` from the `scenes` folder of the `c10_UnwrapUV` project folder.

If the checker pattern is not showing, select CheckerPattern (Checker) from the Edit UVWs dialog box so the pattern shows.

1. Select the alien, go to the Modify panel, and enter Polygon mode of the Unwrap UVW modifier.

2. Select a single polygon on the alien's torso (front or back, it doesn't matter). In the Peel rollout, click the Expand Polygon Selection To Seams icon; this will select all the faces that were included when creating seams for the torso.

3. Click the Pelt Map icon to open the Edit UVWs dialog box and the Pelt Map dialog box. First, click Start Pelt. You will see the UVs moving around. When they stop moving, click the Stop Pelt button.

4. Now, click the Settings button next to the Start Relax button.

5. Make sure the drop-down menu is set to Relax By Polygon Angles. Click Apply, and then close the Relax Tool dialog box.

6. Click the Start Relax button again, and when the UVs stop moving, click Stop Relax.

7. Click the Commit button. The checker pattern on the torso should look organized and even, as shown in Figure 10.18.

For the remaining objects, you don't have to go into the Relax Tool dialog box—just click Start Relax.

FIGURE 10.18 The alien's backside with its UVs pelted and relaxed, showing the checker pattern evenly laid out

8. Now that you have finished with part of the torso, repeat the process on the part of the torso you didn't do in the previous steps.

9. Repeat the process from steps 1–7 until all the remaining body seams on the alien's body are pelted and relaxed.

Save your work before continuing with the next section. To check your work open c10_ex3_unwrap_end.max.

Exercise 10.4: Arranging the Alien's UVs

When the UVs are unwrapped, the squares in the checker pattern on different parts of the alien are different sizes. They need to be set to the same size, showing that the UVs are uniform. Using the Select By Element UV Toggle tool will help with this process. It allows you to select an individual element's full set of UVs so that you can scale and lay them out separately. Give them some space on the flat blank canvas so they can be used later for painting the textures for those parts of the body. Look in the UV Editor and you should see the blue-bordered box. It will look like a mess; these are all the unwrapped UVs piled on top of each other.

The UV layout can vary depending on many factors, as we said earlier. The goal is to fit the UVs into this box without going outside it and without overlapping any of them. Anything outside this box ends up tiling (or having no texture at all), and any overlapping UVs share parts of the texture from another element. Either way, that's not good. Once you have the layout, you can select the UVs and move them around.

Continue with the scene file from the previous section or open c10_ex4_arrange_start.max from the scenes folder of the c10_UnwrapUV project folder.

1. Select the alien and go to the Modify panel; enter Polygon mode of the Unwrap UVW modifier.

2. In the Unwrap UVW modifier ➤ Edit UVs and select Open UV Editor.

3. Click the Select By Element UV Toggle, as shown in Figure 10.19.

FIGURE 10.19 Click the Select By Element UV Toggle.

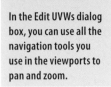

In the Edit UVWs dialog box, you can use all the navigation tools you use in the viewports to pan and zoom.

4. In the Edit UVWs dialog box, click on the "mess"; one part of the alien will be selected, as shown in Figure 10.20.

FIGURE   10.20   Select an element in the Edit UVWs dialog box, and it will appear as selected on the model.

5. In the Edit UVWs dialog box, drag a selection box around all the UVs.

6. From the Arrange Elements rollout on the right side of the Edit UVWs dialog box, change the Padding type-in field to 0.0 and then click the Pack Normalize button, as shown in Figure 10.21. The results of the Pack Normalize command are shown in Figure 10.22.

FIGURE   10.21   The Arrange Elements rollout

FIGURE 10.22   UVs placed within the UV space

7. In the Edit UVWs dialog box, select Tools ➢ Render UVW Template to open the Render UVs dialog box.

8. Click the Render UV Template button in the Render Map dialog box to create an image of your UVs, as shown in Figure 10.23. Remember, the layout of the UV rendered image can vary.

9. Save the UV layout image by clicking the Save Image icon in the Render Map dialog box, as shown in Figure 10.24.

10. In the Save Image dialog box name the UV layout image **Alien UV**, and change Save As Type to TIF Image File (*.tif, *.tiff). Save the UVs in the sceneassets/images folder.

FIGURE 10.23
Use Save Image button to
create UV layout image.

FIGURE 10.24   The UV layout image.

> The more you unwrap UVs for models, the easier it becomes to anticipate how to paint the textures.

Once the UVs are saved, you can close all the UV image boxes and the Edit UVWs dialog box. Now you can open this image in your favorite image editor, and you can use the pieces as guides to paint the alien's textures. Save your work before continuing with the next set of steps. To check your work open `c10_ex4_arrange_end.max` from the `scenes` folder of the `c10_UnwrapUV` project folder.

Build the Material and Apply It to the Alien

With the UV layout image saved, you can go into Photoshop (or the image-editing software of your choice) and create a texture to place on your model. For example, we took the UV image into Photoshop and used painting to create the final map for the alien, as shown in Figure 10.25.

FIGURE 10.25   The final map for the alien

The texture map, as you can see, places painted parts of the alien's body according to the UV layout you just created. For example, you can clearly see the alien's eye socket painted in middle of the texture image file.

Exercise 10.5: Applying the Color Map

Now it is time to use the map you put so much effort into creating. Continue with the scene file from the previous section or open c10_ex5_colormap_start. max from the scenes folder of the c10_UnwrapUV project folder.

1. Open the Slate Material Editor (M).

2. In the Material/Map Browser, expand the Materials rollout, and on the Standard rollout, drag and drop a Standard material onto the View1 window. Double-click the material node title bar to load the parameter into the Material Parameter Editor. Rename the material **Alien**.

3. Double-click the Diffuse Color input socket of the material to open the Material/Map Browser.

4. In the Maps rollout, expand the Standard rollout and double-click Bitmap.

5. When the Select Bitmap Image File dialog box appears, navigate to the \sceneassets\images folder for the c10_UnwrapUV project and select and open the Alien_ColorMap.tif file.

6. Apply the material to the alien, and click Show Shaded Material in Viewport.

The result is shown in Figure 10.26. Now wasn't all that hard UV work worth it? If the blue seams are showing, go back to the Modify panel and select the Unwrap UVW modifier. Go to the Configure rollout and uncheck Peel Seams.

FIGURE 10.26 The alien with the material applied

Save your work before continuing with the next set of steps. To check your work open c10_ex5_colormap_end.max from the scenes folder of the c10_ UnwrapUV project folder.

Exercise 10.6: Applying the Bump Map

Bump mapping makes an object appear to have a bumpy or irregular surface by simulating surface definition. When you render an object with a bump-mapped material, lighter (whiter) areas of the map appear to be raised on the object's surface, and darker (blacker) areas appear to be lower on the object's surface, as shown in Figure 10.27.

FIGURE 10.27 Bump map created in Photoshop by desaturating the original color map to create light and dark areas that conform to the original color texture

You can use this mapping technique to create additional surface detail. Bump maps are simple to create because you can usually take the color map and just desaturate it to make a grayscale image file. You will continue with the Alien material you created in the previous exercise as you add the new map. Continue with the scene file from the previous section or open c10_ex5_bumpmap_start.max from the scenes folder of the c10_UnwrapUV project folder.

1. Double-click the Bump input socket of the material to open the Material/Map Browser.

2. Under the Maps rollout, expand the Standard rollout and choose Bitmap.

3. When the Select Bitmap Image File dialog box appears, navigate to the \sceneassets\images folder of the c10_UnwrapUV project folder and select the Alien_BumpMap.tif file.

4. Double-click the material's title bar to show the main material parameters.

5. In the Maps rollout, set Bump Amount to 30.

The bump map is applied and finished. See Figure 10.28 for an image with the bump map. You may notice that the bump map has created a lot more detail in the alien's body. You will notice the difference even better in your own renders.

FIGURE 10.28   Alien rendered with the bump map

Save your work before continuing with the next set of steps. To check your work open c10_ex6_bump_end.max from the scenes folder of the c10_UnwrapUV project folder.

Exercise 10.7: Applying the Specular Map

Highlights in objects are reflections of a light source. *Specular* maps are maps you use to define a surface's shininess and highlight color, without the complex calculations of reflections in the render. The higher a pixel's value (from black to white, or 0 to 1, respectively), the shinier the surface will appear at that location. You will be adding a specular map to the alien to increase the amount of detail you can get from the render, as shown in Figure 10.29.

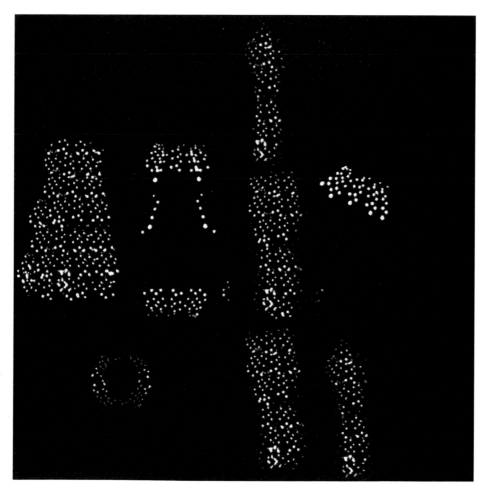

FIGURE 10.29   The specular map for the alien

Continue with the scene file from the previous section or open c10_ex7_spec_ start.max from the scenes folder of the c10_UnwrapUV project folder.

Placing the map into the Specular Color slot allows for iridescence and flexibility.

1. Double-click the Specular Color input socket of the material to open the Material/Map Browser.

2. Under the Maps rollout, expand the Standard rollout and choose Bitmap.

3. When the Select Bitmap Image File dialog box appears, navigate to the \sceneassets\images folder for the c10_UnwrapUV project and select the Alien_SpecularMap.tif file.

4. Double-click the material's title bar to show the main material parameters.

5. In the Specular Highlights group, set Specular Level to 50 and Glossiness to 40.

The final render of the alien is shown in Figure 10.30. You can see the improvement to the appearance of the alien's bumps with the added specular color map.

FIGURE 10.30   Final render of the alien with the specular map applied

Save your work. To check your work open c10_ex7_spec_end.max from the scenes folder of the c10_UnwrapUV project folder.

Now You Know

In this chapter, you learned how to set up the alien model to accept textures properly through a process called UV unwrap, which allowed you to lay out the maps onto the alien's body using the UV unwrap modifier. Once the model was prepared with proper UVs, you saw how to apply the painted maps to the model.

CHAPTER 11

Character Studio: Rigging

At one time or another, almost everyone in the 3D community wants to animate a character. This chapter examines the toolsets used in the process of setting up for character animation using Character Studio, a full-featured package that is incorporated into the Autodesk® 3ds Max® 2014 software and used mostly for animating bipedal characters, including humans, aliens, robots, and anything else that walks on two feet—though you can have characters with more than two feet in certain situations.

In this chapter you'll learn to:

▶ **Utilize Character Studio workflow**

▶ **Associate a biped with the alien model**

▶ **Skin the alien model**

Character Studio Workflow

Character Studio is a system built into the 3ds Max program to help automate the creation and animation of a character, which may or may not be exactly a *biped* (two-footed creature). Character Studio consists of three basic components: the Biped system, the Skin modifiers, and the Crowd system. Biped and Skin are used to pose and animate a single character, and the Crowd system is used to assign similar movements and behaviors to multiple objects in your 3ds Max scene. This chapter covers the Biped and Skin features; the Crowd system is beyond the scope of this book.

The first step in the Character Studio workflow is to build or acquire a suitable character model. The second step is to *skin* (bind) the character model to the skeleton so the animation drives the model properly.

Models should typically be in the reference position known as the Da Vinci pose, where the feet are shoulder width apart and the arms are extended to the sides with the palms down, as shown in Figure 11.1. This allows the animator to observe all of the model's features, unobstructed by the model itself, in at least two viewports.

FIGURE 11.1   A bipedal character in the reference position

In 3ds Max parlance, a *biped* is a predefined, initially humanoid structure. It is important to understand that you animate the biped that is associated with your model and not the model itself. Once the model is bound to the skeleton, the biped structure *drives* the model. You use the Skin modifier to create that relationship between the skeleton and the model.

General Workflow

There are four different biped types you can choose from: Skeleton, Male, Female, and Classic, as shown in Figure 11.2. They all consist of legs, feet, toes, arms, hands, fingers, pelvis, spine, neck, and head. After your model is ready, you will create a biped and, using its parameters and the Scale transform, fit the biped closely to the model.

FIGURE 11.2   Skeleton, Male, Female, and Classic bipeds (from left to right)

Once the biped is fit snugly to the model, you select all the components of the model, not the biped skeleton, and apply the Skin modifier in a process often referred to as *skinning*. It may take a while to properly test and refine the relationship between the model and the biped to get it to an acceptable level.

The final step is animating your character. You can accomplish this by adding to the biped any combination of default walk, run, and jump cycles included with Character Studio; applying any kind of freeform animation to the character; and finally, refining the animation keyframes in the Dope Sheet.

Don't expect the default walk, run, and jump cycles to create realistic motion, though. They are just starting points and must be tweaked to achieve acceptable movements.

The best way to start is to jump in and examine the tools available. In the next sections, you will work with a biped and adjust the parameters and components to modify it.

The better the biped-to-model relationship, the easier the animation will be.

The Dope Sheet displays animation keys over time on a horizontal graph. It simplifies editing animation timing by displaying them in a spreadsheet format.

Associating a Biped with the Alien Model

The purpose of a biped is to be the portal through which you add animation to your model rather than animating the model itself using direct vertex manipulation or deforming modifiers. Any motion assigned to a biped is passed through it to the nearest vertices of the associated model, essentially driving the surfaces of the model. For this reason, it is important that the biped fit as closely as possible to the model.

Exercise 11.1: Creating and Modifying the Biped

In the following steps, you'll create and adjust a biped to fit to a character model. Set your project to the c11_CharacterRigging project available for download from this book's web page at www.sybex.com/go/3dsmax2015essentials. You can then open the c11_ex1_biped_start.max file from the scenes folder of the c11_CharacterRigging project folder. It contains a completed alien model in the reference position.

1. With the alien model file open, select the Perspective viewport, and set the viewport rendering type to Shaded + Edged faces (F4).

2. Select the alien, and use Alt+X to make the model see-through.

3. Right-click in a viewport and choose Freeze Selection. This will prevent you from inadvertently selecting the alien instead of the biped.

VIEWING FROZEN OBJECTS

If your background color is similar to the default shade of gray used to depict frozen objects, the model may seem to disappear against the background. There are several solutions to this situation:

▶ Before you freeze the model go to Object Properties, turn off Show Frozen In Gray, turn on See-Through, and set all viewports to Realistic or Shaded mode.

▶ You can change the viewport background color in the Customize User Interface dialog box (Customize ➢ Customize User Interface ➢ Colors tab).

The first click sets the insertion point. Dragging defines the height of the biped system and defines all of the components. All of the biped's components are sized relative to the Height parameter.

4. From the command panel, select Create ➢ Systems ( ) ➢ Biped. When you click Biped, the parameters will appear below.

5. Go to Body Type, and from the drop-down menu choose Male.

6. In the Perspective viewport, click at the alien's feet and drag to create the biped.

7. Create a biped with a shoulder height the same as the alien's. This will make most of the biped's parts similar in size to those of the alien, as shown in Figure 11.3.

FIGURE 11.3 Create a biped about
the same height as the alien model.

8. With the biped still selected, in the Command panel, click the Motion
   tab ( ), and in the Biped rollout, enter Figure mode, as shown in
   Figure 11.4.

9. Then in the Structure rollout, change the parameters to match
   Figure 11.5. The number of spine links should be set to 3. Change the
   number of toes to 3 and toe links to 3. Change the number of fingers to 4.
   For the alien's nose you will use the Ponytail; set the ponytail links to 3.

Changes to the biped's
features or pose must
be made in Figure
mode to be retained by
the system.

FIGURE 11.4
Enter Figure mode in the
Biped rollout.

FIGURE 11.5 Change the
biped from the Structure rollout.

10. Use the Body Vertical and Body Horizontal buttons in the Track Selection rollout and the Move Transform gizmo to position the biped's pelvis in the same location as the model's pelvis, as shown in Figure 11.6. With the pelvis located properly, scaling the legs or spine to match the model's proportions will be much easier.

Two important factors when creating a biped skeleton: place the joints accurately at the 3D mesh's joints; and modify only one side of the biped and then use Copy/Paste to update the other side.

FIGURE 11.6   Match the positions of the biped's pelvis and the alien's pelvis.

11. Check to make sure the location is correct in all of the viewports.

12. Select Uniform Scale in the main toolbar; make sure the reference coordinate system is set to Local on the View drop-down menu in the main toolbar, as shown in Figure 11.7. This will be set for the Scale tool only.

FIGURE 11.7   Set the reference coordinate system to Local.

13. In the Front viewport, select the pelvis and scale its width so that the biped's legs fit inside the alien's legs. Scale the pelvis in the Left viewport so that it roughly encompasses the alien's lower region, as shown in Figure 11.8.

FIGURE 11.8 Scale the pelvis to fit.

14. Select the biped's left thigh (the blue leg), and then scale it along the X-axis until the knee aligns with the alien's knee. Scale it on the Y- and Z-axes until it is similar in size to the alien's thigh.

15. Select the biped's left calf. Switch to the Right viewport, rotate the calf to match the model (move the calf if necessary), and then scale it on the X-axis until the biped's ankle matches the alien's ankle. Scale the calf to match the proportions of the alien's calf. You may need to select the left foot and use the Move transform, in the Front viewport, to orient the calf to the model.

16. Continue working down the leg by scaling the biped's foot to match the alien's. Be sure to check the orientation of the foot in the Top viewport.

17. Scale and move the biped's toes to match the alien's toes. Be sure to scale the toe links on the Z-axis. The finished leg and foot are shown in Figure 11.9.

FIGURE 11.9 Match the biped's leg, foot, and toes with the alien's.

18. Double-click the left upper leg to select it and all of the objects below it in the hierarchy, from the thigh down to the toes.

19. Open the Copy/Paste rollout.

20. Postures must be saved as collections prior to being pasted. Click the Create Collection button, as shown in Figure 11.10, and then rename the collection from the default Col01 to **Left Leg**.

21. Click the Copy Posture button just below the Posture button to copy the selected posture to the Clipboard. A preview of the copied posture will appear in the Copied Postures area of the command panel, as shown in Figure 11.11.

FIGURE 11.10
Create the collection to paste the left leg hierarchy.

FIGURE 11.11
Copy the posture. The selected objects will appear in red in the preview.

22. Click the Paste Posture Opposite button (). The size, scale, and orientation of the selected objects will be applied to the reciprocal objects on the opposite side of the biped.

Save your work before continuing with the next set of steps. To check your work open c11_ex1_biped_end.max from the scenes folder of the c11_CharacterRigging project folder.

Exercise 11.2: Adjusting the Torso and Arms

Similar to the method used to adjust the legs, you will use the Scale and Rotate transforms to fit the biped to the model. The locations of the arms rely on the scale of the spine links. You can then open the c11_ex2_biped_start.max file from the scenes folder of the c11_CharacterRigging project folder.

1. Select the biped and then access Figure mode if needed.

2. Ctrl+click to select each of the spine links in turn, and then rotate and scale them to fit the alien's torso. Each spine link should be scaled up slightly on the X- and Y-axes in order to move the biped's clavicles to match the model's, as shown in Figure 11.12.

Only the lowest spine link can be moved, and this will move all of the links above it as well.

FIGURE 11.12   Scale the spine links up to place the clavicles in position.

3. Move, rotate, and scale the left clavicle as required, placing the biped's shoulder joint in the proper location.

4. Scale and rotate the left upper arm and left forearm to fit the arm to the model using the same techniques you used to adjust the biped's legs. Pay close attention to the placement of the elbow and wrist joint, as shown in Figure 11.13.

FIGURE 11.13   Arm positioned within the 3D mesh

5. Scale and rotate the left hand as required to fit the model.

6. The hands need only three fingers and one thumb (the fourth finger is actually the thumb) and three links each. Adjust the biped's fingers to match the model's fingers, as shown in Figure 11.14.

FIGURE 11.14   Match the biped's fingers to the model's fingers.

7. When you have finished, create the collection, copy and then paste the posture to the right side of the biped, and make any required changes.

Once the fingers have been adjusted, you cannot go back and change the number of fingers or finger links. If you do, all modifications to the fingers will be lost.

Matching the fingers to the model can be one of the most tedious tasks in character animation, depending on the complexity and orientation of the model's fingers. Take your time and get it right.

Save your work before continuing with the next set of steps. To check your work open c11_ex2_biped_end.max from the scenes folder of the c11_CharacterRigging project folder.

Exercise 11.3: Adjusting the Neck and Head

The neck and head will seem easy to adjust when compared to the hands. You need to make sure the neck links fill the alien's neck area and scale the head to fit. You can then open the c11_ex3_biped_start.max file from the scenes folder of the c11_CharacterRigging project folder.

1. In the Structure rollout, increase the number of neck links to 2.

2. Move, scale, and rotate the neck links to match the proportions of the model's neck.

3. Move and scale the head to the approximate size of the alien's head, as shown in Figure 11.15.

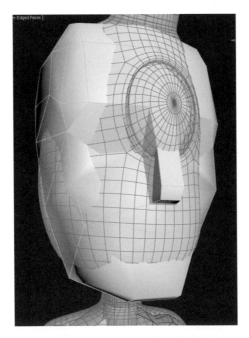

FIGURE 11.15 Matching the head

4. Now for the nose. The ponytail links need to be selected and moved into position at the nose. Using Move, Rotate, and Scale, adjust the ponytail links to match the nose, as shown in Figure 11.16.

FIGURE 11.16 Match the ponytail links with the nose.

That's it. The biped has been created and adjusted to fit the 3D model, and half the battle is over. Next, you will tie the biped to the model and make adjustments to the skinning process. Save your work before continuing with the next set of steps. To check your work open c11_ex3_biped_end.max from the scenes folder of the c11_CharacterRigging project folder.

Skinning the Alien Model

The Skin modifier is the tool used to skin the 3D model to the biped so that all of the biped's animation is passed through to the model. It's important to remember that the modifier is applied to the model and not to the biped.

Exercise 11.4: Applying the Skin Modifier

Continue with the previous exercise's file or open the c11_ex4_skin_start.max file from the scenes folder of the c11_CharacterRigging project folder.

1. Right-click in any viewport and select Unfreeze All from the quad menu to unfreeze the alien model.

2. Select the alien and use Alt+X to exit See-Through mode, and turn off Edged Faces (F4) in all viewports.

3. In the Modify panel, expand the Modifier List and select the Skin modifier.

4. In the Skin parameters, click the Add button next to Bones. From the Select Bones dialog, select all the biped objects and click the Select All button.

Save your work before continuing with the next set of steps. To check your work open c11_ex4_skin_end.max from the scenes folder of the c11_CharacterRigging project folder.

Exercise 11.5: Testing the Model

The most time-consuming part of the process is complete. You have created a biped and adjusted all of its component parts to fit your model. The next step is to add animation that will allow you to test the skinning once it has been applied.

Before we get into fixing the skin, you need to add a little extra animation. Continue with the previous exercise's file or open the c11_ex5_skin_start.max file from the scenes folder of the c11_CharacterRigging project folder.

1. Select the model, right-click again, and from the quad menu choose Hide Selection.

2. Move the time slider to frame 0. Turn on the Auto Key button (Auto) below the time slider.

3. Select the entire biped: The best way to do this is to choose the Select By Name tool ( ) from the main toolbar, and then from the Select From Scene dialog box, click the Select All button ( ) and click OK.

4. Go to the Motion panel ( ), and click the Figure Mode button ( ) to exit.

> You cannot animate a biped in Figure mode.

5. Select the Move tool and move the biped just a bit. The purpose of this is to create a keyframe of this original pose so that when you add animation, this pose won't be lost. The biped should still be in the same position as before—just give the Move tool a wiggle.

6. Select the right upper arm, Ctrl+click the left upper arm on the biped, and then set the reference coordinate system for the Rotate tool to Local, as shown earlier in Figure 11.7.

7. Move the timeline to frame 15, and rotate the arms −55 degrees on the Y-axis (the green wire in the Rotate gizmo).

8. Now select the right and left lower arms on the biped and rotate –55 degrees on the Z-axis.

9. Move the timeline to frame 30 and select the upper arms again, but this time rotate 45 degrees on the Z-axis (blue wire).

10. Now move to frame 50 and select the lower arms and upper arms. In the timeline, Shift+click the keyframe at frame 0, and then drag it to frame 50. This copies the keyframe at frame 0 to frame 50.

11. Add similar keyframes to repeat the animation to fill 100 frames.

Using the same technique, add animation to the legs, chest, and head. The animation does not have to be elaborate. The purpose of the animation is to test the skinning when applied to the model. When you have finished, turn off the Auto Key button, unhide the alien, and play the animation. Most likely you will see some problem with the skin—mostly around the feet, upper arms, and groin, as shown in Figure 11.17.

FIGURE 11.17   The problem areas with the skin

Save your work before continuing with the next set of steps. To check your work open c11_ex5_skin_end.max from the scenes folder of the c11_ CharacterRigging project folder.

Exercise 11.6: Tweaking the Skin Modifier

Each element in the biped has an area of influence, called an *envelope*. It determines which parts of the model it affects. The biped's left foot, for instance, should control the movement of only the model's left foot and the lower part of the ankle. In this case, the envelopes extend to affect some of the vertices on the opposite side.

The biped bone is represented in the viewport as a straight line with vertices at either end. Envelopes are represented by two concentric capsule-shaped volumes; vertices within the inner volume are fully affected by that bone, and then the weighting falls off increasingly for vertices that lie outside the inner volume and inside the outer volume. The weight values appear as a colored gradient using red for the higher weights and blue for the lowest values, with orange, yellow, and green in between.

Continue with the previous exercise's file or open the c11_ex6_skin_start.max file from the scenes folder of the c11_CharacterRigging project. The animation might be a bit different than if you are using your own file, but it will still work to check the Skin modifier.

1. Select the alien model. Then in the Modify panel go to the Skin parameters and click the Edit Envelopes button. You will see a color gradient around the pelvis. The gradient shows how heavily weighted the vertices on your mesh are to a given envelope, as shown in Figure 11.18.

FIGURE 11.18   The alien with the Edit Envelopes button active

2. Select the Bip001 R UpperArm object. You can select the object from the name list in the Skin parameters or just click on the

representation of the bone on the model. Select the vertex at the end of the bone near the elbow and move it toward the clavicle to make the envelope smaller (change the reference coordinate system to Local to make the move easier), as shown in Figure 11.19.

FIGURE 11.19   Select the bone vertex and move it to make the envelope smaller.

3. As the vertex moves, the gradient that represents the influence changes so the yellow-red color moves up the arm. You want the influence to be on the upper arm only. Repeat this step on the other top end of the bone near the clavicle, bringing it in toward the center of the bone.

4. Select the points on the inner envelope and move them in on both ends of the bone.

5. Select the points on the outside envelope and move them in on both sides of the bone, as shown in Figure 11.20.

Select points on the inner and outer envelopes and move them in on both sides

FIGURE 11.20   Make the inside and outside envelopes smaller by selecting and moving the points.

6. Move to frame 30 in the animation. In this frame you can really see the problem with the arm. Even though you edited the envelope for the upper arm, you can't see any improvement in the deformity. The previous exercise showed how to edit the envelope; now let's figure out where the trouble really lies with the upper arm: Bip001Spine2 and Bip001Spine1. Select each one and see how the inner envelope is crossing the upper arm.

7. Select the Bip001Spine2 bone. This bone's envelope is huge! It is influencing almost the whole upper body. Select a vertex on either end of the bone and move it in; immediately you will see the arms reacting. Repeat the process on Bip001Spine1.

8. Now scale down the size of the outer envelope so that the gradient has some yellow on the inside and blue between the capsules, as shown in Figure 11.21.

FIGURE 11.21 The Bip001Spine2 bone after the envelope has been edited

9. Now select and edit the remaining two spine bones. Fixing the remaining bones will also fix the issue with the Bip001 R Forearm bone.

10. Select the BIP001 R UpperArm bone, and in the Mirror Parameters rollout of the Skin modifier, click the Mirror Mode button.

11. Then click the Paste Green To Blue Bones button. This pastes the envelope settings from green bones to blue ( ).

12. In the Skin parameters, click the Edit Envelopes button to exit.

13. Play the animation again, and pay attention to any areas where you see parts of the mesh pulling or distorting.

14. Go back to that area's envelope and edit until you are happy with the results.

Save your work before continuing with the next set of steps. To check your work open c11_ex6_skin_end.max from the scenes folder of the c11_CharacterRigging project folder.

Exercise 11.7: Testing the Alien Model Rig

Continue with the previous exercise's file or open the c11_ex7_skin_start.max file from the scenes folder of the c11_CharacterRigging project folder. The animation might be a bit different than if you are using your own file, but it will still work to check the Skin modifier. Right-click in the viewport and from the quad menu choose Unhide All.

1. To delete any animation, select all the biped bones, drag a selection around the keyframes, and delete them in the timeline.

You cannot be in both Footstep mode and Figure mode at the same time.

2. Select any element of the biped and click the Motion tab of the command panel.

3. Enter Footstep mode (▦). The rollouts change to display the tools for adding and controlling a biped's motion.

4. In the Footstep Creation rollout, make sure the Walk Gait button (🚶) is selected, and then click the Create Multiple Footsteps button (✷) to open the Create Multiple Footsteps dialog box. In the dialog box that appears, you will assign Footstep properties for the number of steps you want, the width and length of each step, and which foot to step with first.

5. Set Number Of Footsteps to 8, leave the other parameters at their default values, and click OK.

6. Zoom out in the Perspective viewport to see the footsteps you just created. Look at the time slider, and note that the scene now ends at frame 123; that's 23 more frames than the 100 frames the scene had at the beginning of this chapter. The 3ds Max software recognized that it would take the biped 123 frames, or just over 4 seconds, to move through the eight steps that it was given.

7. Click the Play Animation button in the Playback Controls area. What happens? Nothing. The biped must be told explicitly to create animation keys for the steps that you have just added to the scene.

8. Stop the animation and drag the time slider back to frame 0.

9. In the Footstep Operations rollout in the command panel, click the Create Keys For Inactive Footsteps button (▦). The biped will drop its arms and prepare to walk through the footsteps that are now associated with it.

10. Select the alien model and right-click to access the quad menu. Choose Hide Unselected; this will hide the biped. Click the Play Animation button again. This time the alien model walks through the footsteps with its arms swinging and its hips swaying back and forth.

Watch the animation play; it won't be perfect. Notice that the arms are in too close to the body and the alien is walking a bit stiffly. Chapter 12 will cover the finer arts of animating with Character Studio. Save your work before continuing with the next set of steps. To check your work open c11_ex7_skin_end.max from the scenes folder of the c11_CharacterRigging project folder.

Exercise 11.8: Controlling the View

Now the problem is that if you zoom in on the biped and play the animation, it walks off the screen so you cannot see the end of the walk cycle. What good is that? Motion cycles can be very linear and difficult to track, so Character Studio contains the In Place mode to follow a biped's animation. In the In Place mode, the biped will appear to stay in place while the scene moves around it in relation. Continue with the previous exercise's file or open the c11_ex8_test_start.max file from the scenes folder of the c11_CharacterRigging project folder.

In Place mode cannot be used in a Camera viewport.

To set up In Place mode follow these steps:

1. Right-click and choose Unhide All; then select a part of the biped. Go to frame 0 and then zoom in on the biped in the Perspective viewport.

2. At the bottom of the Biped rollout, click the Modes And Display text with the plus sign to the left of it. This is a small rollout located inside another rollout that expands to show additional display-related tools. It is hidden and difficult to find, as shown in Figure 11.22.

Click at this position in the Biped rollout.

This will expand the Modes And Displays rollout.

Select the In Place Mode button.

F I G U R E   1 1 . 2 2   In the Biped rollout, click at the bottom to reveal the Modes And Display rollout.

3. In the Modes And Display rollout, click the In Place Mode button (), as shown in Figure 11.22.

4. Click the Play Animation button again. This time the biped will appear to be walking in place while the footsteps move underneath it.

5. Stop the animation playback when you're ready.

6. Select the entire biped by double-clicking Bip001. If it is too difficult to do, use the Select From Scene dialog box (H).

7. Right-click in any viewport and choose Hide Selection from the quad menu to hide the biped and obtain an unobstructed view of the model.

In Place mode helps you work out the way a character moves without having to navigate throughout 3D space. The viewport moves with the character and you can concentrate on how its body is moving.

8. Click the Play Animation button.

Your alien will walk through the scene. It should be similar to the rendered alien shown in Figure 11.23.

FIGURE 11.23   The rendered alien during a walk cycle

The Character Studio tutorials and help system that ship with the 3ds Max program are very thorough, and you should find the information there to expand your skills once you have a solid footing with the basics.

Skinning a character is a detail-oriented task, and it requires lots of experimentation and trial and error—and patience. Character Studio is a complete character-animation package, and we've barely scratched the surface here. There are tools for saving biped configurations and sequences of animation. You can mix animation sequences from different files to create an entirely new motion. When the model does not skin as well as you need, you can use envelopes to refine the skinning process further, define vertices to be excluded from a specific Biped object's influence, or include bulge conditions to define the model's behavior depending on the angle between subsequent biped elements. The list goes on.

It's important to realize that animation requires nuance, and the best animation with the simplest rig and setup will beat a mediocre animation created with a more wonderful, complicated, and ingenious setup. Save your work. To check your work open `c11_ex8_test_end.max` from the `scenes` folder of the `c11_CharacterRigging` project folder.

Now You Know

In this chapter, you were introduced to the basics of Character Studio and the Biped setup for the alien character. The Skin modifier was introduced to apply the Biped setup to the geometry of the alien and was used to adjust the envelopes for the best animation results.

CHAPTER 12

Character Studio: Animation

Character animation is a broad and complex field; in fact, the character-animation computer-generated specialty is one of the toughest specialties to master. To use one word, good character animation comes down to *nuance*. When you animate a character, you have to have a keen eye for detail and an understanding of how proportions move on a person's body. Setting up a computer-generated character to walk *exactly* like a human being is amazingly complicated.

Character systems such as Character Studio make it a breeze to outfit characters with biped setups and have them moving in a walk cycle very quickly.

This chapter introduces you to the basics of using Character Studio and bones for animation. Further investigation into these tools is a must if you want your animation to be full of life and character.

In this chapter, you'll learn to:

▶ **Animate the alien**

▶ **Use freeform animation**

▶ **Modify animating using the Dope Sheet**

Animating the Alien

Bipeds can be animated in several ways, including footstep-driven animation and freeform animation. With *footstep-driven animation,* you add visible Footstep objects to your scene and direct the biped to step onto those footsteps at particular points in time. Footsteps can be added individually or as a set of walk, run, or jump steps; they can be moved or rotated to achieve the desired result and direction. When you use footstep-driven animation, the legs and feet of the biped are not the only things animated; the hips, arms, tails, and all other components are animated as well. However, this approach is rarely the complete solution to your animation needs.

Freeform animation means that you animate the components of the biped manually, as you would animate any other object, such as a bouncing ball.

Animation keys that are added to the selected Biped objects appear in the track bar, just like other objects, where they can be moved, modified, or deleted to adjust the animation.

Exercise 12.1: Adding a Run-and-Jump Sequence

At the end of the previous chapter, you finished rigging the alien model and added footsteps to check the model. New footsteps can be appended to any existing footsteps. In the next exercise, you will add footsteps to the existing animation cycle.

Open the c12_ex1_run_start.max file in the scenes folder of the c12_ CharacterAnimation project on the book's web page at www.sybex.com/go/ 3dsmax2015essentials. This file has most of the biped bones hidden. The objects that are visible in the file are the alien model; Bip001 is the diamond shape that sits at the pelvis area of the alien character and acts as the center for your biped rig,

If you have trouble, you can either press the H key or click the Select by Name icon (⬛) found on the main toolbar, which opens the Select From Scene dialog box.

1. Select the Bip001 object in the Select From Scene dialog box, and click OK.

2. On the Motion panel, choose Footstep mode (🔲).

3. Click the Run icon (🏃) in the Footstep Creation rollout. This will apply a run gait to any footsteps you add to your current footsteps using the Create Multiple Footsteps dialog box.

4. Click the Create Multiple Footsteps icon (🔳) to open the Create Multiple Footsteps dialog box.

5. Change Number of Footsteps to 10 and click OK.

6. In the Footstep Operations rollout, click the Create Keys for Inactive Footsteps icon (🔳) to associate the new footsteps with the biped.

The run sequence meets the definition of a run, but it is far from realistic. In the next exercise, you'll learn how to add to or modify a biped's motion with freeform animation to make a better run cycle.

7. Click the Play Animation button. In this file the In Place Mode icon (🔘) is active. The biped will appear to stay in place while the scene moves around it. The biped walks through the first 8 steps and then runs through the next 10. Click the Stop Animation button to turn off the animation.

8. Click the Jump button in the Footstep Creation rollout, and then click the Create Multiple Footsteps button.

9. In the Create Multiple Footsteps dialog box, set the number of footsteps to 4 and click OK.

10. Click the Create Keys for Inactive Footsteps icon to associate the new jump footsteps with the biped.

11. Click the Play Animation button. The biped will walk, run, and then end the sequence with two jumps, as shown in Figure 12.1.

Because a jump is defined as a sequence with either two feet or zero feet on the ground at a time, four jump steps will equal two actual jumps.

FIGURE 12.1   Alien model with the jump sequence added

The Actual Stride Height parameter in the Create Multiple Footsteps dialog box determines the height difference from one footstep to the next. This is how to make the biped climb stairs.

Save your work before continuing with the next set of steps. To check your work open `c12_ex1_run_end.max` from the `scenes` folder of the `c12_CharacterAnimation` project folder.

Freeform Animation

When you set your keys initially, you will need to edit them to suit good timing and form. When one part of the body is in one movement, another part of the body is in an accompanying or supportive or even opposite form of movement. When you are walking and your right leg swings forward in a step, your right arm swings back and your left arm swings forward to compensate.

You can easily add or modify the biped's existing animation keys with free-form animation using the Auto Key button and the Dope Sheet. The following exercises contain examples of freeform animation.

Exercise 12.2: Moving the Head

The following steps will guide you through the process of creating head movement for your biped. Continue with the previous alien model or open the c12_ ex2_head_start.max file in the scenes folder of the c12_CharacterAnimation project on the book's web page. Because you will be working with the biped a lot in this exercise, the biped components have been unhidden and the alien model has been hidden. If you are using your own file you need to do the same.

1. Select any Biped object, and if necessary, exit Footstep mode by clicking the Footstep Mode icon.

2. Drag the time slider to frame 50, approximately the point when the biped lifts its left foot off footstep number 2.

3. Select the biped's head and note the animation keys that appear in the track bar, as shown in Figure 12.2.

4. In the track bar, select the two keys on either side of the current frame. You can do that using either of the following methods:

   ▶ Drag a selection box around both keys directly on the track bar.

   ▶ Select one key, and then holding the Ctrl key, select the other key.

Footsteps are numbered, starting with the number 0 and initially alternating from the left to the right side. They are also color coded, with blue footsteps on the left and green footsteps on the right.

FIGURE 12.2 Selecting the head of the biped reveals all of that object's animation keys in the track bar.

5. Once the two keys are selected, right-click over either keyframe and then choose Delete Selected Keys, as shown in Figure 12.3.

FIGURE 12.3 Delete the keys on either side of frame 50.

6. Click the Auto Key button or press the N key to turn it on. This will allow you to begin creating the animation.

7. Click the Rotate tool and rotate the head, to the left and up, as shown in Figure 12.4, as if the character sees somebody in a second-floor window off-screen. A new key will be created at frame 50, recording the time and value of the head's rotation.

FIGURE 12.4 Rotate the head to the left and up.

8. Scrub through the time slider by moving it back and forth, watching the head rotate from a neutral position to the orientation that you created and then back to the neutral position.

If animation keys are too close together, the animation could appear jerky.

9. Select all the keys between frame 50 and frame 100 (but not the keys at frames 50 and 100), and delete them. Doing so will make room for the new key that you are about to create.

10. Select the key at frame 50, hold down the Shift key, and drag a copy of the key to frame 90, as shown in Figure 12.5. Use the readout at the bottom of the window to drag the key with precision. Copying the key will cause your biped to hold that neck pose for 40 frames, or about 1 1/3 seconds.

FIGURE 12.5
Drag to copy the key.

11. Scrub the time slider to review the animation.

Save your work before continuing with the next set of steps. To check your work open c12_ex2_head_end.max from the scenes folder of the c12_CharacterAnimation project folder.

Exercise 12.3: Moving the Arms

Continue with the previous alien model or open the c12_ex3_arm_start.max file in the scenes folder of the c12_CharacterAnimation project folder.

1. Select the biped's left upper arm.

The animation keys for the arms define their swing motion.

2. In the track bar, select and delete the key frames between frames 50 and 100. If you scrub the time slider or play the animation, the biped will hold its arm unnaturally stiff for 60 frames because you deleted the animation keys between two points where it moves its hand forward.

3. Move the time slider to frame 60. This is the location for the first new animation key. Now it's time to animate the arms, which are essential components in any walk cycle.

4. Turn on Auto Key (N) and then rotate the upper arm upward, so that it points to the location at which the head is looking.

5. Continue adjusting the biped's left arm, hand, and finger until they appear to be pointing at something, as shown in Figure 12.6.

FIGURE 12.6 Rotate the biped's arm, hand, and finger to assume a pointing posture.

6. Double-click the left upper arm to select it and all of the components below it in the hierarchy.

7. In the track bar, select the key at frame 60, hold down the Shift key, and drag it to frame 90 to create a copy.

8. Drag the time slider and watch the Perspective viewport. The biped will walk for a bit, notice something off-screen, point at it, and drop its arm while looking forward again before breaking into a run and then a jump.

9. Click the Auto Key button to turn it off.

Save your work before continuing with the next set of steps. To check your work open c12_ex3_arm_end.max from the scenes folder of the c12_CharacterAnimation project folder.

Exercise 12.4: Completing the Motion Sequence

Make sure the Auto Key button is turned on to record all the changes that you make as you animate your character.

Continue with the previous alien model or open the c12_ex4_motion_start.max file in the scenes folder of the c12_CharacterAnimation project folder.

For additional practice, add keys to the animation of the biped's arms when it jogs through the run cycle. For example, when the left foot is fully extended and the heel plants on the ground, the right arm should be bent at the elbow and swung forward and slightly in front of the biped's body. As the right foot swings forward during the next step, the right arm should swing backward and assume a nearly straight position. Bend each of the spine links and swing both arms backward to prepare the biped for each of the jumps. Use the Body Vertical button in the Track Selection rollout to lower the pelvis into a prelaunch position, as shown in Figure 12.7, before the biped launches into its upward motion.

FIGURE 12.7   Use the Body Vertical button to position the biped for a jump.

Save your work before continuing with the next set of steps. To check your work open c12_ex4_motion_end.max from the scenes folder of the c12_CharacterAnimation project folder.

Modifying Animation in the Dope Sheet

To change the animation that is generated with Character Studio, you will edit the keyframes of the biped once you are happy with the base animation cycle. For this, you need to use the Track View–Dope Sheet. The Track View–Curve

Editor, as you have already seen in Chapter 5, "Introduction to Animation," is used to edit the function curves between animation keys; however, the Track View–Dope Sheet interface is cleaner and is used to edit the specific value and position of the keys. It is not a different set of keyframes or animation; it's just a different way of editing them.

In the next exercise, you will add individual footsteps and modify the footstep timing in the Dope Sheet to make the biped dance and jump.

Exercise 12.5: Adding Footsteps Manually

For this exercise you will need a file with no animation applied, so start with the c12_ex5_steps_start.max file in the scenes folder of the c12_ CharacterAnimation project folder. This is the rigged and skinned alien biped with no footsteps applied.

1. Select a biped component and enter Footstep mode.

2. In the Footstep Creation rollout, click the Walk button and then the Create Footsteps (At Current Frame) icon ().

3. In the Top viewport, click in several locations around the biped to place alternating left and right footsteps to your liking.

4. Change the gait to Jump, and then click the Create Footsteps (Append) icon to create additional footsteps. Create about 12 footsteps in all.

5. When you have finished, use the Move and Rotate transforms to adjust the footstep locations and orientations as desired. Your Top viewport should look similar to Figure 12.8.

FIGURE 12.8 Manually place the footsteps in the Top viewport.

Access to editing the footstep keys is available only in the Dope Sheet.

6. In the Footstep Operations rollout, click the Create Keys for Inactive Footsteps icon and then play the animation.

Character Studio doesn't have a collision-detection feature, so it is very possible that limbs will pass through one another, which would be quite uncomfortable in real life. If this happens, the footsteps must be modified to eliminate these conditions. If necessary, move any footsteps that cause collisions or other unwanted conditions during the playback. Save your work before continuing with the next set of steps. To check your work open `c12_ex4_steps_end.max` from the `scenes` folder of the `c12_CharacterAnimation` project folder.

Exercise 10.6: Using the Dope Sheet

In Chapter 5, you experimented with the Track View–Curve Editor and learned how to adjust the values of animation keyframes. When the Track View is in Dope Sheet mode, frames are displayed as individual blocks of time that may or may not contain keys. Although you cannot see the flow from key to key that the Curve Editor displays with its curves, the Dope Sheet mode has its advantages. For one, the Dope Sheet has the ability to add Visibility tracks to control the display of an object, as well as Note tracks for adding text information regarding the keys as reminders.

Using the Track View–Dope Sheet, you can adjust the point in time when a foot plants on or lifts off the ground, how long the foot is on the ground, and how long the foot is airborne. Rather than appearing as single-frame blocks in the Dope Sheet as other keys do, footstep keys appear as multiframe rectangles that identify each foot's impact time with the footstep. Continue with the previous alien model or open the `c12_ex6_dope_start.max` file in the `scenes` folder of the `c12_CharacterAnimation` project folder.

1. Make sure you are in Footstep mode. This will select the biped's footsteps.

2. In the main toolbar, choose Graph Editors ➢ Track View–Dope Sheet. The Dope Sheet will open.

3. In the Navigation pane on the left, scroll down until you find the Bip001 Footsteps entry, and expand it.

4. If necessary, click the Zoom Region icon (⬛) in the lower-right corner of the Dope Sheet window and drag a zoom window around the footstep keys, as shown in Figure 12.9. The region will expand to fit the Key pane. Right-click to exit the Zoom Region tool.

The footstep keys appear as rectangles in the Key pane. As expected, the left keys are colored blue and the right keys are colored green.

FIGURE 12.9 Zoom to the footstep keys.

5. Select a few footsteps in the viewport or select the green- and blue-colored rectangles (holding Ctrl to select multiple footsteps). The white dot on the left side of a selected key identifies the frame when the heel of the biped's foot first impacts the footstep. The white dot on the right side of a selected key, as shown in Figure 12.10, identifies when the biped's foot lifts off a footstep. A blue key (rectangle) overlapping a green key (rectangle) indicates that both feet are on the ground. A vertical gray area with no footstep indicates that the biped is airborne and neither foot is on the ground.

FIGURE 12.10 The dots indicate when contact begins and ends. You can drag a dot to change the duration of contact.

6. Select the first key (numbered 0), place the cursor over the right edge of the key, and then drag the dot to the right to extend the length of time the biped's foot is on the ground.

7. Drag the Dope Sheet's time slider to a point in time when the biped is airborne. Increasing the airborne time by increasing the gap between footsteps will also boost the height to which the biped rises, acting against the gravitational force pushing it downward.

The double vertical line in the Dope Sheet's Key pane is another time slider that allows you to scrub through the animation.

You can't move the end of one footstep key beyond the beginning of another one, and you must maintain a one-frame gap between same-side footsteps.

8. Select the last four jump keys and drag them to the right to create a gap approximately 40 frames wide, as shown in Figure 12.11. Doing so will cause the biped to be airborne for about one second.

It is possible to move a footstep beyond the limits of the active time segment in the Dope Sheet. Use the Alt+R key combination to extend the active time segment to include all existing keys.

FIGURE 12.11 Create a key gap to get your biped airborne.

9. Move the time slider to the frame when both feet are planted before the jump starts, and turns on Auto Key mode.

10. Deselect any keys by clicking a blank area in the Key pane.

11. Prepare the biped to leap as follows:

   a. Select the Bip001 object and move it downward, causing the biped to bend its knees more.

   b. Be sure to choose Local as the reference coordinate system for the Rotate transform.

   c. Rotate the spine links, neck, and head to bend the torso forward and tuck the chin.

   d. Rotate both arms backward into a pre-jump posture, as shown in Figure 12.12.

FIGURE 12.12 Prepare your biped to jump.

12. Move the time slider forward until the biped is at the apex of the jump.

13. Rotate the biped's components into positions you like, such as the split shown in Figure 12.13.

FIGURE 12.13 Position your biped in mid-jump.

14. Delete any animation keys that may interfere with your desired motion, and turn off Auto Key.

    The c12_ex6_dope_end.max file in the scenes folder of the c12_ CharacterAnimation project folder contains the completed exercise so you can check your work. This file has the alien model unhidden and the biped hidden.

15. Play the animation and see how it looks; modify where needed.

As you saw, there are several ways to animate a biped, including the footstep-driven method, the freeform method, and a combination of techniques. You can also modify the animation in the track bar, with the Auto Key button, and with Track View–Dope Sheet.

Now You Know

In this chapter, you learned how to animate characters with Character Studio. Using the Biped system, you can quickly create and adjust the substructure that controls a 3D model. Once the Skin modifier associates or skins the model to the biped, character animation can be added using footstep-driven or freeform animation.

CHAPTER 13

Introduction to Lighting: Interior Lighting

Light reveals the world around us and defines shape, color, and texture. Lighting is the most important aspect of computer graphics (CG), and it simply cannot be mastered at a snap of the fingers. The trick to correctly lighting a CG scene is to understand how light works and to see the visual nuances it has to offer.

In this chapter, you will study the various tools used to create light in the Autodesk® 3ds Max® software. This chapter will serve as a primer on this important aspect of CG. It will start you on the path by showing you the tools available and giving you opportunities to begin using them.

In this chapter, you will learn to:

▶ **Recognize 3ds Max lights**

▶ **Light a still life**

▶ **Select shadow types**

▶ **Create atmospheres and effects**

▶ **Utilize the Light Lister tool**

Recognizing 3ds Max Lights

The 3ds Max program has two types of light objects: photometric and standard. *Photometric lights* are lights that possess specific features to enable a more accurate definition of lighting, as you would see in the real world.

Photometric lights have physically based intensity values that closely mimic the behavior of real light. *Standard lights* are extremely powerful and capable of realism, but they are more straightforward to use than photometric lights and less taxing on the system at render time. In this chapter, we will discuss only the standard lights.

Standard Lights

The 3ds Max lights attempt to mimic the way real lights work. For example, a light bulb that emits light all around itself would be an *omni* light in 3ds Max terminology. A desk lamp that shines light in a specific direction in a cone shape would be a spotlight. Each of the different standard lights casts light differently. We will look at the most commonly used lights.

The 3ds Max program has a total of eight light types in its Standard Light collection:

Target spotlight	Omni light
Target direct light	Skylight
Free spotlight	mr area omni light
Free direct light	mr area spotlight

The last two on this list begin with *mr* to signify that they are mental ray–specific lights (see Chapter 15, "mental ray," for more about mental ray). An advanced renderer, mental ray is commonly used in production today. It offers many sophisticated and frequently complex methods of lighting that enhance the realism of a rendered scene. In this chapter, we will cover only the first five standard lights.

Target Spotlight

A *target spotlight*, as shown in Figure 13.1, is one of the most commonly used lights because it is extremely versatile. A spotlight casts light in a focused beam, similar to a flashlight. This type of lighting allows you to light specific areas of a scene without casting any unwanted light on areas that may not need that light. You can control the size of the *hotspot*, which is the size of the beam before it starts losing intensity.

Hotspot/Beam Falloff/Field   Light   Target

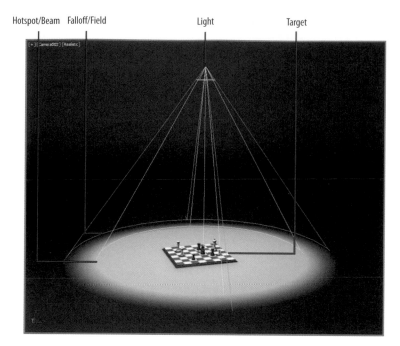

FIGURE 13.1 A target spotlight

The light is created with two nodes: the light itself (*light source*) and the target node, at which the light points at all times. This way, you are easily able to move the light following the subject of the scene, as a spotlight would follow a singer on stage. Select the target and move it as you would any other object. The target spot rotates to follow the target. Similarly, you can move the light source, and it will orient itself accordingly to aim at the stationary target. To see the Spotlight Parameters, select the light source, go to the Modify panel, and open the Spotlight Parameters rollout, shown in Figure 13.2.

FIGURE 13.2 The Spotlight Parameters rollout

The falloff, which pertains to standard lights in 3ds Max software, is represented in the viewport by the area between the inner, lighter yellow cone and the outer, darker yellow cone, shown in Figure 13.2. The light diminishes to 0 by the outer region, creating a soft area around the hotspot circle (where the light is the brightest), as shown in Figure 13.3.

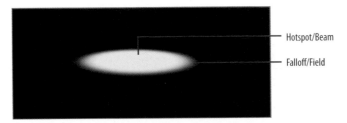

Hotspot/Beam

Falloff/Field

FIGURE 13.3   The falloff of a spotlight

Target Direct Light

A *target direct light* has target and light nodes to help you control the direction of the light. It also has a hotspot and beam, as well as a falloff, much like the target spot. However, whereas the target spot emits light rays from a single point (the light source) outward in a cone shape, the target direct light casts parallel rays of light within its beam area. This helps simulate the lighting effect of the sun because its light rays (for all practical purposes on Earth) are parallel. Figure 13.4 shows a target direct light in a viewport.

▶

Because the directional rays are parallel, the target direct lights have a beam in a straight cylindrical or rectangular box shape instead of a cone.

Light

Target

Falloff/Field

Hotspot/Beam

FIGURE 13.4   A target direct light

You can create and select/move parts of a target direct light in much the same way as a target spot. In the Directional Parameters rollout, you'll find the similar parameters for the target direct light. Although the spotlight and the directional light don't seem to be very different, the way they light is strikingly different, as you can see in Figure 13.5. The spotlight rays cast an entirely different hotspot and shadow than the directional light, despite having the same values for those parameters.

FIGURE 13.5   A target spot (left) and a target direct (right)

Free Spot or Free Direct Light

Free spotlights and *free direct lights* are virtually identical to target spots and target direct lights, respectively, except that the free spot and direct lights have no Target object. You can move and rotate the free spot however you want, relying on rotation instead of a target to aim it in any direction, as shown in Figure 13.6.

FIGURE 13.6   Free spot (left) and free direct (right) lights

Adjusting the length of a free spot or free direct light will not matter when the light is rendered; however, seeing a longer light in the viewports can help you line up the light with objects in the scene.

Another difference between a free spot or direct light and a target spot or direct light is that while the length of the target spotlight is controlled by its target, a free spot or direct light instead has, in the General Parameters rollout, a parameter called Targ. Dist. The default is 240 units.

Free spot and free direct (as well as target spot and target direct) lights are great for creating the main lighting in your scene, because they are very easy to control and give a fantastic sense of direction. In the General Parameters roll-out, there is a drop-down menu allowing you to change your chosen light type to another type. You can also change a free light to a target light by checking the Targeted box.

Omni Light

The 3ds Max *omni light* is a point light that emanates light from a single point in all directions around it. Figure 13.7 shows an omni light. Unlike the spot and directional lights, the omni light does not have a special rollout, and its General Parameters rollout is much simpler.

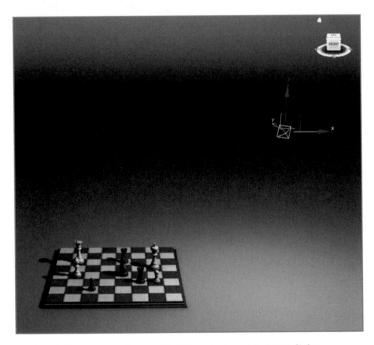

FIGURE 13.7   An omni light is a single-point-source light.

Omni lights are not as good for simulating sunlight as directional lights are. In Figure 13.8, the omni light in the image on the left creates different shadow and lighting directions for all the objects in the scene, and the directional light in the image on the right creates a uniform direction for the light and shadow, as would the sun here on Earth.

FIGURE 13.8   Omni light (left) and directional light (right)

Omni lights are good for fill lights as well as for simulating certain practical light sources.

Lighting a Still Life

Lighting a still life can be approached using the three-point lighting setup. Three-point lighting is a traditional approach to lighting a television shot. After all these years, the concepts still carry over to CG lighting. In this setup, three distinct roles are used to light the subject of a shot. The scene should, in effect, seem to have the following elements:

▶ Only one primary or key light to define lighting direction and create primary shadows

▶ A softer light to fill the scene and soften the shadows a bit

▶ A back light to make the subject pop out from the background

This does not mean there are only three lights in the scene. Three-point lighting suggests that there are three primary angles of light for your shot, dependent on where the camera is located.

Three-point lighting ensures that your scene's main subject for a particular shot is well lit, has highlights, and has a sense of lighting direction using shadow and tone. Figure 13.9 shows a plan view of the three-point lighting layout. The subject is in the middle of the image.

Try to avoid casting shadows with omni lights, because they use a lot more memory than spotlights when casting shadows.

Fill Light   Back Light   Key Light

FIGURE 13.9   A three-point lighting schematic

Exercise 13.1: Basic Light Setup

> The file is a version of the room built in Chapter 3. Models and more materials have been added to beef up the file.

Now that you have an overview of how lights work in a 3ds Max scene, let's put them to good use and light the room from Chapter 9, "Introduction to Materials: Interiors and Furniture," and create a basic light setup for the scene. Set your current project to the c13_IntroLight you copied to your hard drive from this book's web page, www.sybex.com/go/3dsmax2015essentials. Open c13_ex1_basic_start.max from the scenes folder of the c13_IntroLight project folder.

1. Go to the Create panel and select the Lights icon (▨) to bring up the selection of lights you can create.

2. Click the drop-down menu and choose Standard, as shown in Figure 13.10.

FIGURE 13.10
Choose Standard from the Lights drop-down menu.

3. Select Target Spot and go to the Front viewport.

4. Click and drag from the ceiling above the dining room table to the floor below the table. In the command panel, rename the light **Key Light**.

The click will create the light, and the mouse drag places the target.

5. In the Top viewport, use the Move tool to select the light and the target by dragging a selection box around both. Use the Zoom tool if needed to see the light selected.

6. Move them so they are over the dining room table in the Top viewport, as shown in Figure 13.11.

FIGURE 13.11 The spotlight's position in the room

Take advantage of the Nitros display driver that is available; it is turned on by default. It gives the most information in the camera viewport about lights, cameras, and shadows without the need for rendering.

7. Click away from any objects in the scene to deselect the light; then select just the source of the light object. Go to the Modify panel. In the Intensity/Color/Attenuation rollout, set Multiplier to **1.2**.

The multiplier acts as a dimmer switch for the key light. This light will have shadows and give the scene its main source of light and direction.

8. In the Still Life Camera viewport, click the Shading Viewport Label menu to expand it. Choose Realistic from the list.

9. Click the Shading Viewport Label menu again, go down to Lighting and Shadows, and choose Illuminate with Scene Lights, as shown in Figure 13.12. Now the Still Life camera can be used to judge the lights and shadows for this scene.

Keep in mind that rendering a viewport is always the most accurate way of testing lights and shadows.

FIGURE 13.12   The Shading Viewport Label menu

10. Go to the Modify panel and expand the Spotlight Parameters rollout.

11. Set Hotspot/Beam to 40 and Falloff/Field to 100. As you can see in the Still Life Camera viewport, the light spreads out farther toward the walls.

12. Now render by clicking the Render Production button ( ), which is on the main toolbar; the rendered image is shown on the left in Figure 13.13.

The Realistic viewport setting is fairly accurate. The reflections and transparencies that are seen in the rendered image on the right are not shown with the Realistic viewport shading.

FIGURE 13.13   The Still Life Camera viewport set to Realistic, showing new Hotspot/Beam and Falloff/Field settings (left); the rendered scene (right)

Save your file and move on to the next exercise. To check your work, open the c13_ex1_basic_end.max file from the scenes folder of the c13_IntroLight project folder.

Exercise 13.2: Adding Shadows

Using shadows intelligently is important in lighting your scenes. Without the shadows in the scene, the still life would float and have no contact with its environment.

Continue with the file you are working on or open c13_ex2_shadows_start.max from the scenes folder of the c13_IntroLight project folder.

1. Select the key light, if it isn't already selected.

2. In the Modify panel, go to the General Parameters rollout ➤ Shadows area and check the On box.

3. In the Still Life Camera viewport, a low-resolution version of the shadows appears, but a render of the scene will show it more accurately.

4. Render the scene. The result is shown in Figure 13.14.

FIGURE 13.14 It looks good, but the scene shadows are too soft.

5. Go to the Shadow Map Params rollout and change Size to 2048. This parameter adds more pixels to the shadow, which makes it more defined and less diffused.

6. Render the Still Life Camera viewport, as shown in Figure 13.15.

FIGURE 13.15 The render showing more defined shadows

Save your file and move on to the next exercise. To check your work, open the c13_ex2_shadows_end.max file from the scenes folder of the c13_IntroLight project folder.

Exercise 13.3: Adding a Fill Light

In the viewport, the shadow already looks better, but in the render, because the glasses are transparent, the shadow looks a bit weird—too dark and solid for a shadow for a transparent glass. To fix this issue, the shadow's density needs to be lowered. Adding a light to fill in the very dark shadows will correct this issue. A fill light simulates the indirect light seen in the real world. A fill light should not have any shadows or specular highlights; without them you can make sure the render looks as if there is only one light in the room. Continue with the file you are working on or open c13_ex3_fill_start.max from the scenes folder of the c13_IntroLight project folder.

1. In the Create panel, select Lights ≻ Omni, and in the Top viewport, click to create the omni light in the lower-right corner of the dining room.

2. In the Front viewport, move the omni light up so it is just below the ceiling of the dining room, and change the name to **Fill Light**.

3. In the Intensity/Color/Attenuation rollout, change Multiplier to 0.2. By default, shadows are always off, but you must turn off specular highlights manually.

4. With the omni light selected, go to the Modify panel and under the Advanced Effects rollout uncheck Specular.

5. Render again (press F9), and you'll see that the render looks better, but the still life's shadows are still dark, as shown in Figure 13.16. To fix the darkness of the shadow, the density of the shadow needs to be adjusted.

FIGURE 13.16   Interior room with key light and fill light

6. Select the key light, go to the Modify panel, and in the Shadow Parameters rollout change the Object Shadows Dens parameter to 0.8.

7. Render the Still Life Camera viewport again by selecting the Render Production icon (F9) in the main toolbar. The shadows look much better, as shown in Figure 13.17.

Use raytraced shadows when you need highly accurate shadows or when shadow map resolutions are just not high enough to get you the crisp edges you need. You can also use raytraced shadows to cast shadows from wireframe rendered objects.

The Ray Traced Shadow Params rollout controls the shadow. The Ray Bias parameter is the same as the Shadow Map Bias parameter in that it controls how far the shadow is from the casting.

Atmospherics and Effects

Atmospherics provides effects such as parallel beams of fog seen within light rays, and glows. Atmospheric effects with lights, such as fog or volume lights, are created using the Atmospheres & Effects rollout in the Modify panel for the selected light. Using this rollout, you can assign and manage atmospheric effects and other rendering effects that are associated with lights.

Exercise 13.5: Creating a Volumetric Light

Volume Light is a light effect based on the interaction of a light with atmosphere. In the real world, this effect is visible when there's a lot of dust in an enclosed space.

1. Open the c13_ex5_volume_start.max file from the scenes folder of the c13_IntroLight project folder.

2. Go to the Create panel, select Lights, and in the drop-down list select Standard, and then select the Target Direct light.

3. Go to the Left viewport and, clicking from the left outside of the room, position the light at a high angle from the window. Drag toward the living room window and click to set the light on the floor inside the room.

4. Select the Move tool, and then in the Top viewport click the line that connects the light and its target, which will select both easily. Move the light so it is aligned with the living room window, as shown in Figure 13.23.

5. Select the light source only and name the light **Sunlight**.

6. Click the Shading Viewport Label menu to expand it. Choose Realistic from the list. Click the Shading Viewport Label menu again, go down to Lighting and Shadows, and choose Illuminate with Scene Lights.

FIGURE 13.23   The light's position shown in all the viewports

7. Select the Sunlight object and go to the Modify panel. In the General Parameters rollout check On in the Shadows group. Use the default Shadow type, which is Shadow Map.

8. In the Intensity/Color/Attenuation rollout, change the Multiplier to **1.2**.

9. In the Directional Parameters rollout, change Hotspot/Beam to **60.0** and Falloff/Field to **63.0**. Looking at the Chess Set Camera viewport, you will see the light coming in through the window, but it is very dark everywhere else, as shown in Figure 13.24. More lights need to be added.

FIGURE 13.24   Interior room with the direct light in place as the sun

10. In the Create panel, select Lights ➢ Omni, and place the light near the Sunlight's position. Name the light **Fill Light 1**.

11. With the omni light selected, go to the Modify panel, and in the Intensity/Color/Attenuation rollout, change Multiplier to 0.5.

12. In the Intensity/Color/Attenuation rollout, in the Far Attenuation section, check Use and set Start to **150.0** and End to **400.0**.

13. In the Advanced Effects rollout, uncheck the Specular check box. This keeps the light on but does not show any specular highlights from this light.

14. Select the Sunlight light, and from the Modify panel, open the General Parameters rollout.

15. Go to the Shadow Map Params rollout and set the size to 2048 and change Sample Range to 2.0; this will add some sharpness to the shadow's edge and make it more like a daylight shadow.

16. In the Create panel, select Lights ➢ Omni, and place the light behind the Chess Set Camera.

17. Move the light so it is just below the ceiling. Name the light **Fill Light 2**.

18. With the omni light selected, go to the Modify panel, and in the Intensity/Color/Attenuation rollout, change Multiplier to 0.3.

19. In the Advanced Effects rollout, uncheck the Specular check box.

20. In the Intensity/Color/Attenuation rollout, in the Far Attenuation section, check Use and set Start to **48.0** and End to **400.0**.

21. Select the Sunlight light. In the Sunlight's parameters, go to the Atmospheres and Effects rollout.

22. Select Add from the rollout to open the Add Atmosphere or Effect dialog box, select Volume Light, and click OK to add the effect to the light. Volume Light will be added to the rollout.

23. Render the scene. You should see a render similar to Figure 13.25.

24. To adjust the volume light, go back to the Atmospheres and Effects rollout, select the Volume Light entry, and click the Setup button. This will bring up the Environment and Effects dialog box.

FIGURE 13.25   Ooh! Volume light!

25. Scroll down to the Volume Light Parameters section to access the settings for the volume light, as shown in Figure 13.26.

FIGURE 13.26   The Environment and Effects dialog box displays the Volume Light parameters.

You can choose to view or edit all the lights in your scene or just the ones that are selected. When you adjust the values for any parameter in the Light Lister dialog box, the changes are reflected in the appropriate place in the Modify panel for that changed light.

NOW YOU KNOW

In this chapter, you learned the key concepts in CG lighting. You learned about the various types of lights that the 3ds Max program has to offer, from default lights to target spots, and how to use them. You explored the common light parameters to gauge how best to control the lights in your scene before moving on to creating various types of shadows. You ran through a set of short exercises in which you created a volumetric light, and you finished with a peek of the Light Lister window.

CHAPTER 14

3ds Max Rendering

Rendering is the last step in creating your CG work, *but it is the first step to consider when you start to build a scene.* During rendering, the computer calculates the scene's surface properties, lighting, shadows, and object movement and then saves a sequence of images. To get to the point where the computer takes over, you'll need to set up your camera and render settings so that you'll get exactly what you need from your scene.

This chapter will show you how to render your scene using the Scanline Renderer in the Autodesk® 3ds Max® software and how to create reflections and refractions using raytracing.

In this chapter, you'll learn to:

▶ **Navigate the Render Setup dialog**

▶ **Render a scene**

▶ **Work with cameras**

▶ **Raytrace reflections and refractions**

▶ **Render the interior and furniture**

Navigate the Render Setup Dialog

Your render settings and the final decisions you make about your 3ds Max scene ultimately determine how your work will look. If you create models and textures with the final image in mind and gear the lighting toward elegantly showing off the scene, the final touches will be relatively easy to set up.

The Render Setup dialog box is where you define your 3ds Max render output. You can open this dialog box by taking one of the following actions:

► Click the Render Setup icon ( ) in the main toolbar.

► Select Rendering ➣ Render ➣ Render Setup.

► Press F10.

You've already seen how to render ( ) a frame in your scene to check your work. The settings in the Render Setup dialog box are used even when the Render Production button is invoked, so it's important to understand how this dialog box works.

Common Tab

The Render Setup dialog box is divided into five tabs; each tab has settings grouped by function. The Common tab stores the settings for the overall needs of the render—for example, image size, frame range to render, and type of renderer to use. Some of the most necessary render settings are described here:

Time Output   In this section, you can set the frame range of your render output by selecting one of the following options:

>**Single**   Renders the current frame only

>**Active Time Segment**   Renders the current range of frames

>**Range**   Renders the frames specified

Output Size   The image size of your render, which is set in the Output Size section, will depend on your output format—that is, how you want to show your render.

>**Resolution**   By default, the dialog box is set to render images at a resolution of 640×480 pixels, defined by the Width and Height parameters, respectively.

>**Image Aspect**   Changing the Image Aspect value will adjust the size of your image along the Height parameter to correspond with the existing Width parameter. For example, regular television is 1.33:1 (simply called 1.33) and a high-definition (HD) television is a wide screen with a ratio of 1.78:1 (simply called 1.78). The resolution of your output will define the screen ratio.

In the Output Size section of the Render Setup dialog box, there is a drop-down menu for choosing presets from different film and video resolutions. The image quality and resolution of a render affect how long a render will take.

Options   The Options section lets you access several global toggles. You can toggle the rendering of specific elements in your scene. For example, if you are using atmospherics (volume light) or effects (lens flare) and don't want them to render, you can clear the appropriate boxes.

Render Output   Use the Render Output section to indicate that the file should be saved. The image format can be selected to be a single image file or a sequence of image files (such as Targa or TIFF files) that form a sequence, or it can be a movie file such as QuickTime.

Choosing a Filename

To specify a location and file type for the render, click the Files button in the Render Output section. This will open the Render Output File dialog box shown in Figure 14.1. Select the folder to which you want to render, and set the filename. You can set the file type using the Save As Type drop-down menu.

In addition to turning down the resolution for a test render, you can use a lower-quality render or turn off certain effects, such as atmospherics.

Name your rendered images according to the scene's filename. This way, you can always know from which scene file a rendered image was produced.

FIGURE 14.1   The Render Output File dialog box defines how the render saves to disk.

Rendered Frame Window

When you click the Render button at the bottom of the Render Setup dialog box, the Rendered Frame window opens, shown in Figure 14.2.

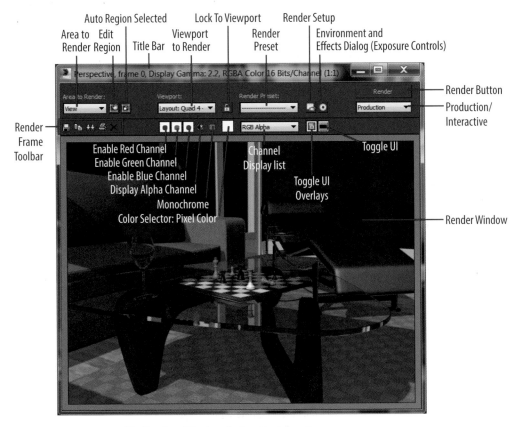

FIGURE 14.2   The Rendered Frame window

The Rendered Frame window shows you how the frames look as the renderer processes through the sequence of frames. A collection of quick-access buttons on the frame is also available in the Render Frame window.

Render Processing

When you click Render, a rendering progress dialog shows what parameters are being used for a scene and a progressing bar, shown in Figure 14.3. This dialog box shows the parameters being used, and it displays a progress bar indicating the render's progress. You can pause or cancel the render by clicking the appropriate button.

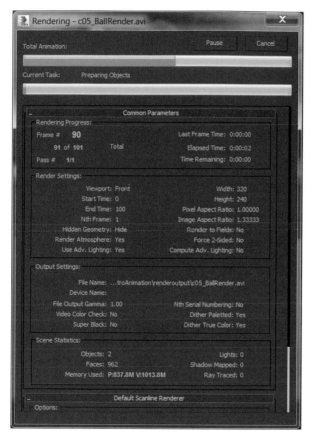

FIGURE 14.3   The Rendering processing dialog shows you everything you want to know about your current render.

Assign Renderer

Five types of renderers are available by default (without any additional plug-ins installed). The Default Scanline Renderer is the default renderer. It is already assigned and appears in the Assign Renderer rollout. To access the Choose Renderer dialog box click the ellipsis button (**...**). Only four renderers appear because the Default Scanline Renderer is already assigned. mental ray rendering is covered in Chapter 15, "mental ray."

Render a Scene

3D rendering is the 3D computer graphics process of automatically converting 3D wireframe models into 2D images with 3D photorealistic effects or non-photorealistic rendering on a computer.

Exercise 14.1: Rendering the Bouncing Ball

Seeing is believing, but doing is understanding. In this exercise, you will render the bouncing ball animation from Chapter 5, "Introduction to Animation," to get a feel for rendering an animation using the 3ds Max program. Just follow these steps:

1. Set your project folder to the c14_Rendering project that you downloaded to your hard drive from the companion web page at www.sybex .com/go/3dsmax2015essentials.

2. Open the c14_ex1_render.max file in the scenes folder. If a File Load: Gamma & LUT Settings Mismatch dialog shows up, select Adopt The File's Gamma And LUT Settings? and then select OK. Now, let's render a movie to see the animation.

3. Open the Render Setup dialog box (), and in the Time Output section, select Active Time Segment: 0 To 100.

4. In the Output Size section, select the 320×240 preset button and leave Image Aspect and Pixel Aspect as is.

5. Leave the Options group at the defaults, and skip down to the Render Output section.

6. Click the Files button to open the Render Output File dialog box, and navigate to where you want to save the output file, preferably into the renderoutput folder in your c14_Rendering project.

7. Name the file **c14_ex1_render**, and click the drop-down menu next to Save As Type to choose MOV QuickTime File (*.mov) for your render file type.

8. After you select MOV QuickTime File and click the Save button, the Compression Settings dialog box, shown in Figure 14.4, opens.

By default, the 3ds Max program renders your files to the renderoutput folder in the current project directory.

Normally, you would render to a sequence of images rather than a movie file; however, for short renders and to check animation, a QuickTime file works out fine.

FIGURE 14.4 QuickTime compression settings affect the quality of the rendered QuickTime video file.

9. Set the parameters for the QuickTime file as indicated:

   ▶ Compression Type: Photo - JPEG

   ▶ Frames Per Second: 30

   ▶ Compressor Depth: Color

   ▶ Quality: High

   Click OK to close the Compression Settings dialog box

10. Select the viewport you want to render in the View drop-down menu. You need to render Quad 4 - Camera01.

11. Click Render.

12. After the render is complete, navigate to your render location (by default, it is set to the renderoutput folder for the c14_Rendering project).

13. Double-click the QuickTime file to see your movie.

Apple's QuickTime movie file format gives you a multitude of options for compression and quality. The quality settings for the QuickTime file are not the same as the render quality settings.

To see an already rendered QuickTime movie of the ball animation and to check your work, navigate to your render location; it is set to the renderoutput folder for the c14_Rendering project.

Work with Cameras

The 3ds Max cameras, as shown in the Perspective viewport in Figure 14.5, capture and output all the fun in your scene. In theory, 3ds Max cameras work as much like real cameras as possible.

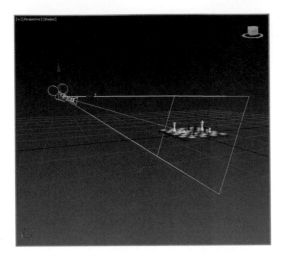

FIGURE 14.5   A camera as seen in the Perspective viewport

The *camera* creates a window through which you can see and render your scene. You can have as many cameras in the scene as you want. You can use the Perspective viewport to move around your scene as you work, leaving the render camera alone.

There are two types of 3ds Max cameras:

Target Camera   A *target camera*, much like a target spotlight, has a Target node that allows it to look at a spot defined by where the target is placed (or animated). A target camera is easier to aim than a free camera because once you position the Target object at the center of interest, the camera will always aim there.

Free Camera   On the other hand, *free cameras* have only one node, so they must be rotated to aim at the subject, much like a free spotlight. If your scene requires the camera to follow an action, you will be better off with a target camera.

You can create a camera by clicking the Cameras icon (📷) in the Create panel and selecting either of the two camera types:

▶ To create a free camera, click in a viewport to place it.

▶ To create a target camera, click in a viewport to lay down the Camera node, and then drag to pull out and place the Target node.

A camera's main feature is the *lens,* which sets the *focal length* in millimeters and also sets the *field of view (FOV),* which determines how wide an area the camera sees, in degrees. By default, a 3ds Max camera lens is 43.456mm long with an FOV of 45 degrees. To change a lens, you can change the Lens or FOV parameters, or you can pick from the stock lenses available for a camera in its Modify panel parameters, as shown in Figure 14.6.

FIGURE 14.6   Stock lenses make it easy to pick the right lens for a scene.

The most interactive way to adjust a camera is to use the viewport navigation tools. The Camera viewport must be selected for the viewport camera tools to be available to you in the lower-right corner of the user interface (UI). You can move the camera or change the lens or FOV.

Exercise 14.2: Creating a Camera

The best way to explain how to use a camera is to create one. Set your project to the c14_Rendering project you have downloaded to your hard drive from this book's web page. Open the c14_ex2_cameras_start.max scene file in the scenes folder.

1. In the Create panel, click the Cameras icon (), select the target camera, and go to the Top viewport. Click from the window inside the room and drag toward the gap between the coffee table and the couch. The camera is created along the ground plane. You need to move the entire camera up.

2. You will need to exit the Create panel and right-click in the Top viewport. Select both the camera and the target to move them as a unit by clicking the line that connects the camera and target in the viewport, and then in the Front viewport use the Move tool to relocate the camera higher in the scene.

3. To see the Camera viewport, select a viewport and press the C key. This changes the viewport to whatever camera is currently selected. In Figure 14.7 you can see Camera001 in all viewports.

You can also change a camera by selecting the Camera object and using the Transform tools, just as you would any other object. The movement depends of the camera type.

This scene is without a camera. Creating a camera is the same as creating a light. It's easier to create a camera in the Top viewport so you can easily orient it in reference to your scene objects.

The first click creates the Camera object. The mouse drag-and-release sets the location of the target, just like creating a target light.

FIGURE 14.7   The camera shown in the Top, Front, Left, and Camera001 viewports.

If there are multiple cameras in your scene and none are selected, when you press C, you will get a dialog box that gives a list of the cameras from which you can choose.

4. Now render the scene—press F9 or click the teapot icon () in the main toolbar—through the camera you just created and positioned.

Now that the camera is set up, take some time to move it around and see the changes in the viewport. To move the camera, select the Camera object. Use the Move tool. Moving a camera from side to side is known as a *truck*. Moving a camera in and out is called a *dolly*. Rotating a camera is called a *roll*. Also change the Lens and FOV settings to see the results. Save the file, and to check your work open the c14_ex2_cameras_end.max file in the c14_Rendering project folder.

Exercise 14.3: Animating a Camera

Zooming a lens (changing the Lens parameter) is not the same as a dolly in or dolly out. The field of view changes when you zoom, and it stays constant when you dolly. They will yield different framing, or they will focus on the subject.

Camera animation is done in the same way as animating any object. You can animate the camera, the target, or both. You can also animate camera parameters such as Lens or FOV. Open the c14_ex3_animate_start.max scene file in the scenes folder in the c14_Rendering project folder.

1. Select the camera.

2. Move the time slider to frame 60.

3. Press the N key to activate Auto Key, or click its button.

4. In the Top viewport, use the Move tool to move the camera farther away from the chess set; watch the Camera001 viewport to be sure you don't go outside the room. The direction or distance doesn't really matter just as long as it is different than the previous camera position.

5. Look in the Camera001 viewport, and then move the time slider through the animation. Press the N key again to turn off Auto Key. The camera should just move away from the chess set parallel to the window, as shown in Figure 14.8. Don't worry if your camera position isn't the same as in the figure.

FIGURE 14.8 Move the camera in the Top viewport.

Save the file, and to check your work open the c14_ex3_animate_end.max file in the c14_Rendering project folder.

Clipping Planes

In a huge scene, you can exclude, or *clip*, the geometry that is beyond a certain distance from the camera by using *clipping planes*. This helps minimize the amount of geometry that needs to be calculated. Each camera has a clipping plane for distance (Far Clip), as shown in the left image in Figure 14.9, and for the foreground (Near Clip), as shown in the right image. The near clipping plane clips geometry within the distance designated from the camera lens.

If you find that a model or scene you have imported looks odd or is cut off, check to make sure your clipping planes are adjusted to fit the extent of the scene.

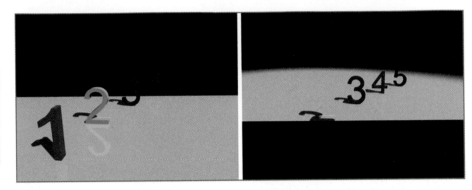

FIGURE 14.9 A far clipping plane cuts off the distant extents of a scene (left). A near clipping plane cuts off the extents directly in front of a camera (right).

To enable clipping planes, click the Clip Manually check box and set the distances needed. Once you turn on manual clipping planes, the camera displays the near and far extents in the non-camera viewports with red plane markers.

Exercise 14.4: Safe Frames

Safe Frames allow you to see the portions of your rendered output within a viewport. Safe Frames display a series of rectangular frames in the viewport. This is particularly useful when you are rendering to output that doesn't match the viewport's aspect ratio. Open the c14_ex4_safe_start.max scene file in the scenes folder in the c14_Rendering project folder.

1. In the Camera001 viewport, click the General Viewport Label menu ([+]) and choose Configure Viewports near the bottom of the menu.

2. In the dialog box, choose the Safe Frames tab. This tab contains settings for frame types, as shown in Figure 14.10.

FIGURE 14.10 The Safe Frames tab in the Viewport Configuration dialog box

3. The default is to show only the Live Area Safe Frame. To have the other Safe Frames show, you check the boxes in the Safe Frames tab.

The keyboard shortcut to toggle Safe Frames is Shift+F.

The Live Area Safe Frame is the extent of what will be rendered. The Action Safe area is the boundary where you should be assured that the action in the scene will display on most if not all TV screens. The Title Safe area is where you can feel comfortable rendering titles in your frame. Finally, the User Safe setting is for setting custom frames, as shown in Figure 14.11.

FIGURE 14.11 Safe Frames shown in the Camera001 viewport

Save the file, and to check your work open the `c14_ex4_safe_end.max` file in the `c14_Rendering` project folder.

Raytraced Reflections and Refractions

As you saw in Chapter 9, "Introduction to Materials," you can apply a Raytrace map to a material's Reflection parameter to add a reflection to the object. To get a true reflection of the other objects in the scene, you will need to use the raytracing methodology. There are essentially two ways to create raytraced reflections in a scene:

▶ By using a Raytrace map

▶ By using a Raytrace material

In many cases, the Raytrace map looks great and saves tons of rendering time as opposed to using the Raytrace material.

▶

Keep in mind that the amount of control you will have with a Raytrace map is significantly less than with the Raytrace material.

Exercise 14.5: Raytrace Material

In the following steps, you will learn how to use the Raytrace material to create reflection in a scene using the room built in Chapter 3 and Chapter 4. Open the c14_ex5_raytrace_start.max scene file in the scenes folder in the c14_Rendering project folder.

1. Open the Material Parameter Editor; in the Material/Map Browser, select Materials ➤ Standard and drag Raytrace material into the active view.

2. Double-click on the node title area to load the parameters into the Material Parameter Editor, and change the material name to **New Dark Wood**.

3. The parameters to create reflections are available through the Raytrace Basic Parameters rollout. Leave most of these parameters at their default values, but change the Reflect color swatch from black to white. This sets the reflection of the material all the way to the maximum reflectivity.

4. In the Material/Map Browser, choose Maps ➤ Standard and drag Bitmap to the Diffuse input socket of the Raytrace material. This will bring up the Select Bitmap Image File dialog box; you should see the images folder of the c14_Rendering project folder.

5. Choose DarkWood_Grain.jpg and then click Open.

6. Apply the New Dark Wood Raytrace material to the coffee table legs in the scene. Render the Camera001 viewport. The coffee table leg is very reflective; it looks like a mirror, as shown in Figure 14.12.

7. Go back to the Raytrace Basic Parameters rollout, select the color swatch next to Reflect, and change the Reflect color (RGB sliders only) so that R = 20, G = 20, and B = 20, which is a darker gray and will lessen the reflections.

FIGURE 14.12   The Raytrace material with reflections set to the maximum

8. In the Specular Highlight area, change Specular Level to 80 and Glossiness to **70**. This will change how clear the reflection appears.

9. Go to the Raytracer Controls rollout, and in the Falloff End Distance area check the box next to Reflect and change the value to **50**. This parameter will fade the reflection over distance, which is more accurate. Select the Camera001 and render, as shown in Figure 14.13.

FIGURE 14.13   More accurate reflections are added to the coffee table legs.

Save the file. To check your work open the c14_ex5_raytrace_end.max file in the c14_Rendering project folder.

Exercise 14.6: Raytrace Mapping

You use Raytrace map as you do other maps. This means you can add raytraced reflections or refractions to any kind of material. In this case, you will assign a Raytrace map to the Reflection map channel of a material to get truer reflections in the scene and at a faster render time than when using the material as you just did. Continue with your file or open the c14_ex6_raytrace_start.max scene file in the scenes folder in the c14_Rendering project folder.

1. In the Material Parameter Editor and in the Material/Map Browser, select Materials ➤ Standard and drag a Standard material to the view area. Load the materials into the Material Parameter Editor and change the name to **Hardwood Floors**.

2. In the Material/Map Browser, choose Maps ➤ Standard and drag a Raytrace map into the Reflection input socket.

3. In the Material/Map Browser, choose Maps and drag a Bitmap map into the Diffuse Color input socket.

4. From the Select Bitmap Image File dialog box, choose Hardwood_honey.tif from the images folder.

5. In the Maps rollout, change Reflection Amount to **50**.

6. Apply the Hardwood Floors material to the Floor object in the scene by dragging from the output socket to the Floor object in the Camera001 viewport.

7. In the Material Parameter Editor toolbar, select the Show Shaded Material in Viewport button (🖼).

8. Render the Camera001 viewport; the floors look good but too reflective, and a falloff needs to be added.

9. Double-click the Raytrace Map node to load the parameters into the editor.

10. In the Attenuation rollout, change Falloff Type to Linear, and then change Ranges: End to **50**. Render the Camera001 viewport; the results are shown in Figure 14.14.

FIGURE 14.14 The reflection map with falloff

Take a look at the images created with reflections using the Raytrace material and those created using the Standard material with the Raytrace map applied to reflection. They look almost the same. However, there is slightly better detail in the reflections created with the Raytrace material but with longer render times. Save the file. To check your work open the c14_ex6_raytrace_end.max file in the c14_Rendering project folder.

Exercise 14.7: Refractions Using the Raytrace Material

Creating raytraced refractions in glass can be accomplished using the same two workflows, as for the raytraced reflections from the previous sections. The Raytrace material renders better, but it takes longer than using a Raytrace map for the refraction map in a material. Continue with your file or open the c14_ex7_raytrace_start.max scene file in the scenes folder in the c14_Rendering project folder. This file has a rug in it.

Keep in mind that render times are much slower with refractions—so don't freak out.

1. For this section you are going to create a new camera. Start by changing the Camera001 viewport to a Perspective viewport:

   a. Select the Camera001 viewport and press P on the keyboard.

   b. Select the wineglass in the scene and then press Z on your keyboard. This will frame the wineglass in the Perspective viewport.

    c. Use Ctrl+C, which is a shortcut, to create a camera from a Perspective viewport.

    d. Name the camera **Wine Glass Camera**.

2. In the Material Parameter Editor, drag a Raytrace material from the Material/Map Browser into the area. Name it **Wine Glass**, and apply the material to the wineglass.

3. Go to the Raytrace Basic Parameters rollout, and change the color swatch for Transparency from black to white.

Black is opaque and white is fully transparent.

4. Uncheck the box next to Reflect and change that spinner to 10. This sets a slight reflection for the material.

5. Take a look at the Index Of Refr parameter. This value sets the index of refraction (IOR) value that determines how much the material should refract. The value is already set to 1.55. Leave it at that value.

6. Go to the Extended Parameters rollout, shown in Figure 14.15. The Reflections section is at the bottom.

FIGURE 14.15 The Extended Parameters rollout for the Raytrace material

7. Select Additive and change Gain to **0.7**. This gives a bit of reflective brightness for the clear wineglass.

8. Render the Wine Glass Camera viewport. The render shows the Raytrace material on the wineglass refracting and reflecting, but you may notice the jagged edges or artifacts around the reflected objects. What you're seeing is aliasing in the reflections.

9. Clone this rendered image by pressing the Clone Rendered Frame Window icon (), which is found in the Rendered Frame Window toolbar. This allows you to compare the before and after shots of the rendering.

10. Go to the SuperSampling rollout and uncheck Use Global Settings.

11. Check Enable Local Supersampler and keep it set to Max 2.5 Star. Leave the other parameters at their defaults, as shown in Figure 14.16. Render the Wine Glass Camera viewport.

> SuperSampling is an extra pass of anti-aliasing. By default, the 3ds Max program applies a single SuperSample filter pass over all the materials in the scene.

FIGURE 14.16   The SuperSampling rollout

12. In the Specular Highlight group, change Specular Level to 98 and Glossiness to 90. Figure 14.17 shows these changes.

FIGURE 14.17   The wineglass with default SuperSampling (left); the SuperSampling modified (right)

13. Render the Wine Glass Camera viewport.

You will see a very nice wineglass render. Change the Index of Refr parameter on the material to 8.0 and you will see a much greater refraction, as shown in

Figure 14.18. That may work better for a heavy bottle, but it is too much for the glass. An Index Of Refr parameter between 1.5 and 2.5 works pretty well for the wineglass.

FIGURE 14.18 A much more pronounced refraction is rendered with an IOR of 8.0.

Save the file. To check your work open the `c14_ex7_raytrace_end.max` file in the `c14_Rendering` project folder.

Exercise 14.8: Refractions Using Raytrace Mapping

If the Reflection Map setting is enabled, it will take a long time to render the image. If you have a slower computer or perhaps are in a rush, uncheck the Reflection Map box in the Maps rollout of the reflection.

▶

Just as you did with the reflections, you will now use a Raytrace map on the Refraction parameter for the Wine Glass material. Open the `c14_ex8_raytrace_start.max` scene file in the `scenes` folder in the `c14_Rendering` project folder.

1. In the Material Parameter Editor, drag a Standard material from the Material/Map Browser into the view area. Name it **Wine Glass 1**.

2. Drag the Raytrace map from the Material/Map Browser into the Refraction input slot.

3. Drag the Raytrace map from the Material/Map Browser into the Reflection input slot.

4. Go to the Maps rollout and change Reflection Amount to **6**. This will reduce the amount of reflection.

5. Go to the SuperSampling rollout and uncheck Use Global Settings, check Enable Local Supersampler, and keep it as Max 2.5 Star.

6. In the Specular Highlights group, change Specular Level to 98 and Glossiness to 90.

7. Apply the material to the Wine Glass object in the scene and render as shown in Figure 14.19. In the Raytrace map, you can control the IOR through the material parameters in the Extended Parameters rollout, in the Advanced Transparency section, as shown in Figure 14.20.

FIGURE 14.19 Use the Raytrace map on the Refraction parameter to create refraction in the wineglass.

FIGURE 14.20 The Advanced Transparency section in the Extended Parameters rollout

The raytracing reflections and refractions slow down the render quite a bit. You can leave out the reflections if you'd like, but that will reduce the realistic look of the wineglass. Save the file. To check your work open the c14_ex8_ray-trace_end.max file in the c14_Rendering project folder.

Render the Interior and Furniture

The Raytrace map calculates reflections as they work in the real world, reflecting the object's environment. Let's take a quick look at rendering the short 30-frame sequence of the scene you did earlier in the chapter. You'll need to tweak a few of the scene settings, such as setting the furniture and the interior materials to have raytraced reflections for maximum impact. Let's go!

Exercise 14.9: Adding Raytraced Reflections

Open the c14_ex9_raytrace_start.max scene file in the scenes folder in the c14_Rendering project folder.

1. In the Slate Material Editor, at the bottom left of the view area, is an icon of a pair of binoculars. This is a search feature. Click it, and a type-in area appears.

2. Then type **Light Wood for Chess** in the type-in area and press Enter. The material will be zoomed in on the active view, as shown in Figure 14.21.

FIGURE 14.21 Frame the material using the Zoom To Results feature in the Material Parameter Editor.

3. In the Material/Map Browser, select Maps ≻ Standard, drag a Raytrace map into the area, and then drag from the output socket of the Raytrace map into the input socket of the reflection map, as shown in Figure 14.22.

FIGURE 14.22 Plug the Raytrace map into the Reflection input socket of the Light Wood for Chess material.

4. Double-click the title of the Light Wood for Chess material to load the parameters into the Material Parameter Editor, and in the Maps rollout, change the Amount value for Reflection to **20**.

5. Render a frame, and you should see some reflections of the room.

6. Go through the materials in the Material Parameter Editor to add a Raytrace map to the material's Reflection channels.

Save the file. To check your work, open the `c14_ex9_raytrace_end.max` file in the `c14_Rendering` project folder.

Exercise 14.10: Outputting the Render

You need to render out the entire 30 frames of the camera move. As you saw with the bouncing ball render earlier in the chapter, rendering out a sequence of images is done through the Common tab of the Render Setup dialog box. Open the `c14_ex10_raytrace_start.max` scene file in the `scenes` folder in the `c14_Rendering` project folder.

If you want the reflective objects in the scene to have a higher amount of reflection, go back to the Maps rollout and make the Amount value for Reflection higher than 20.

1. In the Time Output section, click to select Range and change it to read 0 to 60, as shown in Figure 14.23.

FIGURE 14.23   The Time Output section setup for a range from 0 to 60

The resolution of the render is set in Output Size. The default resolution is 640×480.

If your computer isn't a powerful one, drop the size to 320×240, half the default size, and it will cost you one-fourth of the higher resolution's time to render.

2. Go to the Render Output section of the Render Setup dialog box and click Files to open the Render Output File dialog box. Typically, animations are rendered out as a sequence of images, but for simplicity's sake, you will render it out to an AVI.

3. In the Render Output File dialog box, choose where you want to store the rendered file and pick a name for the movie (**Room_Raytrace.avi**, for example).

4. Then, in the Save As Type drop-down menu, choose AVI File (*.avi) and click Save. The AVI File Compression Setup dialog box will appear.

Again, it is generally preferable to render to a sequence of images rather than a movie file; however, in this case, an AVI movie file will be best.

5. In the AVI File Compression Setup dialog box, select MJPEG Compressor for the compressor type, and set the Quality slider to 100. This Quality setting applies only to the compression of the AVI file and not to the render itself.

6. Click OK to return to the Render Output File dialog box, and click Save to return to the Render Setup dialog box.

7. It's a good idea to save your scene file. You are ready to render! Just click Render in the Render Setup dialog box.

To check your work, open the c14_ex10_raytrace_end.max file in the c14_ Rendering project folder.

Now You Know

Rendering is the way you get to show your finished scene to the world, or whoever will stop and look. Nothing is more fulfilling than seeing your creation come to life, and that's what rendering is all about. In this chapter, you learned how to set up and render your scenes out to files. In addition, you took a tour of raytracing and cameras.

Rendering may be the last step of the process, but you should travel the entire journey with rendering in mind, from design to models to animation to lighting.

mental ray

This chapter will show you how to create materials and render your scene using the Autodesk® mental ray® renderer.

In this chapter, you'll learn to:

▶ **Navigate the mental ray renderer**

▶ **Navigate the Final Gather parameters**

▶ **Navigate mental ray materials**

▶ **Use photometric lights with mental ray**

▶ **Use the Daylight System**

Navigate the mental ray Renderer

mental ray is a popular general-purpose renderer that has fantastic capabilities. One of mental ray's strengths is its ability to generate physically accurate lighting simulations based on *indirect lighting* principles. *Indirect lighting* occurs when light bounces from one object in a scene onto another object. In addition, incandescence or self-illumination from one object can light other objects in the scene. *Direct lighting*, such as from an omni light, is not necessarily required. Another thing to consider is that mental ray's reflections and refractions take on very real qualities when set up and lighted well.

Exercise 15.1: Enabling the mental ray Renderer

Set your project to the c15_mental ray project folder that you downloaded to your hard drive from the companion web page at www.sybex.com/go/3dsmax2015essentials. Open the c15_ex1_assign_start.max file in the scenes folder. You'll render a movie to see the animation. To enable mental ray, follow these steps:

1. Choose Rendering ➤ Render ➤ Render Setup or select the icon in the main toolbar (🖼) or use the shortcut, F10, to open the Render Setup dialog box.

2. On the Common tab, scroll down to the Assign Renderer rollout. Click the Assign Renderer rollout bar to expand it. Select the ellipsis button for the Production entry, as shown in Figure 15.1. This opens the Choose Renderer dialog box.

FIGURE 15.1   The Assign Renderer rollout

3. In the Choose Renderer dialog box, highlight NVIDIA mental ray, and then click OK.

Save the file. To check your work you can open the c15_ex1_assign_end.max file in the c15_mental ray project folder.

mental ray Sampling Quality

Once the mental ray renderer is enabled, click the Renderer tab in the Render Setup dialog box. The following is a brief explanation of the render settings most useful for you in your work.

Under the Sampling Quality rollout, shown in Figure 15.2, are the settings that let you control the overall image quality of your renders.

In the Sampling Mode drop-down list, there are three options to choose from. Unified/Raytraced (Recommended) is the default. This mode raytraces the scene using the same sampling method for both anti-aliasing and calculating motion blur. This results in far quicker rendering than the Classic/Raytraced method.

▶

Once the NVIDIA mental ray renderer is assigned, you can make it the default renderer by clicking the Save As Defaults button on the Assign Renderer rollout. If mental ray is set as the default, the Render Setup dialog box opens with the mental ray controls in tabs. You will not need to do this for the exercises in this chapter.

FIGURE 15.2 The Renderer tab shows mental ray's common settings.

Quality essentially sets the "noise level" at which the renderer stops sampling. Higher quality implies less noise. The Quality parameter sets the quality of rendering. The lower the values, the faster the render, but the render is much grainier, as shown in Figure 15.3. The higher the value, the smoother the images, as shown in Figure 15.4, but they take longer to render.

FIGURE 15.3 A Quality setting of 0.01 renders a noisy image.

FIGURE 15.4   A Quality setting of 20.0 renders a smooth image.

Navigate the Final Gather Parameters

A popular feature in mental ray is *indirect illumination*—the simulation of bounced light (explained in the next section). Click the Global Illumination tab at the top of the Render Setup dialog box. There are four rollouts, the second of which we will explore further:

▶ Skylights & Environment Lighting (IBL)

▶ Final Gathering (FG)

▶ Caustics & Photon Mapping (GI)

▶ Reuse (FG And GI Disk Caching)

▶

This type of rendering can introduce artifacts or noise in the render. Finding the right settings to balance a clean render and acceptable render times is an art form all its own and is rather difficult to master.

Final Gather is a method of mental ray rendering for estimating global illumination (GI). In short, *global illumination* is a way of calculating indirect lighting. This way, objects do not need to be in the direct path of a light (such as a spotlight) to be lit in the scene. mental ray accomplishes this by casting points throughout a scene. These light points are allowed to bounce from object to object, contributing light as they go, effectively simulating how real light photons work in the physical world.

Figure 15.5 shows the Final Gathering (FG) rollout. Some of the Final Gather options, including how to deal with quality and noise, are explained next.

FIGURE 15.5 The Final Gathering (FG) rollout in the Global Illumination tab of the Render Setup dialog box

Basic Group

These are the most important parameters in the Basic group of the Final Gathering (FG) rollout; they set the accuracy and precision of the light bounces, thereby controlling noise:

FG Precision Presets Slider   Sets the accuracy level of the Final Gather simulation by adjusting settings for the renderer such as Initial FG Point Density, Rays Per FG Point, and Interpolate Over Num. FG Points. Use this slider first in setting how well your render's lighting looks. In the left image in Figure 15.6, three spheres are rendered with the Draft setting for Final Gather, while the right image is set to High. Notice that the right image is a cleaner render, and it also shows more of the background and the spheres than does the Draft quality in the left image. This slider will adjust the settings for several of the values covered in the following list.

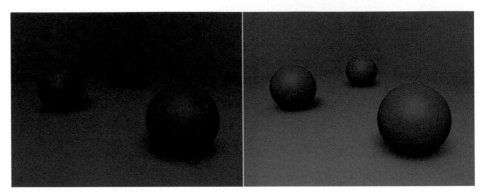

F I G U R E   1 5 . 6   The Draft setting produces a test render of the spheres (left). The High setting produces a better-quality render of the spheres (right).

Initial FG Point Density   This multiplier controls the density for the Final Gather points. This is one of the settings adjusted by the FG Precision Presets slider, but it can also be set manually. This value sets the quantity and density of FG *points* that are cast into the scene. The higher the density of these points, the more accurate the bounced light appears, at a cost of render time.

Rays Per FG Point   This value is controlled by the FG Precision Presets slider but can also be manually set. The higher the number of rays used to compute the indirect illumination in a scene, the less noise and the more accuracy you gain, but at the cost of longer render times.

Interpolate Over Num. FG Points   Interpolation is controlled by the FG Precision Presets slider as well as manual input. This value is useful for getting rid of noise in your renders for smoother results. Increasing the interpolation will increase render times but not as much as increasing the Initial FG Point Density or Rays Per FG Point values.

Diffuse Bounces   The number of bounces governs how many times a ray of light can bounce and affect objects in a scene before stopping calculation. If you set the number of bounces higher, the light simulation will be more accurate, but the render times will be costly. A Diffuse Bounces setting of 1 or 5 is adequate for many applications. Figure 15.7 shows the same render of the spheres as Figure 15.6, but with a Diffuse Bounces value of 5. This render is brighter and also shows color bleed from the purple spheres onto the gray floor.

FIGURE 15.7   More diffuse bounces mean more bounced light.

Advanced Group

The Advanced group of settings gives you access to additional ways of controlling the quality of your Final Gather renders. Some are described next, in brief. You should experiment with different settings as you gain more experience with Final Gather to see what settings work best for your scenes.

Noise Filtering (Speckle Reduction)   This value essentially averages the brightness of the light rays in the scene to give you smoother Final Gather results. The higher the filtering, the darker your Final Gather simulation, and the longer your render times will be. However, the noise in your lighting will diminish.

Draft Mode (No Precalculations)   This setting allows you to turn off a good number of calculations that mental ray completes prior to rendering the scene. Enabling this setting results in a faster render for preview and draft purposes.

Max. Reflections   This value controls how many times a light ray can be reflected in the scene. A value of 0 turns off reflections entirely. The higher this value, the more times you can see a reflection. For example, a value of 2 allows you to see a reflection of a reflection.

Max. Refractions   Similar to Max. Reflections, this value sets the number of times a light ray can be refracted through a surface. A value of 0 turns off all refraction.

The mental ray Rendered Frame Window

When you render a scene using the Autodesk® 3ds Max® program, the Rendered Frame window opens, displaying the image you just rendered. When you render with mental ray, an additional control panel is displayed under the Rendered Frame window, as shown in Figure 15.8.

FIGURE 15.8   The Rendered Frame window now shows several mental ray controls.

This control panel gives you access to many of the most useful settings in the Render Settings dialog box so you can adjust render settings easily and quickly.

Navigate mental ray Materials

For the most part, mental ray treats regular 3ds Max maps and materials the same way the Default Scanline renderer does. However, a set of mental ray–specific materials exists to take further advantage of mental ray's power. The mental ray Arch & Design material works great for most hard surfaces, such as metal, wood, glass, and ceramic. It is especially useful for surfaces that are glossy and reflective, such as metal and ceramic. To showcase these materials, let's retexture a few of the features from the room from Chapter 9, "Introduction to Materials."

Exercise 15.2: Setting Up the Material Editor

Set your project to the c15_mental ray project folder that you downloaded from the web page at www.sybex.com/go/3dsmax2015essentials. Open the c15_ex2_materials_start.max file from the scenes folder from the c15_mental ray project folder. This file has NVIDIA mental ray already assigned as the renderer. The scene includes the room and the textured furniture. There are no lights in the scene, but because NVIDIA mental ray is the assigned renderer, it utilizes the default lights to generate a lighted scene, as shown rendered in Figure 15.9. mental ray renders the materials from the previous chapter; some look the same, but others don't look so good.

FIGURE 15.9   The file rendered with mental ray

1. Open the Slate Material Editor, and then look at the top of the active view. You will see a tab called View 1; it holds all the materials that were created for the scene.

2. To keep the new materials that will be created separate and organized, create another tab for the mental ray materials. To create a new tab, right-click in the blank area next to the tab, as shown in Figure 15.10, create a new view, and name it **mental ray**.

FIGURE 15.10   Create a new view.

Save the file. To check your work you can open the c15_ex2_materials_end .max file in the c15_mental ray project folder.

Exercise 15.3: Using Arch & Design Material Templates

In the Material/Map Browser, you will see an additional rollout, mental ray. This gives a whole new set of materials, including the Arch & Design materials. Arch & Design materials have a special feature: templates. *Templates* provide access to already created materials and parameters for different types of materials, such as wood, glass, and metal. These templates can also be used as a starting point for material creation. Open the c15_ex3_materials_start.max file from the scenes folder from the c15_mental ray project folder. You will use one to create the material for the tabletop and wineglass in the following steps:

1. Drag an Arch & Design material to the new active view from the mental ray material section of the Material/Map Browser.

2. Double-click the title of the node; this will display the Arch & Design material in the Material Parameter Editor.

3. Name the material **Thick Glass**.

4. From the Material Parameter Editor, in the Select a Template drop-down menu, choose Glass (Solid Geometry), as shown in Figure 15.11.

FIGURE 15.11   Arch & Design Glass (Solid Geometry) from the template drop-down menu

5. Drag a wire from the Thick Glass material's output socket to the wineglass object.

6. Render the Room Camera viewport to see the new material on the coffee table top. There is some blue in the glass; this is from the Refraction color.

7. Select the Refraction Color swatch and change the color to achieve a colored tint to the glass. Change the color to white to get a clear glass.

8. Render the scene, as shown in Figure 15.12.

Another Arch & Design material template is the Chrome template. You will use it to replace the chrome that already exists on the side table and lounge chair frames.

FIGURE 15.12   Refraction color changed to white to achieve clear glass

9. Press the C key on the keyboard. This will bring up the Select Camera dialog box, which includes a list of cameras in the scene.

10. Select the Lounge Chair/Table Camera. Click OK to close the dialog box.

11. In the Material Parameter Editor, create a new Arch & Design material and choose Chrome from the template list. Name it **Chrome**.

12. Select the pieces of the side table and lounge chair that need to be chrome, which are all the pieces of the table except the glass, as well as the frame of the lounge chair. When you apply the material, you will get an error message, as shown in Figure 15.13, telling you

that a material with the same name already exists. This material is a Standard material that was previously applied.

FIGURE 15.13 The message warns you about assigning a material with a duplicate name to an object.

13. Select the *Replace It?* radio button.

14. Render to see the new Chrome material applied to the side table and lounge chair frame, as shown in Figure 15.14.

FIGURE 15.14 The new Chrome material applied to the chair frame and side table

Save the file. To check your work, open the c15_ex3_materials_end.max file in the c15_mental ray project folder.

Exercise 15.4: Creating Arch & Design Materials

Using the Arch & Design material, you will create a new material for the floor. There is a template called Glossy Varnished Wood, but you are going to create the floor material from scratch. Open the c15_ex4_materials_start.max file from the scenes folder of the c15_mental ray project folder.

1. Switch from the Lounge Chair/Table Camera to the Floor Camera using C to bring up the Select Camera dialog.

2. Open the Material Parameter Editor if it isn't already open, and drag an Arch & Design material to the new active area from the mental ray rollout of the Material/Map Browser.

3. Double-click the title of the node to display the Arch & Design material parameters in the Material Parameter Editor. Name the material **Hardwood Floors**.

4. Drag a bitmap from the Maps rollout to the Diffuse Color Map input socket of the Arch & Design material. This will bring up the Select Bitmap Image File window.

5. Choose the Hardwood_honey.tif file. Leave all the other parameters at the default.

6. Apply the material to the floor. You will get an error window telling you that there is a material with the same name already applied. Select *Replace It?* from the dialog. If the Hardwood Floors material doesn't show up in the viewport, click the Show Shaded Material In Viewport button ( ). Render the Floor Camera viewport. The results are shown in Figure 15.15.

FIGURE 15.15   Floor with the Arch & Design material applied

7. In the Material Editor, in the Reflection group, leave Reflectivity at 0.6 and change Glossiness to 0.6.

8. Render the camera to see the results, as shown in Figure 15.16.

FIGURE 15.16 The Hardwood Floors material showing the change in the reflections

By default, Arch & Design materials have reflection enabled. The area below the Diffuse group in the Material Parameter Editor of the Slate Material Editor is the Reflection group of parameters. Reflections for this material are calculated using the Reflectivity and Glossiness values. The higher the Reflectivity value, the clearer the reflections. The Glossiness value controls the blurriness of the reflections from sharp (a value of 1) to completely blurred (a value of 0). When you blur your reflections, the blurrier they are, the noisier they will be in the render. You can use the Glossy Samples value to increase the quality of the blurred reflections once you set Glossiness to anything less than 1. The floors should not be so reflective.

You can use the same techniques for creating Arch & Design materials for the other objects in the scene, like the base of the coffee table and the couch. Save the file. To check your work open the c15_ex4_materials_end.max file in the c15_mental ray project folder.

Exercise 15.5: Using the Multi/Sub-Object Material and Arch & Design

You can use the same technique for the window that you used in Chapter 9, but the difference is that you will use the Arch & Design material instead of the Multi/Sub-Object material. The window is divided into two materials: shiny white for the frame and a shiny transparent material for the glass. Another way to apply a Multi/Sub-Object material is to apply the material to the selected sub-objects. Open the c15_ex5_materials_start.max file from the scenes folder of the c15_mental ray project folder.

1. Switch from the Floor Camera to the Window Camera by pressing C to bring up the Select Camera dialog box.

2. Select the window and go to the Graphite Modeling Tools tab ➢ Polygon Modeling ➢ Convert to Poly.

3. Enter Polygon mode (�), and select all the polygons for the window frame. The simplest way to do this is to select the Window object, hold down Alt, and click just the window glass; this will deselect the glass. There are front and back Window objects.

4. In the Slate Material Editor, you'll create a shiny white material: Drag an Arch & Design material to the mental ray active area, and change the Diffuse color to R = 1.0, G = 1.0, B = 1.0 and rename it **White Window Frame**. Based on what you know about reflections from the previous steps, the default reflections are too high, especially for the frame on the window.

5. In the Reflection group, change Reflectivity to 0.4 and Glossiness to 0.4.

6. Apply the material to the selected sub-objects using the Assign Material To Selection button (🔳).

7. Now go to the main toolbar ➢ Edit menu and choose Select ➢ Select Invert; this will deselect the window frame and select the window glass.

8. Back in the Material Parameter Editor, drag an Arch & Design material to the mental ray active area.

9. Double-click the title bar of the new Arch & Design material to load it into the Material Parameter Editor.

10. In the Select A Template drop-down menu, choose Glass (Thin Geometry), and select the Show Background In Preview icon (🔳). This will place a checker pattern behind the sample sphere to make the transparency easier to edit. Rename the material **Window Glass**.

You can see that the window and frame look very similar to the Standard materials, but the coffee table and floor look significantly better than with their previous Standard material. When you're using mental ray, Arch & Design materials are superior. Sometimes the look of a particular object can change depending on the camera angle and lighting. Keep an eye on the window to see if the look maintains the realism you are after.

The Arch & Design material type is an elaborate construct of mental ray shaders, and with proper lighting it can make any render look special. If you open the c15_ex5_materials_end.max file, you will see several examples of materials beyond what you created in the previous exercise, as shown in Figure 15.17.

Save the file. To check your work, open the c15_ex5_materials_end.max file in the c15_mental ray project folder.

FIGURE 15.17   The final render of the mental ray materials

Use Photometric Lights with mental ray

Photometric lights simulate real lighting by using physically based energy values and color temperatures. Many of the parameters for photometric lights are the same as or very similar to the standard lights you looked at in Chapter 13, "Introduction to Lighting: Interior Lighting."

Exercise 15.6: Using Photometric Lights in mental ray Renderings

Here you see the parameters that are specific to photometric lights. To learn about photometric lights, follow these steps:

1. Open the c15_ex6_ light_start.max file from the scenes folder of the c15_mental ray project folder from the book's web page.

2. To create a light, one method is to go to the main menu bar and choose Create ➤ Lights ➤ Photometric Lights ➤ Target Light to create a photometric target light.

3. When you click on the Target Light, you will get a pop-up, Photometric Light Creation, recommending that you use the mr Photographic Exposure Control, as shown in Figure 15.18. Click Yes.

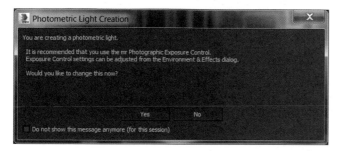

FIGURE 15.18 Select *Yes* in the Photometric Light Creation dialog box.

4. In the Left viewport, click to create the light, and then drag from the ceiling down to the floor. Make sure you stay within the room.

5. You will need to move the light into the room. Both the light source and target need to be selected. The easiest way to select both the light and the target is to select the blue string that runs between the two objects.

6. Switch to the Top viewport, and with the Move tool move the light and its target so they are above the coffee table.

7. Change the viewport rendering type to Realistic in the Room Window Camera viewport.

8. Select the light source and go to the Modify panel.

9. The first rollout under the modifier stack is Templates. Then in the Select A Template drop-down menu, select Recessed 75W Wallwash (Web). When you add a template to a photometric light a new rollout appears. Figure 15.19 shows a photometric light rollout with a "web" distribution essentially defining the light's behavior and the light it casts.

Template rollout gives you access to several light type presets to save you time in creating a light.

Lighting manufacturers provide web files that model the kinds of lights they make, so using these distribution patterns as templates will give you a lot of options in simulating real-world lights, such as this 75-watt recessed lamp.

FIGURE 15.19 The Distribution (Photometric Web) rollout

You originally created a targeted light, but when you used the template, it took away the target. Having a target on a light makes it easier to edit the light's position.

The preview may show as either very bright or very dark at first. If so, the preview function will work perfectly once you render a frame for the first time.

10. You need to take care of some basic stuff now, so with the light still selected, open the General Parameters rollout and check the Targeted box. Checking this box turns the target back on for the light.

11. Click the Shadows On box to turn it on. From the drop-down menu, choose Ray Traced Shadows.

12. Choose Rendering ➢ Exposure Control, and click the Render Preview button in the Exposure Control rollout, as shown in Figure 15.20.

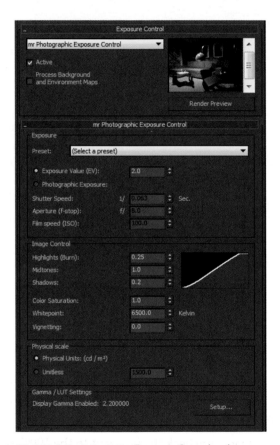

FIGURE 15.20 Exposure Control and mr Photographic Exposure Control rollouts in the Environment and Effects dialog box

13. Under the mr Photographic Exposure Control rollout, select Exposure Value (EV) if it isn't already selected.

14. Set some different values for the EV and see what happens in the Render Preview window. The higher the EV number, the darker the scene will be; when you change the exposure value, the Render Preview window updates. Set the EV to 3 and render the Room Window Camera. Then render the Room Window Camera viewport, as shown in Figure 15.21.

FIGURE 15.21 The room so far

15. You can continue to work with the EV to experiment with the luminance level. When you've finished experimenting, be sure to set the EV to 3 and close the Environment and Effects dialog box.

16. With the 75W light still selected, go to the Modify panel, and in the Color group in the Intensity/Color/Attenuation rollout, click the radio button next to Kelvin and change the value to **5600**. This will give the light a bit more warmth by adding more yellow/red.

17. In the Dimming group, uncheck the box next to the 100% spinner under Resulting Intensity to enable the Intensity parameter.

18. In the Intensity group, select cd, as shown in Figure 15.22, and set the cd amount to **200**. This will brighten things up a bit.

Exposure controls adjust output levels and the range of colors of a rendering. These controls are similar to real-world film exposure settings on a physical camera.

FIGURE 15.22
Intensity/Color/Attenuation
rollout showing the changed
parameters

19. Render the scene. The result is shown in Figure 15.23. The scene still looks a bit dark and the shadows are very dark; they look like black holes. You will use Final Gather to brighten up the overall render.

Most of the controls in the Final Gather panel also have a home in the Render Setup dialog box, and changing the value in one area updates the corresponding value in the other area.

When you are rendering with mental ray, the mini Final Gather panel in the Rendered Frame window is available for quick changes.

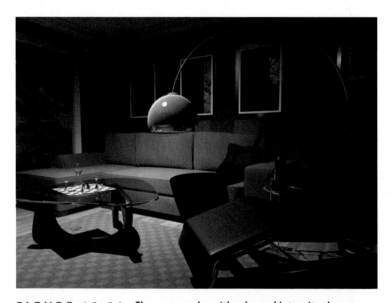

FIGURE 15.23   The room render with color and intensity changes

20. In the mini panel below the Rendered Frame window, shown in Figure 15.24, change FG Bounces to 7.

FIGURE 15.24   This mini panel gives you access to Final Gather controls to adjust your render easily.

21. Render the scene and compare the resulting render shown in Figure 15.23 to Figure 15.25. Figure 15.25 shows the final render.

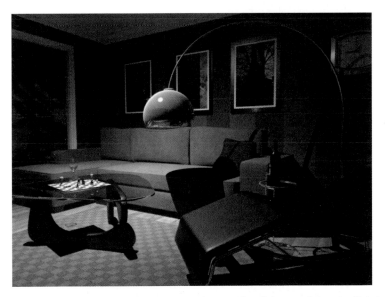

FIGURE 15.25   The final mental ray render of the room's interior lighting

Save the file. To check your work, open the c15_ex6_materials_end.max file in the c15_mental ray project folder.

Photometric Light Parameters

Now let's look in the command panel at the photometric light's Intensity/Color/Attenuation rollout for the 75W light.

The Color group of parameters controls the color temperature of the light, which you can set either with a color value or in Kelvin units, just as with real-world photographic lights. In the drop-down menu, there are different color/temp settings. The default is D65 Illuminant (Reference White).

The Intensity group of parameters controls the strength or brightness of the lights measured in lm, cd, or lx.

lm (lumen)   This value is the overall output power of the light. A 100-watt general purpose light bulb measures about 1750 lm.

cd (candela)   This value shows the maximum luminous intensity of the light. A 100-watt general-purpose light bulb measures about 139 cd.

lx at (lux)   This value shows the amount of luminance created by the light shining on a surface at a certain distance.

The parameters in the Dimming section are also used to control the intensity of the light. When the Resulting Intensity box is checked, the value specifies a multiplier that dims the existing intensity of the light and takes over control of the intensity.

Use the Daylight System

The Daylight System simulates sunlight by following the geographically correct angle and movement of the sun over the earth. You can choose location, date, time, and compass orientation to set the orientation of the sun and its lighting conditions. You can also animate the date and time to achieve very cool time-lapse looks and shadow studies.

Exercise 15.7: Using the Daylight System in mental ray Renderings

In essence, this type of light works really well with mental ray and Final Gather. In this exercise, you will use it in the most basic way, using all of its defaults.

1. Open the c15_ex7_daylight_start.max file from the scenes folder of the c15_mental ray project folder.

2. Choose Create ➢ Lights ➢ Daylight System.

3. A Daylight System Creation warning will appear, as shown in Figure 15.26, asking if you want to change the exposure controls to suit the Daylight System. Click Yes.

Daylight System Creation

You are creating a Daylight system.

It is recommended that you use the mr Photographic Exposure Control set to an Exposure Value of EV = 15. Exposure Control settings can be adjusted from the Environment & Effects dialog.

Would you like to change this now?

Yes   No

☐ Do not show this message anymore (for this session)

FIGURE 15.26 The Daylight System Creation warning

4. In a Top viewport, click and drag at the center of the scene. This will create a compass that is attached to the Daylight System. Make it the size of the room.

5. When you release the mouse button, move the mouse so the light is placed outside the walls of the room. The Daylight System is supposed to simulate the sun and sky, so it needs to be outside the room.

6. With the light still selected, open the Modify panel, and in the Daylight Parameters rollout, change the drop-down menus under both Sunlight and Skylight to mr Sun and mr Sky, respectively.

7. When you change the Skylight parameter, a mental ray Sky warning will appear, asking if you want to place a mr Physical Sky environment map in your scene. Click Yes.

8. Also in the Daylight Parameters rollout, under the Position rollout, select Manual. This will allow you to use the Move tool to move the light to where you want it. The default position represents noon.

9. Move the light so it is going through the window, as shown in Figure 15.27.

The lower the light is to the horizon in your scene, the more it will simulate darker skies at sunset.

FIGURE 15.27 Move the Daylight System light so it will shine through the window.

10. Select the Room Window Camera viewport and render. As you can see, it is too dark. You are trying to simulate a sunny day, and beyond the direct light coming through the window, it's pretty dark, as shown in Figure 15.28.

A good tool to use in this situation is mr Sky Portal. It gives you an efficient way of using a scene's existing sky lighting within interior scenes that do not require costly Final Gather or Global Illumination.

FIGURE 15.28 This scene is too dark.

11. Choose Create ➤ Lights ➤ Photometric Lights ➤ mr Sky Portal.

12. In the Front viewport, drag the mr Sky Portal so it fits the window size in the wall.

13. Then in the Top viewport, move the mr Sky Portal back so it is aligned with the opening of the window outside the room. Make sure the arrow is pointing into the room, as shown in Figure 15.29. Figure 15.29 is shown with just the walls, window, Daylight System, and mr Sky Portal.

A portal gets its brightness and color from the environment already in your scene.

FIGURE 15.29 Move the mr Sky Portal to the window in the wall in the Top viewport.

14. Render the Room Window Camera viewport again. That helps, but it is not enough; it is still too dark, so it's time to play with exposure controls.

15. Choose Rendering ➤ Exposure Control. Click Render Preview.

16. In the mr Photographic Exposure Control rollout, change Exposure Value (EV) from 15 (the default) to 9. You should see the render preview change to show the update.

17. Render the Room Window Camera viewport again to see the difference. It looks good but is still a bit dark, so it's time to add Final Gather bounces.

18. In the Rendered Frame window, change FG Bounces to **5**. Render the viewport again.

That's it! If you want to play around some more, try moving the light for a more dramatic shadow on the floor. Moving the light can have a dramatic effect on the luminance levels, so be prepared to edit FG Bounces and Exposure Controls. The last render is shown in Figure 15.30. Don't be surprised if it takes a while to render.

FIGURE 15.30   The final render

Open the c15_ex7_daylight_end.max file to compare it to your file.

Now You Know

In this chapter, you learned the basics of mental ray. mental ray is used for lighting, material creation, and rendering. You saw the quality settings and how they could help you with better renders. Finding the right balance of settings for a clean render is an art all to itself. We introduced the Arch & Design material, and you learned the basics of navigating and applying it. You also started lighting with Final Gather using photometric lights and the Daylight System.

Autodesk 3ds Max Certification

Autodesk certifications are industry-recognized credentials that can help you succeed in your design career—providing benefits to both you and your employer. Getting certified is a reliable validation of skills and knowledge, and it can lead to accelerated professional development, improved productivity, and enhanced credibility.

This Autodesk Official Press guide can be an effective component of your exam preparation for the Autodesk® 3ds Max® 2015 certification exam. Autodesk highly recommends (and we agree!) that you schedule regular time to prepare, review the most current exam preparation road map available at www.autodesk.com/certification, use Autodesk Official Press books, take a class at an Authorized Training Center (find ATCs near you at www.autodesk.com/atc), take an assessment test, and use a variety of resources to prepare for your certification—including plenty of actual hands-on experience.

Certification Objective

Table A.1 is for the Autodesk 3ds Max 2015 Certified Professional exam and lists the topics, exam objectives, and the chapter where the information for each objective is found—and in the chapters, you'll find certification icons like the one in the margin here to indicate where objectives are covered. This book will give you a foundation for the basic objectives covered in the exam, but you will need further study and hands-on practice to complete and pass the Professional exam.

Please refer to www.autodesk.com/certification for the most current exam road map and objectives. Good luck preparing for your certification!

TABLE A.1: 3DS MAX 2015 EXAM OBJECTIVES

Topic	Exam Objective	Chapter
Animation	Create a path animation and evaluate an object along the path	Not covered
	Identify Controller types	Chapter 5
	Identify playback settings	Chapter 5
	Locate the value of keys in the Time Slider	Chapter 5
	Use a Dope Sheet	Chapter 12
Cameras	Differentiate camera types	Chapter 14
	Edit FOV (Field of View)	Chapter 14
	Data Management/Interoperability	Chapter 1, 14
	Differentiate common file types and usages	Chapter 1
	Use the import feature to import model data	Chapter 3
Effects	Use atmosphere effect	Chapter 13
	Identify particle systems	Not covered
	Identify Space Warp types	Not covered
Lighting	Compare Attenuation and Decay	Chapter 13
	Differentiate light functions in a scene	Chapter 13
	Identify parameters for modifying shadows	Chapter 13
	Use the Daylight System	Chapter 15
	Use the Light Lister	Chapter 13
Materials/Shading	Identify Shader parameters	Chapter 9
	Identify standard materials	Chapter 9
	Use the Material Editor	Chapter 9, 10, 15

Topic	Exam Objective	Chapter
Modeling	Differentiate reference coordinate systems	Chapter 1, 8
	Differentiate workflow	Chapter 2-4,
	Differentiate standard versus extended primitives	Chapter 2-3
	Identify Clone types	Chapter 2-4, 7
	Identify Vertex types	Chapter 2
	Use object creation and modification workflows	Chapter 2-4, 7 & 8
	Use polygon modeling tools	Chapter 2-4, 7-10
	Use ProBoolean	Not Covered
Rendering	Differentiate Renderers	Chapter 14
	Identify rendering parameters	Chapter 14
Rigging	Use Character Studio for rigging	Chapter 11
	Create simple Bipeds	Chapter 11
	Use the Skin modifier	Chapter 12
UI/Object Management	Describe and use object transformations	Chapter 1, 2, 5
	Identify Selection Regions	Chapter 2, 7, 8
	Use Viewports	Chapter 1, 2
	Set up and use Scenes	Chapter 1, 2

Index

Note to the Reader: Throughout this index boldfaced page numbers indicate primary discussions of a topic. *Italicized* page numbers indicate illustrations.